DISCIPLING
Nurturing
AND RECLAIMING

NURTURE AND RETENTION SUMMIT

Foreword by G. T. Ng, Ph.D.

PUBLISHED BY: Review and Herald® Publishing Association

PRINTED BY: Editorial Safeliz,S.L.
Pradillo,6, Pol. Ind. La Mina, E-28770 Colmenar Viejo, Madrid (España)
admin@safeliz.com, www.safeliz.com

COVER DESIGN: Erika Miike
INTERIOR DESIGN & LAYOUT: Regina Reaves
COPY EDITORS: James and Ida Cavil

EDITED BY: General Conference Nurture and Retention Committee:
Geoffrey G Mbwana, Gerson P Santos, Rachel Bustamante, Torben Bergland, Gary T Blanchard, Marcos F Bomfim, Ramon J Canals, Cheryl Doss, Sherri Ingram-Hudgins, Anthony R Kent, Linda Mei Lin Koh, Gary D Krause, Elbert Kuhn, Duane McKey, Willie Oliver, Karen J Porter, Heather-Dawn K Small, David Trim, James M Howard, Galina Stele

Ex-officials: Ted N C Wilson, G T Ng, Juan R Prestol-Puesan

Printed in China.

ISBN: 978-0-8280-2871-4

BIBLE CREDITS

Table of Contents

Note from the Editors

Dear Reader,

Addressing low church member retention is long overdue. Very often this issue has been brought up to the General Conference Executive Committee meeting by the Secretariat and the Office of Archives, Statistics, and Research (ASTR). One of the initiatives of the General Conference (GC) of Seventh-day Adventists to address this matter is to hold Nurture and Retention (N&R) global summits. The first one met November 18–20, 2013, at the Adventist Church World Headquarters under the title "Discipling, Retaining & Reclaiming." It was organized by the GC N&R Committee and ASTR. Division N&R coordinators, church leaders, departmental directors, and Adventist researchers discussed retention challenges, shared research data and division reports, and brainstormed recommendations to the world Church *(see Appendix 1)*.

In April 5–7, 2019, a second N&R summit was held. This time the N&R committee proposed to cover three important related areas: Discipling, Nurturing, and Reclaiming. Summit presenters focused on these themes, trying to suggest practical solutions to existing problems. The summit recommendations, approved by the 2019 Annual Council, can be found in Appendix 2. Presentations from both summits were posted on the ASTR website at https://www.adventistresearch.org/research-conferences) and are expected to be a helpful tool for all who are involved in the work of discipling, nurturing, and reclaiming church members.

The primary purpose of this publication is to preserve and disseminate the content of the seminars/workshops offered during the 2019 N&R summit. The secondary, and probably most important, long-term goal is to keep the conversation running and to continue to share and develop best practices to be more effective and efficient in God's mission.

A special note of gratitude to Dr. G. T. Ng, General Conference Executive Secretary, always pushing us to the edge of creativity and innovation to deal with hot issues as we pursue effectiveness in mission. In his foreword, Dr. Ng highlights the importance of having a balance approach to evangelism and discipleship, "winning and keeping must go hand in hand... there is no question that mission must march on unabated. Discipleship and nurture must follow baptism."

Another note of appreciation to Elder G. Mbwana, General Vice President, for his leadership and insights as chair of the GC N&R Committee. In his introduction, Elder Mbwana stressed our need "to cooperate with the Holy Spirit in making disciples for Christ."

The content of this volume is organized following the team of presenters at the 2019 summit. Even though there are no specific sections in the book, the articles were organized following three main areas. First, we presented the articles about membership, discipleship, and mission. Second are the articles regarding Adventist families, Christian education, and young people. Lastly, there are the articles analyzing how to build healthy relationships in the church, how to connect with new members and reclaim former members.

At the end of the book, in Appendices, you will find recommendations from both the 2013 and 2019 N&R summits and a sample survey for the local church for self-assessment of the implementation of the 2019 summit recommendations.

We believe these topics will give you enough insight about the need to develop more efficient ways to attract and equip new members, as well as sending them to fulfill God's work to "make disciples of all nations" (Matt. 28:19, NIV) .

Lose None and Disciple All

G. T. NG, Ph.D.

THIS BOOK IS A COLLECTION of papers about nurture, retention, reclamation, discipleship, and mission. Volumes could be written about each of these topics. But the genius of the book is in treating these vital subjects wholistically and weaving them into a composite picture of disciple-making that is at the very heart of Jesus' Great Commission in Matthew 28:18–20. This book is the work of the General Conference Nurture and Retention Committee under the leadership of Geoffrey Mbwana as the chair and Gerson Santos as the secretary. The committee has worked tirelessly and heroically, highlighting nurture and retention as an intrinsic part of the mission of the church.

APOSTASY

Research conducted by the General Conference Office of Archives, Statistics, and Research (ASTR) has revealed a disturbing trend of membership loss through the years.

Since 1965, 40,421,554 people have been members of the Seventh-day Adventist Church. Of those, 16,240,069 have chosen to leave. Our net loss rate is 40 percent. In other words, four of every 10 church members have left the church.

Nobody likes bad news. We would rather not know or talk about it. Bearers of evil tidings are sometimes branded as killjoys. But the bad news of huge membership loss is not just about statistics. It is about lives God has created and redeemed.

ENGINE NOISE

A huge Boeing 777 was thundering down the runway picking up speed and ready to take off. Suddenly the pilot aborted the takeoff, turned the plane around, and returned to the gate. After a two-hour delay the plane finally took off.

A worried passenger asked the flight attendant, "What was the delay all about? Was there a problem?"

The flight attendant explained, "The pilot was bothered by a noise he heard in the engine, so he returned to the gate."

"Did they manage to find the problem with the engine?"

"No, they never did. But it took them two hours to find a new pilot."

What do you do when you have an engine problem? Fix the engine or change the pilot?

RESPONSE

How should the church respond to the crisis of apostasy?

The logical and responsible response should be to take the bull by the horns and find ways to rectify the problem. Unfortunately, we either bury our heads in the sand, refusing to deal with the problem (ostrich syndrome), wash our hands and go on with business as usual (Pilate syndrome), or delay confronting the problem until a more convenient time (Felix syndrome).

Turning a blind eye to huge perennial membership losses is biblically indefensible, ethically irresponsible, morally inexcusable, and spiritually untenable. But when we start taking responsibility as a church, we follow the same passion of Jesus in looking for lost souls.

LOST SHEEP, LOST COIN, AND LOST SON

Luke 15 records a string of three parables told by Jesus: the lost sheep, the lost coin, and the lost son. All three parables paint a poignant picture of the imperative and urgent searching for the lost. The parable of the lost sheep is especially riveting. The shepherd is courageous. He looks for the lost sheep at great risk to himself. No mountain is too steep to climb, no valley is too deep to explore, and no precipice is too dangerous to survey. He leaves no stone unturned. He is focused. He has 99 sheep, but he concentrates on that one straying sheep that needs help. It is a do-or-die situation. The shepherd is relentless. He is doggedly determined to find that one sheep. Nothing else matters. The shepherd is tenacious. The search has been arduous, but retreat is not an option. He is unstoppable, indomitable, and invincible because to him the lost sheep is priceless. He goes "after the one which is lost until he finds it" (Luke 15:4, NKJV).

|

The Good Shepherd is none other than Christ Himself looking for lost humanity. Ellen White writes:

"These souls whom you despise, said Jesus, are the property of God. By creation and by redemption they are His, and they are of value in His sight. As the shepherd loves his sheep, and cannot rest if even one be missing, so, in an infinitely higher degree, does God love every outcast soul. Men may deny the claim of His love, they may wander from Him, they may choose another master; yet they are God's, and He longs to recover His own. He says, 'As a shepherd seeketh out his flock in the day that he is among his sheep that are scattered; so will I seek out My sheep, and will deliver them out of all places where they have been scattered in the cloudy and dark day.' Ezekiel 34:12 ."[1]

"Angels pity these wandering ones. Angels weep, while human eyes are dry and hearts are closed to pity."[2]

What have we learned from the parable of the lost sheep? First, every lost individual is significant and must be accounted for. Like the Good Shepherd, we must spare no effort to redeem the lost. Second, behind every loss is a person and not just a number, a person whom Christ has died for and redeemed. Statistics can mask the sanctity of human life; each one must be treated as a person, not as a statistic.

MISSIOLOGICAL BLACK HOLE

Beyond the statistics of the appalling loss rate of 40 percent lies an enigma that has persisted for years. How has this happened? What has accounted for this tragic and unnecessary attrition? What are the factors that could have possibly precipitated membership hemorrhage on such a staggering scale? No simple answer can adequately explain the phenomenon. But there are some clues about what may have contributed to the colossal missiological black hole.

Hasty Harvest

Too often individuals are baptized before they are ready. They have at best only a rudimentary knowledge of the Adventist faith. They have not been properly grounded in the faith. They eventually wither away because they have no root (Matthew 13:6). Others come to the church with intellectual or doctrinal knowledge, but their hearts have not been changed, because Christ's method[3] of ministry has been ignored or neglected.

Postbaptismal Care

Sometimes public meetings are hit-and-run events. In the exhilaration of altar calls, people are baptized with little preparation. When meetings are over and candidates have been baptized, what then? Without follow-up plans, the newly baptized are left to teeter and wobble, especially those in mass baptisms where individuals are not always taken into account. Whose obligation is it for postbaptismal care? Some say it is the evangelist's responsibility. Others argue it is the obligation of the church pastor. While arguments ensue, more newly baptized members languish and spiritually die.

The Great Commission

Matthew's version of the Great Commission is considered the most comprehensive of the accounts in the Synoptic Gospels. There is only one grammatical imperative in Matthew 28:18–20, and that is "make disciples." The goal of the Great Commission is to make disciples. This is clearly spelled out in the mission statement of the Seventh-day Adventist Church:

"Make disciples of Jesus Christ who live as His loving witnesses and proclaim to all people the everlasting gospel of the Three Angels' Messages in preparation for His soon return (Matthew 28:18–20; Acts 1:8; Revelation 14:6–12)."

The commission is not only to go, baptize, or teach, but also and specially to make disciples. Going, baptizing, and teaching are tools to achieve the ultimate goal of making disciples. The commission is not to baptize; it is to baptize to make disciples. Baptism is absolutely vital in the process of making disciples. But baptism is not the end goal of the commission. Rather, it is a means to an that end. Discipling is a process. Nurturing and discipling begin before a person is baptized, and continue after baptism.

The role of the pastor is especially critical in the process of discipleship. According to the commission, teaching is also a postbaptismal activity. Newly baptized believers must be nurtured and taught to become disciples. Pastors must double up as teachers and educators. The Spirit of Prophecy has never been more unequivocal:

"Christ intends that His ministers shall be educators of the church in gospel work. They are to teach the people how to seek and save the lost." [4]

"Let the minister devote more of his time to educating than to preaching. Let him teach the people how to give to others the knowledge they have received." [5]

The Lord of the Great Commission, in the final analysis, is interested in disciples, not simply baptism. Praise God that embedded in the commission is the perfect formula for nurture and retention! Evangelism and nurture are not mutually exclusive. Winning and keeping must go hand in hand.

Does disciple-making ever come to an end? To answer that question, we must first ask another question: "What is the fruit of an apple tree?" The fruit, or legacy, of an apple tree is another apple tree! Apples don't produce apples, but apple trees do. One author describes it this way: "When the evangelized becomes the evangelizer, the work of disciple-making has been accomplished." Newly baptized members must be taught and trained until they become fruit-bearing Adventists capable of reproducing themselves.

I once attended a highly inspirational convention in Mexico where a local conference celebrated the success of small-group ministry in a stadium. Local churches came with hundreds of exuberant small groups bringing with them the fruits of their labor—individuals who were ready for baptism. After the baptism service was over, I noticed each newly baptized person was given a Bible, a baptismal certificate, and a sash. My curiosity was piqued about the sash being placed on the shoulder of each person. "What does the sash say?" I asked my translator.

He replied, "The sash says 'Today I have been born as a missionary.'"

The statement was almost a direct quote from Ellen White: "Every true disciple is born into the kingdom of God as a missionary."[6] Indeed, baptism marks the beginning of one's missionary career. The journey of discipleship has just begun.

The Numbers Game

Unfortunately, the imperative of discipling souls is too often debased into baptism numbers. Individuals get caught up in a numbers game whereby success is measured by baptisms, to the exclusion of other equally important gauges.

Numbers typically signify status, recognition, and sometimes promotion. The numbers game is both competitive and addictive. Unfortunately, baptism has been held up as a reward system.

All organizations are under pressure to maintain performance. Having reasonable pressure is a good motivation for better results. But undue fixation with numbers tends to impair judgment and compromise integrity, and it is the beginning of a slippery slope to "ethical collapse," claims author Marianne M. Jennings. She writes:

"In this first sign of a culture at risk for ethical collapse, there is not just a focus on numbers and results, but an unreasonable and unrealistic obsession with meeting quantitative goals."[7]

Who is guilty of such ethical collapse? Both for-profit and nonprofit organizations are just as liable, according to Jennings. God forbid that we should play the numbers game as a religious organization. The numbers game is not about numbers. It is about people—souls that have been lost twice!

Baptism is absolutely critical as the basis of disciple-making. Baptism, however, is only the beginning of the process of discipleship. It was never meant to be a means to an end.

Perhaps it is time to tweak our monthly report. Pastors who nurture and equip the newly baptized have no way to report that. Since nurture and disciple training are not generally reportable, there is little incentive to train new believers. Pastors in their many pressing duties find it easier to concentrate on winning souls rather than discipling, educating, and training. If the reporting system is rewarding the wrong things, a change of the reporting system is in order. Even more is needed—a change of focus. Get out of the numbers game and embark on the biblical model of disciple-making that is embodied in the mission statement of the church.

THE WAY FORWARD

So far statistics have not been in our favor, but thankfully much can be done to remedy the unfortunate loss of members from our ranks.

Scientists have developed elaborate systems for tracking dolphins and snow leopards. What about church members, who are indefinitely more valuable than animals?

The Iglesia ni Cristo religion based in the Philippines has an ingenious member tracking system. This is an indigenous church with a membership of about 3 million. Each church building has a uniform architecture. Situated in the foyer near the front entrance is a large board with the members' names written on discs. When worshippers attend church, they look for their name. Once their names are identified, they turn the discs inside out, signifying their presence in church. After worship is over, deacons jot down the names of absentees and visit them on the same afternoon. Such a membership care system is very rare.

The South American Division has an innovative tracking system through the office of local church clerks in conjunction with elders, pastors, and members. Aside from their regular duties, church clerks double up as member-care coordinators and are members of the membership audit committee. Working through Sabbath School units and small-group ministry, the committee tracks members' attendance, visits missing members, and nurtures and retains members who may have become discouraged. The committee even organizes a special annual "homecoming" event to welcome back former believers. Such an intentional approach in member-care has been most heartening.

Samuel Johnson has been credited to have said, "People need to be reminded more often than they need to be instructed." Perhaps we need to be reminded as a church that we are our brothers' keepers (Genesis 4:9). In the United States from the late 1960s through the late 1980s, there was this public service announcement on every radio and television: "It's 11:00. Do you know where your children are?" The announcement was a simple message to parents to keep their children off the streets. Perhaps we need a similar remind every Sabbath, "It's 11:00 a.m. Do you know where your members are?"

Desmond Thomas Doss (1919–2006) was well known as an American war hero. He enlisted voluntarily in the Army as a combat medic in 1942 during World War II. Being a faithful Seventh-day Adventist, he refused to kill an enemy soldier or carry a weapon into combat. He was the first U.S. conscientious objector to receive the Medal of Honor, which was presented by President Harry Truman.

Doss was noted for his audacious bravery in saving the lives of wounded soldiers. In 1945 a fierce battle was waging at Hacksaw Ridge, on the island of Okinawa, Japan. The terrain was treacherous, and the plateau was defended by a large force of heavily armed Japanese soldiers. Thousands of American and Japanese soldiers perished. While gunfire and explosions were raging around him, Doss crawled on the ground from wounded soldier to wounded soldier and dragged them one by one to the edge of the ridge, tied a rope around their bodies, and lowered them down to other medics below. Desmond Doss is credited with saving 75 soldiers during one of the bloodiest battles of World War II. He was reported to have said, "I was praying the whole time. I just kept praying, 'Lord, please help me save one more.'"

As we think of the heavy losses among those who have been baptized, may our prayer be, "Lord, please help me save one more!" There is nothing more precious to Jesus than souls He has redeemed. They are not mere numbers. They are "peculiar treasures."[8] "Lord, let me save one more, be they lost Gentiles or lost Adventists!"

Yes, the leaky bucket should be fixed, because every newborn member deserves to live!

Winning and keeping must go hand in hand. Winning and keeping are not mutually exclusive. They are two sides of the same coin.

There is no question that mission must march on unabated.

Discipleship and nurture must follow baptism. Mission without nurture is incomplete and irresponsible. May our motto be "Lose None and Disciple All."

April 2020

ENDNOTES

1. Ellen G. White, *Christ's Object Lessons* (Washington, D.C.: Review and Herald Pub. Assn., 1900, 1941), p. 187.
2. *Ibid.*, p. 192.
3. "Christ's method alone will give true success in reaching the people. The Savior mingled with men as one who desired their good. He showed His sympathy for them, ministered to their needs, and won their confidence. Then He bade them, 'Follow Me'" (Ellen G. White, *The Ministry of Healing* [Mountain View, Calif.: Pacific Press Pub. Assn., 1905], p. 143).
4. Ellen G. White, *The Desire of Ages* (Mountain View, Calif.: Pacific Press Pub. Assn., 1898, 1940), p. 825.
5. Ellen G. White, *Testimonies for the Church* (Mountain View, Calif.: Pacific Press Pub. Assn., 1948), vol. 7, p. 20.
6. E. G. White, *The Desire of Ages*, p. 195.
7. Marianne M. Jennings, *The Seven Signs of Ethical Collapse* (New York: Martin's Press, 2006), p. 17.
8. "What compassion, what matchless love, has God shown to us, lost sinners, in connecting us with Himself, to be to Him a peculiar treasure!" (Ellen G. White, *Patriarchs and Prophets* [Mountain View, Calif.: Pacific Press Pub. Assn., 1890, 1908], p. 289).

Introduction

GEOFFREY MBWANA

MORE THAN 2,000 YEARS AGO Jesus said, "And I, when I am lifted up from the earth, will draw all people to myself" (John 12:32, NIV). We are witnesses to the fulfillment of this reality as thousands of people are choosing to follow Jesus, accepting the three angels' messages. God has appointed us to cooperate with the Holy Spirit in making disciples for Christ. It is a noble responsibility that warrants us taking time to pray and study on how best we can efficiently carry our role.

The making of disciples involves soul winning, nurture, retention, and reclamation. As a body, disciples of Jesus are the church of God. God owns the church by creation and redemption; it is holy; He loves it and cares for it like "the apple of His eye." God challenges the shepherds of God's church, whom God has appointed, to take loving care of his church (Jeremiah 3:15; 23:4; Ezekiel 34:23). In his letter to Ephesian elders the apostle Paul urged them to "keep watch over yourselves and all the flock of which the Holy Spirit has made you overseers" (Acts 20:28, NIV). Being our brothers' keepers, we believe that someday we will be confronted with a question from the owner of the flock—where is that beautiful flock?

The General Conference (GC) Nurture and Retention Committee organized a discipleship summit for GC officers, division officers, and GC departmental directors. Presenters were invited from around the world to make presentations and share experiences on disciple- making. The summit was of great benefit to church leaders who attended. This book is a compilation of the presentations that were made during the summit.

We are very thankful to the various individuals who took time to prepare and make presentations on discipleship and its various elements.

We value the precious time they took to prepare and make available manuscripts of their presentations, which are now being presented as a book for wider circulation and use.

We are very grateful to the leadership of the General Conference, world divisions, and GC departmental directors for their participation in the summit. The global leadership of the church has given great importance to this subject. We believe every church leader and church member will find these presentations useful as we carry the mandate of Jesus Christ in its totality.

May God bless you abundantly as you read these presentations. May your disciple-making endeavor grow to be even stronger as you joyfully participate in carrying out the mission of Jesus Christ.

It is our hope that through these summits we will see increased interest, focus, and engagement in disciple-making in the church globally. Together we desire to see every soul that accepts Jesus become a true disciple of Christ. May God bless you.

On behalf of the GC Nurture and Retention Committee

New Member Discipleship

Disciple-making Principles
and the *Discipleship Handbook*

JAMES HOWARD

THE MISSION OF THE CHURCH is "Go . . . and make disciples" (Matthew 28:19).[1] We cannot afford to make anything less. Many churches have mistakenly assumed that baptizing new converts is equivalent to bringing them safely into the fold. Yet the startling number of members who have left the church over the past 50 years tells a different story. The truth is that baptism is only one of many steps toward becoming a mature disciple of Christ. And it is this, becoming a mature disciple, that is needed to help members grow stronger and keep them faithful to Christ.

So what is needed in order to fulfill the commission to make disciples, and not mere members? This article will begin by establishing principles that are important to remember when making disciples. It will then explain how these principles can be applied in an intentional and systematic new member discipleship plan using such tools as the *Discipleship Handbook*. The first principle is that the *process* of discipleship is the growth cycle. Second, the *instruments* of discipleship are people. Third, the *goal* of discipleship is Christlikeness. And last, the *power* of discipleship is from God.

THE PROCESS OF DISCIPLESHIP

When Jesus described the evangelistic mission of the church, He often used the analogy of the agricultural growth cycle to describe the growth of the kingdom of God: "A sower went out to sow" (Luke 8:5). "The fields . . . are already white for harvest" (John 4:35). "The seed is the word of God" (Luke 8:11). "The harvest truly is plentiful, but the laborers are few" (Matthew 9:37).

The farmer must *prepare* the soil, *plant* the seed, *cultivate* the growing plants, *harvest* the crop, *preserve* the harvest, and then repeat the cycle using the seed reaped in the previous harvest. Similarly, the gospel sower must prepare the soil of the heart with friendship and service, plant the seed of God's Word with literature or spiritual conversations, cultivate spiritual interest with ongoing Bible studies, harvest decisions for Christ with personal and public appeals, and preserve the harvest of souls with a systematic and intentional discipleship plan for new members *(see figure)*.

Figure:

The GROW Model. Learn more at https://grow.adventist.org. The top icon represents the first step of preparing the soil of the heart. Continuing clockwise, the second icon represents planting the seed of truth, the third icon represents cultivating spiritual interest, the fourth icon represents harvesting decisions for Christ, and the fifth icon represents preserving the harvest with ongoing discipleship. The continuous circle represents the cyclical and multiplying nature of discipleship.

The key principle taught by Jesus in His agricultural analogy is that making disciples is a ***process,*** not an event. Far too often we describe the mission of the church in narrow terms. We consider evangelistic outreach to be isolated from nurture, and we view numerical growth as separate from spiritual growth. Yet we discover that discipleship, when properly understood, is a process that includes both! Notice the following statements by Ellen White: "When souls are converted, set them to work at once. And as they labor according to their ability, they will grow stronger."[1] "The more one tries to explain the Word of God to others, with a love for souls, the plainer it becomes to himself."[2] "Let ministers teach church members that in order to grow in spirituality, they must carry the burden that the Lord has laid upon them—the burden of leading souls into the truth."[3] "Those who are most actively employed in doing with interested fidelity their work to win souls to Jesus Christ are the best developed in spirituality and devotion."[4]

DISCIPLING, NURTURING, AND RECLAIMING

From these inspired statements we discover a beautiful synergy between evangelistic labor and personal spiritual growth. It is by laboring for souls that we grow spiritually ourselves. Outreach and nurture are two sides of the same coin. Whether we call that coin evangelism, discipleship, or soul winning, a true and comprehensive definition will include every phase of disciple-making. It will include ministering to people's needs, introducing them to Bible truth, engaging in ongoing Bible studies, leading them to follow Christ and be baptized, and then nurturing and training them as they grow into well-rounded and active disciples of Christ.

We have only one mission. It is both the best strategy for church growth and, at the same time, the best strategy for the nurture and retention of our members. Discipleship is one continuous process that begins before baptism, continues after baptism, and leads the disciple to become more like Jesus and to carry on His mission of winning souls. The process of discipleship is the growth cycle taught by Jesus.

THE INSTRUMENTS OF DISCIPLESHIP

When Jesus said, "Go therefore and make disciples" (Matthew 28:19), He was talking to His disciples. While it is true that books, classes, and sermons may be helpful in the discipleship process, we must always keep in view that it is *people who make disciples.* True discipleship requires relationships, time, and a living example. The reason Jesus was so effective at making disciples was that He understood this principle and therefore invested significant time and energy in developing the Twelve. They learned to pray by watching Jesus pray. They learned to depend upon the Scriptures when they saw how Jesus depended on the Scriptures. They learned how to sacrifice and deny themselves by how Jesus denied Himself. They learned how to minister to others' needs and teach the gospel by watching the Master Healer and Teacher.

Paul also understood this principle. He wrote to the young minister Timothy: "And the things that you have heard from me among many witnesses, commit these to faithful men who will be able to teach others also" (2 Timothy 2:2). Christ and certain representatives of the church taught Paul, Paul taught Timothy, Timothy was to teach faithful men, and these faithful men were to teach others also. That's four generations of discipleship in one verse!

The important takeaway from this discipleship principle is that we can't simply hold a class or give someone a book and call this discipleship. New members learn how to be disciples by spending time with Jesus, but they also learn from the example of more experienced church members who are willing to invest time in them. For this reason both Paul and Peter emphasize the importance of being a godly example (see 1 Peter 5:2, 3; 1 Corinthians 11:1; Philippians 3:17; 1 Thessalonians 1:5-7). Ellen White concurs, stating that "one example is worth more than many precepts."[5]

Since the primary instruments of discipleship are people, the quality of the new disciples we make will to a great degree be dependent upon the quality of the disciple-makers! For this reason the first step for church leaders in establishing a new member discipleship plan should be to prepare and train godly mentors.

THE GOAL OF DISCIPLESHIP

Jesus explained the ultimate goal of discipleship when He declared, "A disciple is not above his teacher, but everyone who is perfectly trained will be like his teacher" (Luke 6:40). The goal of discipleship is to be like Jesus—*Christlikeness* in character and behavior. Jesus had a lot to say about what it meant to be a disciple, but in every case He was simply calling on His followers to be like Him.

A few of Jesus' statements are sufficient in order to grasp the primary aspects of this goal of Christlikeness in His followers: "By this all will know that you are My disciples, if you have love for one another" (John 13:35). "If anyone desires to come after Me, let him deny himself, and take up his cross, and follow Me" (Matthew 16:24). "Follow Me, and I will make you become fishers of men" (Mark 1:17).

Jesus explained that those who follow Him were to become loving, self-denying, soul winners—just like Him. This is a high calling indeed. It is also a compelling reason we can't afford to cease our labors for new converts immediately after they are baptized. Does a newly baptized member understand how to be a loving, self-denying, soul winner—a disciple who makes other disciples? We are not truly fulfilling the mission unless we are leading our new members to be not merely consumers, but producers. We must encourage and help them to become loving, obedient, active fishers of men and women.

Jesus instructed His disciples to not only baptize new believers, but to continue "teaching them to observe all things that I have commanded you" (Matthew 28:20). Discipleship includes practical instruction in Christ's way of living. This begins with His habit of communion with God in prayer, His study and dependence on Scripture, His bold witness to the truth, and His loving ministry to the needs of humanity. It also includes many other practical areas of biblical instruction, such as baptism,

Sabbathkeeping, reverence, stewardship, health, modesty, marriage, and family.

It should also be noted that discipleship in the last days will reflect the unique message of the Seventh-day Adventist Church as the remnant church of Bible prophecy. This message, entrusted by God to His people and firmly established in the Bible, is the foundation of faith and practice for end-time disciples. With a wealth of guidance through the Bible and the prophetic counsel of Ellen White, our Lord Jesus Christ desires that His disciples in the last days will follow in His footsteps and reflect His image.

THE POWER OF DISCIPLESHIP

While it is true that people are the primary instruments in making disciples, it must always be remembered that the power required for true discipleship comes from God. No matter how much we love people, build friendships, establish confidence, provide godly examples, or show sympathy, none of these has power to convert or transform the soul. We must connect people to Christ and His Word. It is through the foundational spiritual habits of prayer, Bible study, and witnessing that the Christian beholds and experiences divine power.

When surveys are taken of those who have left the church, reasons such as conflicts, hypocrisy, lack of love and care, or offensive attitudes are often cited to explain why they left. While we must take these seriously, we should also not fail to discern and address the more fundamental reasons that are rarely recognized or expressed. More often than not, the reason new members leave the church is that they failed to establish or continue in spiritual habits that would have given life and power to their spiritual walk with God. Without these spiritual habits, they become easily discouraged, distracted, tempted, or offended.

Ellen White writes of the spiritual habit of prayer: "Prayer is the breath of the soul. It is the secret of spiritual power. No other means of grace can be substituted and the health of the soul be preserved.... Neglect the exercise of prayer, or engage in prayer spasmodically, now and then, as seems convenient, and you lose your hold on God."[6] Rarely will someone who leaves the church state that the reason they left is that they stopped praying regularly. They may not even recognize this. Nevertheless, the neglect of this habit causes many to lose their hold on God. This is the hidden but true reason we lose many members out the back door.

Another essential spiritual habit is spending regular time in the Bible. Jesus boldly declared, "Unless you eat the flesh of the Son of Man and drink His blood, you have no life in you.... The words that I speak to you are spirit, and they are life" (John 6:53-63). It is often the case that new members come to a Bible study or evangelistic meeting and are convicted and compelled by the inspiring biblical preaching and teaching. However, when the meetings are over and after they are baptized, they gradually lose their inspiration. What happened? They had been genuinely changed by the Word being taught to them in the meetings, but they never learned how to regularly feed *themselves.* New members must be taught that unless they consistently read the Word, they will not be able to maintain a spiritual life. The Bible is not like other books. It is not merely informational, but transformational. It is through the living and powerful Word of God that we are converted, or born again, and the same Word is needed for power to live a victorious Christian life (see Hebrews 4:12; 1 Peter 1:23; Matthew 4:4). For this reason Ellen White warns, "Satan well knows that all whom he can lead to neglect prayer and the searching of the Scriptures will be overcome by his attacks."[7]

Because of the creative power in God's Word, we should make its study foundational to any discipleship plan for new members. This plan should include five different levels of Bible study: (1) encourage the spiritual habit of personal daily Bible reading, (2) give Bible studies to share the full Adventist message for the first time, (3) give baptismal preparation studies to ensure readiness for baptism, (4) give discipleship studies after baptism to integrate new members into the life and mission of the church, and (5) review our message with more in-depth Bible studies that prepare new members to give Bible studies to others. By saturating the discipleship process in the Word of God, divine power will be imparted to the new disciples. For the five levels of Bible study listed above, the General Conference Sabbath School and Personal Ministries Department has developed resources to aid churches in their discipleship training. To encourage daily Bible reading, the *Discipleship Handbook* contains a daily Bible and Spirit of Prophecy reading plan. The resource *Fundamentals of Faith* is specifically designed for use in baptismal preparation studies. The main portion of the *Discipleship Handbook,* which will be discussed later in this article in greater detail, can be used for discipleship studies after baptism. And the *Bible Study Handbook* can be used to prepare and train members to give Bible studies to others.[8]

Just before ascending to heaven, Jesus told His disciples, "But you shall receive power when the Holy Spirit has come upon you; and you shall be witnesses to Me in Jerusalem, and in all Judea and Samaria, and to the end of the earth" (Acts 1:8). When we share the gospel of Christ with others, we join God in His work and experience His power. While the power of prayer and Bible study is familiar to most Christians, the power of God experienced through witnessing is far less common. Even so, nothing solidifies new disciples in their faith like sharing God's Word with others. When we engage in this vital work, the power of the Holy Spirit strengthens our convictions, increases our faith, grows our knowledge, and expands our love for souls.

In the great mission of making disciples, we must always remember that our job is not merely to connect with people, but to connect people to Christ: "If we can awaken an interest in men's minds that will cause them to fix their eyes on Christ, we may step aside, and ask them only to continue to fix their eyes upon the Lamb of God."[9] Jesus is the Master, and we are all His disciples. All power resides in Christ and His Word. In order for us to make disciples and retain them in the church, a discipleship plan must focus on developing in new members the foundational "power" habits of prayer, Bible study, and witnessing.

NEW MEMBER DISCIPLESHIP
AND THE *DISCIPLESHIP HANDBOOK*

When we understand that the discipleship process follows the growth cycle, that the primary instruments of discipleship are people, that the goal of discipleship is Christlikeness, and that the power of discipleship comes from God, we are ready to establish a new member discipleship plan that will improve both member involvement and retention rates. The General Conference Sabbath School and Personal Ministries Department has developed the *Discipleship Handbook,* which may be used as the foundation of a new member discipleship plan in any local church. The remainder of this article will use the *Discipleship Handbook* to show how a local church can apply the principles of discipleship in a practical way to disciple new members.

But first, why would we want to use a book for new member discipleship if true discipleship is based on relationships more than books, classes, or programs? While it is true that books don't make disciples, they *do* equip disciple-makers! Ellen White had these wise words to say regarding the thinking of many church members: "Many would be willing to work if they were taught how to begin."[10] There are a few important things to remember about the practical application of making disciples: (1) discipleship happens at the local church, (2) church members, and not pastors, are the primary disciple-makers, and (3) even most experienced members are not familiar with how to mentor new members. In light of these realities, and Ellen White's counsel that church members need taught "how to begin," it becomes vitally important that tools and resources be provided to equip church members with a simple process and clear direction for the discipleship of new members. This is the purpose of the *Discipleship Handbook.*

HOW TO USE THE *DISCIPLESHIP HANDBOOK*

It is important to make the distinction that the *Discipleship Handbook* is not merely a book about discipleship. Rather, it is a local church discipleship tool that can be used in the discipleship process of every newly baptized church member. When considering the five phases of the disciple-making process (prepare, plant, cultivate, harvest, preserve), the *Discipleship Handbook* fits in the final phase—the nurture and training of new members for preserving the harvest. The book contains 26 chapters, which correlate to 26 weekly meetings (six months) between mentors and new members.

To begin, local church leaders should read through Appendix A, "The Discipleship Plan," to understand how to implement a simple discipleship plan for new members. They should then give a copy of the book to as many members as possible, asking them to read and familiarize themselves with the book in preparation for using it to mentor newly baptized church members. Because every member is to engage in the work of making disciples, every member should be preparing for a time in the future when they will serve as a local church discipleship mentor for someone newly baptized. Alternatively, only a small group of experienced members already willing to serve as mentors could be asked to read the book to familiarize themselves with the new member discipleship process.

The process for using the *Discipleship Handbook* is straightforward and simple. When new members are baptized, each one is paired with a more experienced member called a mentor. Both new members and mentors are given a *Discipleship Handbook* if they don't already have one. Beginning immediately after baptism, mentors and new members meet weekly to review one chapter of the *Discipleship Handbook* together. This may be done individually or in a small group. It may be ideal to meet before prayer meeting or after church, thus merely adding an hour to a day when the mentor and new member already plan to be in the same place. In Appendix A, "The Discipleship Plan," one-page meeting outlines are provided to guide the mentor in what to do during the weekly meetings. These outlines include discussion questions for the chapter being read that week. More important than this, however, are the activity ideas given to mentors to integrate the new members into the life and mission of the church. Activities such as introducing new members to members they haven't yet met, arranging for Sabbath lunch and fellowship with other members, inviting new members to experience family sundown worship, taking new members on outreach activities, and many other recommended activities are suggested in the weekly outlines. These activities, or similar substitutes, are essential for training new members and for integrating them into the life of the church.

In the second weekly meeting, which focuses on the topic of the Bible in the devotional life, the new member is encouraged to begin using the Bible and Spirit of Prophecy reading plan found in Appendix B of the *Discipleship Handbook.* This reading plan consists of daily readings of 15 to 20 minutes per day. As the new members are guided to a Bible passage to read during their daily devotional time, they are also asked to read a correlated passage in the writings of Ellen White. Each week, when mentors and new members meet, they are encouraged in the weekly outlines to begin their meeting by sharing one insight gained from their devotional time that week. By doing this, support and accountability are provided to help nurture the daily devotional habit in the new member. Of course, in order for the new member to follow the reading plan, the mentor will need to provide the necessary Ellen White books, or point them to free access versions on apps or websites.

It is important that the local church personal ministries leader, or someone appointed as a discipleship ministry leader, provide active oversight of the new member discipleship process. Biweekly or monthly mentor meetings are one way to do this. Alternatively, the discipleship ministry leader may make personal contact every few weeks with each mentor. The reason this support and accountability is so important is that it is often the case that new member discipleship breaks down because the mentors are not fully committed. They may allow difficulties in schedules or distractions in their lives to prevent them from gaining any momentum with weekly meetings. If the meetings between mentors and new members don't happen weekly, it greatly reduces the quality of the disciple-making.

Over the course of the six-month process, mentors and new members will study many important topics. The 26 chapters in the *Discipleship Handbook* cover discipleship, the Bible, the Spirit of Prophecy, personal prayer, character development, family worship, Adventist mission and identity, personal witnessing, church attendance, church ordinances, church organization, Adventist history, Adventist ministries, lifestyle, Sabbath observance, reverence, stewardship, health, modesty, entertainment, marriage and family, the evangelism cycle, preparing the soil of the heart, planting the seed of truth, cultivating spiritual interests, and harvesting and preserving decisions for Christ with ongoing discipleship.

FOUNDATION PRINCIPLES
AND THE *DISCIPLESHIP HANDBOOK*

We began this article with certain foundation principles of disciple-ship, the first being that disciple-making is a process that follows the growth cycle. This is reflected in the *Discipleship Handbook* in various ways: (1) the last five chapters provide instruction in the evangelism cycle and all five phases of disciple-making, (2) the weekly outlines encourage the mentor to engage in several hands-on soul-winning activ-ities with the new member, and (3) at the conclusion of the book, the new member is encouraged to use the book in the future to mentor someone even newer to the faith.

The second principle was that the instruments of discipleship are people. This is reflected in the discipleship plan outlined in the *Discipleship Handbook* by the pairing of each new member with a more experienced mentor. This vital relationship is built by incorporating weekly meetings as well as activities they experience together outside the meetings. In addition to the relationship between the new member and the mentor, there is also an intentional effort to connect the new member to both the worldwide church (e.g., history, organization, ordi-nances, etc.) and the local congregation (e.g., meeting attendance, social life, mission, etc.).

The third principle was that the goal of discipleship is Christlikeness. This principle can be seen in the *Discipleship Handbook* in various ways. The very first chapter, "To Be Like Jesus," establishes this as the goal of discipleship. The fifth chapter, "By Beholding," focuses on becoming like Jesus by beholding Him in prayer and the reading of His Word. Various aspects of practical, Christlike living are also reflected in the Christian lifestyle chapters.

Fourth and last is the principle that the power of discipleship is from God. This principle is applied from the outset of the *Discipleship Handbook,* with an introduction in the first chapter to the eight spiritual "power" habits of consistent prayer, Bible study, family worship, Sabbath School attendance, church attendance, prayer meeting or small group attendance, personal witnessing, and involvement in church ministries. Several chapters are dedicated to giving practical guidance and strong encouragement to developing these spiritual habits. The Bible and Spirit of Prophecy reading plan is also introduced to equip new members with a simple plan that can help them discover the power of a consistent devotional life.

CONCLUSION

Whether you utilize the *Discipleship Handbook* or something similar, waste no time in employing an intentional and systematic plan to disciple every new member in your church or territory. With the four discipleship principles outlined in this chapter as your foundation, aim to develop every member into a loving, self-denying, soul winner—like Jesus. By doing this, you will not be limited to the plan of addition, but will experience the abundant joy of the plan of multiplication. "One soul, won to the truth, will be instrumental in winning others, and there will be an ever-increasing result of blessing and salvation."[11]

JAMES HOWARD

Jim Howard is associate director of the General Conference Sabbath School and Personal Ministries Department. His 17 years in pastoral and administrative ministry were preceded by a 12-year career in corporate accounting. He is married to Sonya, his wife of 24 years, and has two daughters—Kayla, 22, and Lindsey, 19. Throughout Howard's ministry of preaching, teaching, training, and developing resources for soul winning and discipleship, his burden has been to lead every member to a closer walk with Jesus through communion with God, fellowship with the church, and active involvement in both personal and public outreach.

ENDNOTES

1 Bible texts in this chapter are from the New King James Version.
2 Ellen G. White, *Evangelism* (Washington, D.C.: Review and Herald Pub. Assn., 1946), p. 355.
3 Ellen G. White, *Christ's Object Lessons* (Washington, D.C.: Review and Herald Pub. Assn., 1900, 1941), p. 354.
4 Ellen G. White, *Christian Service* (Washington, D.C.: Review and Herald Pub. Assn., 1925), p. 69
5 E. G. White, *Evangelism*, p. 356
6 E. G. White, *Christian Service*, p. 59.
7 Ellen G. White, *Prayer* (Nampa, Idaho: Pacific Press Pub. Assn., 2002), p. 84.
8 Ellen G. White, *The Great Controversy* (Mountain View, Calif.: Pacific Press Pub. Assn., 1911), p. 519.
9 The resources mentioned are currently available with the exception of the *Bible Study Handbook*, which is currently planned to be published by the end of 2021.
10 Ellen G. White, *Maranatha* (Washington, D.C.: Review and Herald Pub. Assn., 1976), p. 99.
11 E. G. White, *Christian Service*, p. 59.

Membership or Discipleship

What You Aim for is What You Get

LEIGH RICE, D.Min & GLENN TOWNEND

PREMISE

1. If we aim to make disciples, we will have disciples, but if we aim to make believers, we may not have disciples.
2. The evangelism approach we use will determine whether we make disciples or believers.

INTRODUCTION

After Jesus healed the blind man in Mark 8, he told him to "not return" to the village but go directly home. Jesus did not use the opportunity to attract the crowded village to himself. The disciples then declare him to be Messiah, but "he sternly ordered them not to tell anyone about him" (Mark 8:30, NRSV). Why? This presentation provides an opportunity to reflect on Jesus' approach to making disciples.

GUIDING PRINCIPLES

Guiding Principle 1—The Goal and the Process
Determine the Outcome

Jesus' aim was to make disciples and not just believers. His approach was to work with a small group intensely. He modeled life and disciple-making to this small group. He taught the ways of God and faith. He corrected their failings and pointed them toward holiness. He instructed them in the processes of disciple-making. He asked questions to challenge their faulty thinking. Yes, He often talked to crowds, but He knew that on Sunday they could believe in Him as king and on Friday believe that He needed to be crucified.

If we focus on telling people about Jesus and His message and life in crowds, we end up with believers. If we focus on Jesus' model of self-discovery and doing things in small groups, we end up with disciples. In the South Pacific Division we are committed to following Jesus' method to make disciples in relational groups focusing on self-discovery.

Guiding Principle 2—Disciple-making Is a Process, Not an Event

Discipleship is a lifelong journey. There may be significant events along the way, but unless discipleship is seen as a process and not an event, we will fail to make disciples who are "faithful to the end." The first awakening to the reality and presence of God, the first contact with a Christian person, saying yes to Jesus as Savior and Lord, and sharing the gospel with a friend are all significant events. Being mentored in good spiritual habits, developing the life of a steward, being trained in sharing faith, also form part of the discipleship journey.

Guiding Principle 3—Disciple-making Is Everyone's Responsibility

The Great Commission (Matthew 28:16-20) was given to the original 11 disciples, but its scope is global, embracing the entire globe and for all time. Paul teaches that leaders are to train all for the work of ministry (Ephesians 4:12), and Peter affirms that we are a royal priesthood (1 Peter 2:9).

Guiding Principle 4—Relationships Are Key

The union Sabbath School and personal ministries director who guided my (Leigh) early ministry used to say, "We don't make strangers disciples. We make strangers friends and introduce our friends to Jesus." Relationships are key to disciple-making.

Guiding Principle 5—Relationships and Involvement Ensure Retention

At the center of the church's focus on friendship evangelism in the 1980s was research that indicated that the number of friends within the congregation was predictive of whether new converts stayed in the church or not. Almost all new members with no or one friend in the congregation left. Almost all new members with 10 friends in the church stayed. Making disciples using strong relational connections will address much of the retention problem.

Guiding Principle 6—New Disciples Do Better in New Churches

The longer a church has existed, the harder it is for new believers to integrate into the congregation. Conversely, new disciples do better in new groups. As Jesus said: "You do not put new wine into old wineskins" (see Matthew 9:17). Since networks in new groups are less established, it is easier for new disciples to connect and become involved in the life of the congregation. Ministry opportunities are available for new as well as established believers. Experience confirms that involvement is important in nurture and retention.

SOUTH PACIFIC DIVISION (SPD) PROCESS

A Compelling Vision

The SPD has defined a clear and compelling vision for the church. The vision is *A thriving Adventist movement living our hope in Jesus and transforming the Pacific.* By Adventist movement SPD means a disciple-making church-planting movement reflecting the growth of the early Adventist Church. This vision is driven by the command of Jesus in the Great Commission: "I have been given all authority in heaven and on earth. Therefore, go and **make disciples** of all the nations, baptizing them in the name of the Father and the Son and the Holy Spirit. Teach these new disciples to obey all the commands I have given you. And be sure of this: I am with you always, even to the end of the age" (Matthew 28:16-20, NLT).

We have defined what a disciple is, so the church in SPD knows exactly what we are seeking in our discipleship process. *A disciple is a person who in every way is becoming more like Jesus Christ.* This definition grows out of Ephesians 4:15.

In line with the General Conference we have *Our Mission: Make disciples of Jesus Christ who live as His loving witnesses and proclaim to all people the everlasting gospel of the three angels' messages in preparation for His soon return* (Matthew 28:18-20; Acts 1:8; Revelation 14:6-12) as our mission statement.

Align Structure and Finance With Vision

The SPD executive has been intentional in aligning structure and finances to the vision of creating a disciple-making church-planting movement. Historically about 3 percent of the SPD budget was for strategic purposes focusing on disciple-making; since 2015, 20 percent of the budget funds disciple-making strategy. The discipleship ministries team was created at the same time to bring into one unit all the ministries whose primary focus would impact the local congregation, as each ministry of the local church is intended to be a part of a unified disciple-making strategy. So the SPD process is: maximizing *health and media ministries with a focus on disciple-making in the big cities by aligning finances and other church activities to making better and more disciples.*

Membership Versus Discipleship

SPD has been intentional on prioritizing discipleship over membership. Disciples will be members, but members may not be disciples. In the stories of Andrew and Phillip in John 1 and the Samaritan woman in John 4 we find two characteristics of disciples. They have met Jesus and have a story to tell, and they invite others to "come and see" Jesus.

In a presentation to the General Conference leaders meeting in the Caribbean in February 2019, the president of the West Africa Division contrasted member and disciple. Some of these contrasts follow.

MEMBER	DISCIPLE
Has head knowledge	Has heart knowledge
Depends on the pastor	Involved in ministry
Likes to be complimented	Is a living sacrifice
Gives a portion of his finances	Gives her life
Gives prayer requests	Prays for others
Influenced by the world	Transforms the world
Wants to be in heaven	Works for others

The experience in many parts of SPD has convinced leadership that the focus needs to be on disciples rather than members. They say that large-scale public evangelistic programs contribute little to making disciples and fail in making members who stay.

The Central Papuan Conference president describes these large events as "backslider factories," and the Port Moresby elders have decided that there will be no more big events in the city. When hosting evangelists in the city these days, the evangelist will preach in one church, and the meeting is livestreamed to other churches in the city. This approach gives the local church greater involvement in the process and the ability to nurture the new contacts and integrate them into the ministry of the local congregation. These elders reflected that they could identify only a few hundred of the many thousands who have been baptized in these large campaigns during the past 10 years. However, in recent public evangelistic programs that are streamlined to different venues, each venue can care for the five, 12, or 43 new members. The church people know the newly baptized and can relationally disciple them. When adding the number of baptisms in each venue, the number of new converts is similar to previous mass baptisms, but the retention is greater.

The Trans Pacific Union Mission president is not inviting visiting evangelists from outside the SPD into the TPUM because it inhibits the union in equipping local elders, women, and youth to lead small public evangelism programs throughout their territory. They want to build the local church leadership in the evangelism process of disciple-making.

CLEAR FRAMES TO GUIDE THE DISCIPLE-MAKING PROCESS

A number of clear frames have been developed so members can understand and easily remember the process for making disciples and multiplying churches.

Clear Frames—Farming Cycle (Mark 4:1-9, 26-29)

The dominant frame is the farming cycle, which grows out of Jesus' parables in Mark 4. It clearly shows that disciple-making is a process that results in multiplication "30, 60, even 100 times." No multiplication will occur without practicing the process of preparing, sowing, cultivating, harvesting, and multiplying. This frame enables both churches and individuals to plan for and assess the integrity of their disciple-making process. Unless there is preparation and sowing, there will be little harvesting of new disciples into the kingdom of God.

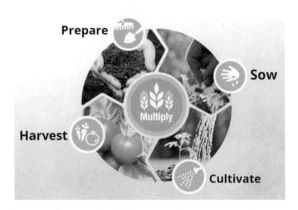

Churches and individuals can populate the five steps of the process with activities that are appropriate in their local church context or with the people in their relational streams.

In Jesus' second farming parable (Mark 4:26-29) He emphasis the power of the Word and the work of the Holy Spirit in the process of making disciples, and the role of the church in gathering new believers into kingdom groups. The farmer plants the seed, but it grows "all by itself" (verse 28, NIV). The challenge of the disciple-maker is to share the story of Jesus into people's lives in such a way that it can grow "all by itself" whether the disciple-maker is present or not. Discovery Bible Reading is one tool that enables this "all by itself" principle.

Clear Frames—Five Invitations of Jesus

Jesus modeled disciple-making. We notice that He invited people to become His disciples through a series of questions that led them into a deepening experience and commitment—*becoming more like Jesus in every way*. To Andrew and Philip He said, "Come and see" (John 1:39, NKJV). The next day He invited Philip to "follow Me" (verse 43, NKJV). Philip went to find Nathanael, and invited him to come. Some 18 to 20 months later Jesus invited Peter and Andrew, and James and John, to "fish with Me" (see Matthew 4:19). Jesus then took them on a fishing journey and modeled to them disciple-making. His fourth invitation is found in a series of challenging invitations in the Sermon on the Mount. Love your enemies, turn the other cheek, and other commands that called these followers to "sacrifice with me." His final invitation, "receive the Spirit," is in Acts 1:8.

These five invitations guide the journey of each disciple and also gives insights to disciple-makers. As one ascertains where a person is on their journey, the disciple-maker will know which is the appropriate invitation to extend to the person to move them along in the disciple-making process.

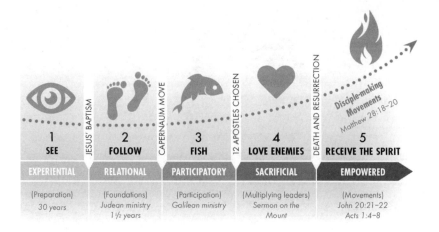

1		2		3		4		5
SEE	JESUS' BAPTISM	FOLLOW	CAPERNAUM MOVE	FISH	12 APOSTLES CHOSEN	LOVE ENEMIES	DEATH AND RESURRECTION	RECEIVE THE SPIRIT
EXPERIENTIAL		RELATIONAL		PARTICIPATORY		SACRIFICIAL		EMPOWERED
(Preparation)		(Foundations)		(Participation)		(Multiplying leaders)		(Movements)
30 years		Judean ministry 1½ years		Galilean ministry		Sermon on the Mount		John 20:21–22 Acts 1:4–8

Clear Frames—Luke 10:1-9

In Luke 10 we see Jesus multiplying leadership as he sends out the 70/72 on their disciple-making trip. Principles of prayer, working in teams, having relational skills, identifying places and finding the person of peace are apparent. As he sends them out he says, "Eat their food, heal their sick and tell them the Kingdom of God is near you" (Luke 10:9). Eating their food allows the disciple-maker to hear the story of the person. They discover the pain and sickness in their life and can offer healing. The healing process will be both practical and spiritual. Sharing your story of how God has healed you will be a part of this healing. As the Spirit prepares their heart, there will be opportunity to share God's story, that Jesus is the Christ who died and rose again and to invite them into the kingdom of God through repentance, belief, and following Jesus.

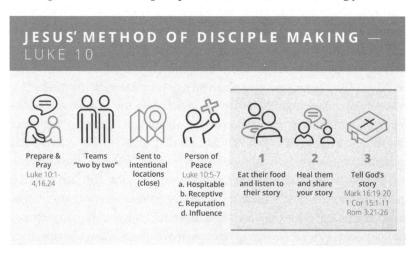

JESUS' METHOD OF DISCIPLE MAKING — LUKE 10

Prepare & Pray	Teams "two by two"	Sent to intentional locations (close)	Person of Peace	1	2	3
Luke 10:1-4,16,24			Luke 10:5-7 a. Hospitable b. Receptive c. Reputation d. Influence	Eat their food and listen to their story	Heal them and share your story	Tell God's story Mark 16:19-20 1 Cor 15:1-11 Rom 3:21-26

Clear Frames—Revelation 14:6-13

Revelation 14:6-13 is not only our message but gives us insights into the methods we should use in sharing the story of scripture. Since the messages of the three angels are to go "to every nation, tribe, language, and people" (verse 6, NIV), disciple-makers must take into consideration the *context* of the people. The first angel flies with the *eternal gospel,* so the stories of Jesus and the message of the gospel must be shared first. Notice Ellen White's words: "In order to be rightly understood and appreciated, every truth in the Word of God . . . must be studied in the light that streams from Calvary."[1] "There should not a sermon given unless a portion of that discourse is to especially make plain the way that sinners may come to Christ and be saved."[2]

The call of the angel is to "fear God" and "give Him glory." This is *practical Christian living.* Ellen White writes, "Speak to them, as you have opportunity, upon points of doctrine on which you can agree. Dwell on the necessity of practical godliness. Give them evidence that you are a Christian, desiring peace, and that you love their souls. Let them see that you are conscientious. Thus you will gain their confidence; and there will be time enough for doctrines."[3]

The first angel introduces *Adventist distinctives,* with a call to worship God as Creator because the hour of His judgment has come. Here we see Creation, the Sabbath, and Christ's heavenly ministry taught. Ellen White's instruction mirrors this process. "But while we have many things to say, we may be compelled to withhold some of them for a time, because the people are not prepared to receive them now."[4] "You should not feel it your duty to introduce arguments upon the Sabbath question as you meet the people. If persons mention the subject, tell them that this is not your burden now. But when they surrender heart and mind and will to God, they are then prepared candidly to weigh the evidence in regard to these solemn, testing truths."[5]

The second and third angels introduce the major prophetic themes. Once again, Ellen White is instructive. "[Brother ———] is in some per-plexity. . . . He wished to know how to present the truth in entering new fields. . . . I told him that the best and wisest plan would be to dwell upon subjects that would arouse the conscience. He could talk to them upon practical godliness; devotion and piety; and present the self-denial, self-sacrificing life of Jesus as our example until they will see the contrast in their self-indulgent life, and become dissatisfied with their unchris-tian lives. Then present to them the prophecies."[6] She also cautions about what we say about the Roman power and the Papacy.[7]

Our reflection on the three angels continues into verse 13, where the *multiplication* stage appears. Before moving on from the three angels, a voice from heaven calls them blessed, "for their good deeds follow them."

This frame enables disciple-makers to know when and how to introduce a new person to the teachings of Scripture. You do not give a stage 5 answer to a person who is not yet in stage 2. So when a person asks, "What is this about the antichrist and the mark of the beast?" (a stage 5 question), but they are not yet following Jesus (stage 2), you could respond, "I would love to tell you about the antichrist, but before you can understand the antichrist you need to know the Christ." You could then invite them on a Discovery Bible Reading journey to become a follower of Jesus. So Revelation 14:6-13 is both our message and our method.

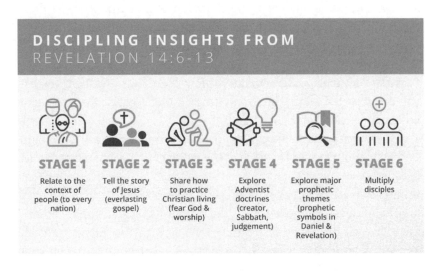

DISCIPLING INSIGHTS FROM REVELATION 14:6-13

STAGE 1	STAGE 2	STAGE 3	STAGE 4	STAGE 5	STAGE 6
Relate to the context of people (to every nation)	Tell the story of Jesus (everlasting gospel)	Share how to practice Christian living (fear God & worship)	Explore Adventist doctrines (creator, Sabbath, judgement)	Explore major prophetic themes (prophetic symbols in Daniel & Revelation)	Multiply disciples

SIMPLE, REPRODUCIBLE, ANYONE-CAN-DO SKILLS AND AT NO COST

Central to mobilizing large numbers of church members to become disciple-makers and church planters is to re-create in the minds of pastors and church leaders that their primary role is to equip God's people "for the work of ministry" (Ephesians 4:12, NKJV). Such simple skills as Discovery Bible Reading, sharing your testimony, and presenting the gospel enable many members, including new disciples, to become disciple-makers. The New Testament records the rapid multiplication of church plants led by natural leaders immediately after becoming converts to Christianity. These natural leaders were often coached by Paul's associates, and instructed and encouraged by Paul's letters and occasional visits.

Discovery Bible Reading

Discovery Bible Reading is a simple, reproducible, anyone-can-do skill that can be used by large numbers of members and at no cost. Members invite friends, neighbors, work colleagues, and fellow students to Discovery Bible Reading groups. These can happen in homes, workplaces, in cafés and parks. They can happen anywhere. See the story of Nathan in Port Moresby, Papua New Guinea, at https://vimeo.com/258195171 and Leighton at the Central Coast Adventist School in Australia at https://vimeo.com/274600460. Discovery Bible Reading grows out of the belief that the Word of God is "quick, and powerful, and sharper than a twoedged sword" (Hebrews 4:12, KJV) and that "where two or three are gathered" in the name of Jesus (Matthew 18:20, NKJV), the Spirit is there to guide.

We encourage groups to start with the Gospel of Mark. It is short and gets straight into the stories of Jesus and His ministry. Groups start at the beginning and read one story at a time. One person reads the story once, a second person reads the story through again, and a third person summarizes the story in their own words.

Then the group discusses the story using five questions: 1. What is new? 2. What surprises you? 3. What don't you understand? 4. What will you obey or apply? and 5. What will you share with someone this week? Leaders of the group do not need to be experts. For those parts of the story that people don't understand, we encourage a simple response, such as "Let's keep reading. I sure we will find the answer as we read more of the stories of Jesus." The group arranges the time to meet again where they will share how they went at applying the teaching to their own lives and what happened when they shared with another person. The process has new believers following a discipleship process of applying Scripture to their lives and sharing it with someone else. These Discovery Bible Reading groups (called Branch Sabbath Schools in some territories of SPD) become the basis of new church plants.

Member-led House Churches

One of the features of movements is believers gathering in natural, affordable (or at little or no cost) venues. The cost of land and building in many places restricts the rapid expansion of church plants. An expectation that a congregation will have its own pastor or at most shared with one other is not sustainable if we are expecting a rapid multiplication of churches. Lounge rooms, garages, school classrooms, parks, and cafés could all serve as places for new churches to meet. This is the pattern in the New Testament. See Nathan's experience in Port Moresby,

PNG (https://vimeo.com/258195171) and Simelli and Josephine's experience in Lautoka, Fiji (https://vimeo.com/257057066). Other resources are found at https://vimeo.com/spddiscipleship and http://discipleship.adventistchurch.com/resources/.

These experiences have been repeated among young adults in South Queensland and in youth groups in Sydney, Australia. It confirms that these simple reproducible skills work across cultures, in both developed and developing countries and in city and rural settings.

Vanuatu Experience

Perhaps the best example of all of these principles coming together is in the Vanuatu Mission.

In preparation for a citywide public evangelistic program in Port Vila, Efate, Vanuatu, two churches committed to prayer-walk for a whole year around Fresh Water Oval, the proposed venue. One church prayer walked around the oval on a Wednesday lunchtime and the other at opening Sabbath time. When the program started in September 2014, thousands came to hear Jean Noel Adeline, the public evangelist, and Dr. Chester Kuma speak on health. By the end of the program, 12,000 were at the oval and others were connecting on Hope Channel TV and Hope Radio.

While the public programs ran in the evening, Adeline led in a prayer meeting at 5:00 a.m. in the Epauto church. More than 1,000 people participated, where they sang praises and prayed as if God were right there with them. A revival broke out. The leaders of those who had separated from the official church in the 1990s to form independent Sabbathkeeping churches came to the prayer meetings to criticize. However, they experienced the power of God and repented. They asked to rejoin the Seventh-day Adventist Church. God's grace enabled this to happen. Dozens of churches and thousands of people came back. In the final weekend of the program, 2,957 people were baptized. The church in Port Vila then focused on discipling all of these new members with discipleship workshops and giving them World Changer Bibles. Some learned how to start new groups and churches.

In March 2015 Cyclone Pam devastated Efate Island—everyone suffered loss. However, the Adventists were quick to respond by taking water, tarpaulins, food, clothes, and other necessities to people in need all over the island. Such practical ministry was the focus for the year. At the time, about a third of villages in Efate had a Seventh-day Adventist presence. Today every village has an Adventist presence. The revival led to ongoing church growth and personal discipleship.

On Friday, November 2, I had the privilege of opening the largest building in Vanuatu, with Maveni Kaufononga, the TPUM president, and Nos Terry, the Vanuatu Mission president. The new Epauto Adventist Multipurpose Centre in Port Vila seats about 5,000 people. On Sabbath morning it was filled beyond capacity. God is certainly creating a thriving Adventist discipleship movement in Vanuatu.

CONCLUDING REFLECTIONS

The approach that the SPD has been taking has a strong philosophical foundation. A focus on disciple-making to fulfill the gospel commission. Clearly aligned vision, structure, and finances. Redefining the role of pastors and church leaders as equippers of the church for ministry. Training large numbers of members with simple reproducible skills, such as Discovery Bible Reading and gospel presentations. Starting small member-led churches for new disciples.

Anecdotal evidence says that it is working. The task ahead for the SPD is to evaluate the process with more rigorous analytical research, which is planned as part of the 2019-2020 initiatives.

LEIGH RICE, D.Min.

Leigh Rice is the discipleship ministry team leader for the South Pacific Division. Leigh is a pastor at heart, who has served in both departmental and administrative roles. An Australian by birth, he has spent more than half of his 44 years of ministry abroad. Leigh is married to Barb, a daughter of missionary parents. They have a son, a daughter, and nine grandchildren. Leigh Rice holds a Doctor of Ministry degree from Andrews University.

GLENN TOWNEND

Glenn Townend is the president of the South Pacific Division. He is an experienced local church pastor, departmental director, and administrator —all in the SPD. His wife of 33 years, Pamela, and he have three married children and four grandchildren.

ENDNOTES

1 Ellen G. White, *Evangelism* (Washington, D.C.: Review and Herald Pub. Assn., 1946), p. 190.
2 *Ibid.*, p. 188.
3 Ellen G. White, *Gospel Workers* (Washington, D.C.: Review and Herald Pub. Assn., 1915), p. 120.
4 E. G. White, *Evangelism*, p. 200.
5 *Ibid.*, p. 228.
6 *Ibid.*, p. 226.
7 *Ibid.*, p. 577.

SigaMe (Follow Me)

An Experience in Creating
a Culture of Discipleship

KLEBER D. GONÇALVES, Ph.D.

INTRODUCTION

"Follow Me, and I will make you fishers of men" (Matthew 4:19, NKJV).

By the Sea of Galilee Jesus Christ offered to two brothers a new path for their lives. Peter and Andrew were invited into a life-transforming experience that would take them from a humble lifestyle as basically unknown fishermen to becoming the very first disciples of the One who called Himself the Son of God. On that day a new and extraordinary process began. Jesus then established the pattern for the first 12 disciples that was later accepted for all who would embrace His passionate invitation: "Follow Me."

The reality found in many Christian churches, however, is a remarkably different approach from what Jesus Christ experienced with His initial disciples. In today's reality, typically after a short cognitive "teaching" based on doctrinal and denominational instruction, the prospective "member" is then invited to join the church through baptism with the assumption that the new believer will spontaneously become a committed and devoted disciple. Unfortunately, a purposeful and experiential discipleship process, such as the one modeled by Christ with the first disciples, is generally overlooked. Most Christian communities miss the "in-depth, extensive orientation to being a 'student of Christ' in order to be a well-prepared, inspired 'follower of Christ.' "[1] It should not surprise us that the direct consequence is the sad reality of nonfunctional church members, who tend to become mere consumers of "religious goods," usually during a few hours in just one day of the week, within the four walls of a church building. In other words, very few committed, fully devoted followers of the Master can be found in the disciple-making mandate found in the Scriptures.

We don't need to be rocket scientists to notice that "something is missing" in many of our churches. There seems to be a disruption between membership and active involvement in ministry. After all, how to develop a significant, active, relevant life as real disciples following the footsteps left by the Master? Besides, if we accept that Christ has already given us an effective and meaningful discipleship model to follow, why not embrace it and fully benefit from its original purpose? How can disciple-making be a transformational and intentional process in every church, focusing every member and permeating every ministry? "Should not disciple-making be the primary goal of the church evangelistic efforts, instead of generally focusing on numerical growth?"[2]

With the above issues in mind, this chapter will first look at the historical roots of the master-disciple relationship, then explore the biblical/theological basis for discipleship with selected passages from the New Testament, and finally introduce the *SigaMe* (FollowMe) Forum as a case study in developing a culture of discipleship at the local church level.

DISCIPLESHIP: A HISTORICAL JOURNEY[3]

All of us would agree that from the earliest days of life on earth, the more skilled have taught the less experienced. This was the way knowledge, abilities, competences, and character were passed through the generations. This concept is clearly seen in the Bible. A significant example is the connection between Paul and Timothy. Timothy was quite young and inexperienced when he first met his mentor. Paul, in turn, openly instructed Timothy how to proceed: "What you heard from me, keep as the pattern of sound teaching, with faith and love in Christ Jesus. Guard the good deposit that was entrusted to you—guard it with the help of the Holy Spirit who lives in us." "And the things you have heard me say in the presence of many witnesses entrust to reliable people who will also be qualified to teach others" (2 Timothy 1:13, 14, NIV; 2:2, NIV). The instruction was clear: Timothy should keep Paul's teachings to himself but also intentionally pass on to others what he had learned from his mentor.

This was just an example of how, throughout history, mentors or spiritual guides have helped others maintain spiritual focus and keep a godly life. These relationships involved nurture, skills training, obedience, and intentional search for wisdom.[4] Even though this process is found in most ancient civilizations, the concept of discipleship in the Greco-Roman and in the first-century Jewish cultures is important as a background to better understanding its use, especially in the New Testament period.

DISCIPLESHIP IN THE GRECO-ROMAN CULTURE

Greece is commonly recognized as the birthplace of Western civilization, and in many aspects discipleship was part of the Greek life. The Greek word μαθητής (*mathētēs*) was used by Herodotus, Plato, and Socrates centuries before Jesus.[5] The term appears frequently in classical Greek literature with three main meanings:[6]

Learner/trainee: the earliest use of *mathētēs* referred to a person who was a learner in different fields, such as dancing, wrestling, music, astronomy, and so on. Therefore, the "learner" was acquiring knowledge or skill from an expert to a particular activity.

Pupil/apprentice: the term then progressed from learner to pupil, thus including the concept not just of learning but also of commitment to an individual teacher. For instance, the disciples of Plato or Socrates were not just learning skills; they were also fervently devoted to their master. Therefore, discipleship during this period became more than just acquiring education.

Disciple/adherent: additionally, in a deeper level *mathētēs* also indicated a person who made a significant, personal, life commitment. After the practices were learned, they were to be demonstrated in practical ways. For instance, becoming a disciple of a particular culture now meant that one's lifestyle should reflect that culture. Taking into consideration the commitment involved, Wilkins notices: "The type of adherence was determined by the master, ranging from being the follower of a great thinker and master of the past like Socrates, to being the pupil of a philosopher like Pythagoras, to being the devotee of a religious master like Epicurus."[7]

In common use, however, a *mathētēs* was not a committed follower of a particular master. Direct interaction with a famous teacher, nevertheless, was not a precondition to follow his teachings. For instance, "one could follow the teachings of Socrates simply by adopting the way of life promoted by the person of Socrates as developed in the writings of Plato. A disciple could also conform their habits to a way of life that exemplified the virtues of a particular culture or city."[8] Toward the end of the Hellenic era the focus gradually shifted to the kind of relationship that demanded a devotion having the potential to affect the follower's life entirely. In the New Testament period, religious adherents were ultimately called disciples. Learning was minimised in these contexts, where the main focus was the religious devotion and imitation of the master's life and character. Imitation of the teacher's conduct became crucial. The emphasis increasingly moved from learning a basic skill to imitation of character and conduct.

DISCIPLESHIP IN THE FIRST-CENTURY JEWISH CULTURE

Similar to the meaning of "disciples" in the Greco-Roman classical era (up to the New Testament period) there were people called disciples in the Judaism of the first century. Such individuals were committed to well-known teachers or movements—independently of their philosophical schools, religious observances, and/or political preferences. Nevertheless, true Jews would call themselves disciples of Moses, regardless of sectarian commitments. Various subgroups had their own followers. For instance, the Pharisees and their disciples openly professed to be Moses' disciples (John 9:28, 29). They were the precursors of the later relationship between a disciple and a master that evolved into a formal system centered on the teaching of the Torah.

Prophets also had their disciples based not only on learning but also on righteousness and piety. John the Baptist had his own disciples who followed his teachings and practiced his austere lifestyle (Mark 2:18; Luke 11:1; John 3:25; Acts 19:1-7). Qumran also had social structures that could be described as master/disciple within their community.

In general terms, in first-century Judaism, boys were trained in community, having the Torah as the central focus of their "home-schooling" learning process. Primarily the father had the responsibility to teach the Torah to his children. During Jesus' time evidences suggest that primary schools were established to diminish Hellenistic influences.[9] However, after 13 years of age boys would no longer receive this kind of formal training. If further education was desired, they had to become a disciple under the orientation of a recognized Torah scholar.[10] This was the proper way to master the Mosaic law, Jewish traditions, and the interpretations associated with them. For instance, Paul's experience was a perfect example of a young man who was sent to study the Torah under Gamaliel, a renowned Rabbi in Jerusalem, thus leaving behind his hometown, Tarsus of Cilicia, for that purpose (Acts 5:34; 22:3).

Especially among Jewish contexts of the first century there is clear evidence that one-to-one discipleship was a common practice. During that period it is possible to find several examples of discipleship as an experience of individuals fully committed to follow a prominent teacher, carrying on his teachings, and imitating his life.

A striking shift, however, in comparing the Greek with the first-century Jewish approach to discipleship is clearly perceptible. In the Hebrew context, *discipleship was much more than just a cognitive exchange, but included one's life experience—within the context of community, starting in the family and then with others.* In other words, it indicated not only the acceptance of the master's values and embracing his principles, but ultimately reproducing his ideas and beliefs in practical ways.

DISCIPLESHIP IN THE OLD TESTAMENT

The apparent lack of specific discipleship terminology is a remarkable aspect that stands out when we go to the Old Testament seeking to find the foundations of the discipling-making process. For instance, the Greek word *mathētēs* does not occur in the Septuagint.[11] (Rausch 2003:71). This fact, however, does not mean that the notion and practical aspects or different words are not found. On the contrary, two terms, *talmîdh* and *limmûdh*—although found together only seven times in the whole Old Testament—express the same concept.

The Terms "Disciple" in the Old Testament

Talmîdh is the Hebrew equivalent of *mathētēs*. Just as *mathētēs* (disciple, learner) comes from the verb *manthanō* (to learn), so *talmîdh* comes from the Hebrew verb *lāmadh* (to learn), meaning "the taught one."[12] *Talmîdh* as such is used only once in the Old Testament: "Young and old alike, teacher as well as student [*talmîdh*], cast lots for their duties" (1Chronicles 25:8, NIV). Wilkins points out that "within a classification of musicians, the noun indicates a pupil in contrast to a teacher (*mebhîn*), or a novice in contrast to a master. . . . Some have understood this to mean that a formal school existed in Jerusalem for the training of temple musicians."[13] The text of 1 Chronicles 25:8, therefore, should be seen and understood in the simplest way: a *talmîdh* is someone who is committed to the learning process or an apprentice learning a specific skill.

The adjective *limmûdh* (taught), in turn, occurs only six times in the Old Testament, in the books of Isaiah (8:16; 50:4 [twice]; 54:13) and Jeremiah (2:24; 13:23). This adjective also comes from the verb *lāmadh.* In Jeremiah it has the meaning of "accustomed to" something: "Can the Ethiopian change his skin or a leopard its spots? Neither can you do good who are *accustomed to* doing evil" (Jeremiah 13:23, NIV). Here it clearly points to the reality of someone who has been "discipled" or taught to do evil things.

In the book of the prophet Isaiah *limmûdh* means "taught" or "instructed."[14] The occurrences of *limmûdh* in Isaiah are important, especially because scholars have given to the adjective in these passages the connotation of "taught, as disciples," or "disciple, follower."[15] The text of Isaiah 8:16 declares: "Bind up this testimony of warning and seal up God's instruction among my disciples" (NIV). Here *limmûdh* indicates that a group of disciples were gathered around the prophet Isaiah, listening to the words of God through him. It may also imply that Isaiah personally trained these disciples who could then transmit the prophet's teachings to others. In other words, while Isaiah may not have had a formal school under his responsibility—such as in Elisha's case (1 Kings 20:35; 2 Kings 2:3-15; 4:1-38)—he nevertheless gathered a special group of men to share his teachings with them.

Furthermore, Isaiah 50:4, reads: "The Lord God has given Me the tongue of disciples, that I may know how to sustain the weary one with a word. He awakens Me morning by morning, He awakens My ear to listen as a disciple" (NASB).This text implies a familiar category of persons in Israel known as "disciples/taught ones," who were assumed to have the ability of speaking and attentive listening. Isaiah 54:13, in turn, records that the sons of Zion will be directly instructed by the Lord: "All your children will be taught by the Lord, and great will be their peace" (NIV). The context does not designate the content of the instruction, but the picture indicates those who will be characterized as "God-taught." This is the same as affirming that they have been committed disciples of God.[16]

It is critical to observe, however, that even tough direct discipleship terminology is very scarce in the Old Testament; discipleship relation-ships are unmistakably present. They include, for instance, the experiences of Moses-Joshua, Elijah-Elisha, Mordecai-Esther, Jeremiah-Baruch. Apparently these relationships were not intended to build the case for discipleship. They were in fact unique relationships to fulfill a special work of God in a given circumstance. Yet—perhaps unwittingly—individual master-disciple relationships enabled leadership functions to be passed from one leader to the next. Among the examples of disci-ple-master relationship in the Old Testament we can emphasize three groups: the prophets, the scribes, and the wise men.

The Prophets

The Old Testament indicates that some prophets had followers or disciples. As we have seen above, Isaiah mentions his disciples (Isaiah 8:16). Samuel had groups of "student prophets" around him (1 Samuel 10:5-10) and apparently he was a mentor to his pupils (1 Samuel 19:20-24). In this case the established disciple-master relationship had no connec-tion with a formal school structure but as a community of "prophets" recognizing Samuel as their spiritual mentor.

In a different role, Elijah mentored Elisha, and Elisha later led the "company of the prophets." With this special group Elisha also established his mentorship (cf. 1 Kings 20:35; 2 Kings 2:3, 5, 7, 15; 4:1, 38; 5:22; 6:1; 9:1). These prophets "were not prophets in training but were rather gathered around Elisha for guidance in performing their own prophetic activities . . . a master-disciple relationship in mutual commitment to service of God."[17] These men were evidently influenced and learned from Elisha's example and teachings.

Other prophets reveal a master-disciple interaction with monarchs. Hull writes, "Prophets also seemed to have a special relationship with kings: Isaiah with Hezekiah, Nathan with David, and Samuel with Saul. While not always pleasant for the kings, these odd relationships were often necessary for the spiritual direction of the kings."[18] Concomitantly, the direction the king took had direct consequences to the whole nation. Nevertheless, leaders of Israel were evaluated according to whether or not they were following God's instructions. Individual discipleship, therefore, became the basis for national discipleship, since all discipleship relationships were designed to lead individuals and Israel as a nation into a closer walk with the Lord.

The Scribes

In a similar way, the scribes also displayed features of the discipleship process. Taking into consideration the very nature of their profession, the scribes would obviously be involved in the student type of training into their daily and basic activities (e.g., reading, copying, and so on). Different abilities were also linked with the scribes. For instance, they got involved in political duties as counselors to members of the monarchy and also in their attempts to fulfill God's purposes through their services (cf. 2 Samuel 8:16-18; 20:23-25; 1 Kings 4:1-6).

For instance, after the Exile Ezra's responsibilities as scribe focused on the teaching of the law (Nehemiah 8:1), but such responsibility was also in evidence prior to the Exile (cf. Jeremiah 8:8, 9). Wilkins writes, "Much of the training for these various scribal responsibilities appears to have occurred within the family and clan, which would speak of disciple-master training in these skills being from father to son."[19] In all of these developments relationships centered in the discipleship processes were not only implied but also essential.

The Wise Men

The existence of a professional class of thinkers in the Old Testament

DISCIPLING, NURTURING, AND RECLAIMING

to carry on the development of wisdom literature has been a reality for centuries. The need of this occupation was seen crucial in at least three areas: wisdom was a world outlook, a teaching opportunity, and a tradition to be kept. If seen from this point of view, wisdom developments required master-disciple relationships, varying of course in form and function depending on the type of relationships.[20]

A wisdom school is often suggested as being behind this nationwide wisdom organization. Evidence of wisdom emphasis at the royal court gives some weight to this suggestion. But the nonexistence of a "wisdom school" suggests that the master-disciple association was more suitable to be found in family contexts, in elder-leader training, and among "wise men" who were authorities in the wisdom tradition.[21]

Even with the relative lack of discipleship terminology, the essence of the work done by the prophets, the scribes, and the wise men point out to the need of the master-disciple connection in the Old Testament experience. These relationships were crucial for the continuation of the discipleship process that would come in the New Testament period.

DISCIPLESHIP IN THE NEW TESTAMENT

As we have seen so far, discipleship experiences often demanded devotion to the instructions of an outstanding teacher or lessons carried on by a particular cultural context. In the New Testament, however, we find a broader understanding and application of discipleship.

The Greek word μαθητής and its variations appear 263 times in the New Testament: 235 times in the Gospels and 28 times in Acts.[22] The first disciples in the Gospels were actually followers of John the Baptist. The Gospel of John clearly points out that the Baptist recognized his role essentially as someone who would pave the way for the expected Messiah (John 1:23). When Jesus begins His public ministry, John immediately leads two of his disciples to Christ (verses 35-39). After this first encounter Jesus continued His work in gathering the 12 around Him. Gradually Jesus then becomes the great master in the Gospels.

As a direct result of this process, the first disciples of Jesus followed Him wherever He went. On these experiences they observed how Christ reacted in His daily relationships with the multitudes and also with the religious leaders of Israel. They also carefully paid attention to Jesus' teachings about these interactions and the issues involved.

The cultural understanding of discipleship in the Gospels, therefore, was clearly evident in those who would follow Him. Yet the distinction of Jesus' ministry from that of the religious leaders was also related to some cultural aspects. For instance, Jesus said: "The teachers of the law and the Pharisees sit in Moses' seat. So you must be careful to do everything they tell you. But do not do what they do, for they do not practice what they preach. They tie up heavy, cumbersome loads and put them on other people's shoulders, but they themselves are not willing to lift a finger to move them" (Matthew 23:2-4, NIV). Thus, to become a true disciple of Christ meant to intentionally follow Him, in words *and* actions.

In order to further understand this dimension of the Christian discipleship process, I now turn to three of the most important discipleship passages found in the teachings of the Master.

Make Disciples

> *"Then the eleven disciples went to Galilee, to the mountain where Jesus had told them to go. When they saw him, they worshiped him; but some doubted. Then Jesus came to them and said, 'All authority in heaven and on earth has been given to me. Therefore go and make disciples of all nations, baptizing them in the name of the Father and of the Son and of the Holy Spirit, and teaching them to obey everything I have commanded you.*
>
> *And surely I am with you always, to the very end of the age'"*
> (Matt 28:16-20, NIV).

This is the biblical mandate, commonly identified as the Great Commission, in which Jesus instructs His followers to move outward and make disciples, teaching them in faith, and initiating them into fellowship. The basic components of Matthew 28:16-20 can be seen as follows:

1. Jesus commands His disciples to go to Galilee to be with him (verses 16, 17)
2. Jesus comes to them declaring His authority and sovereignty (verse 18)
3. Jesus then commissions His disciples to a specific task (verses 19, 20)
   a. Making disciples is the primary focus of the commission.
   b. Going to everyone, baptizing, and sharing Jesus' teachings to the whole world are the characteristics of the discipleship process.
4. Jesus promises to be with His disciples until the end (verse 20)

DISCIPLING, NURTURING, AND RECLAIMING

The Background of Discipleship— Verse 16. The phrase "the eleven disciples" just confirms the tragic end of Judas' experience, followed by suicide (Matthew 27:5). In the attitude of the 11 of going where Jesus had told them, we see—one more time—one of the most important elements of a true discipleship experience: obedience. Looking at the geographical context, Jesus' ministry finishes where it had started: in Galilee (Matthew 4:15, 16). It sets the context to the fact that Jesus was about to communicate vital instructions to his disciples.

The Reality of Discipleship—Verse 17. When Jesus suddenly appears to His disciples, worship and doubt were expressed. But how was it possible? Are these reactions mutually exclusive, or could both be realities that happened at the same time within the disciples? Was there another group beyond the 11 at this mountaintop? These are some of the questions this passage brings. A first possibility is that the Gospel of Matthew presents the responses of two different groups among the 11 disciples. It means that among the 11 some worshipped Jesus, but some showed doubt.[23] A second possibility indicates that those who worship and those who doubt are, in fact, the same people. In this case the verb "doubted" might indicate uncertainty rather than disbelief.[24] The disciples' doubt is therefore not unbelief but another case of "little faith" (Matthew 14:31, NIV). This might also indicate that a disciple still faces situations with a certain level of tension. Somehow, faith cannot exist without the possibility of doubt.

The Basis of Discipleship—Verse 18. Jesus now affirms that "all authority" has been given to Him. However, before the upcoming commission of the subsequent verse, Jesus assures His disciples of His sovereign dominion over heaven and earth. Several scholars believe that this verse is at least an echo of Daniel 7:13, 14. Nolland affirms that this connection "is very likely, but it implies newly gained authority only if the allusion is not simply to the status of the one like a son of man/humanity, but to that status as having just been acquired."[25] A common understanding, nevertheless, is that a newly acquired authority came to Jesus after His death and resurrection. "It is the investiture of the risen Christ with such unrestricted, universal sovereignty, that Jesus now claims and which, especially within a few days, that is after his ascension to heaven, he is beginning to exercise. That is the reward upon his labors."[26] The term "all" is also a key word in the Great Commission, as it is used not only to describe the greatness of Jesus' authority—in heaven, over spiritual forces, on earth, and over His disciples[27]—but also to reveal distinctive dimensions that come three more times in the subsequent verses: "all the nations"; "to observe all"; "all the days" (verses 19, 20a, 20b, YLT).

The Goal of Discipleship—Verses 19, 20a. Literally the original says, "Having gone, therefore, make disciples . . ." The "therefore" gives to the commission its foundation on what has just been presented on the previous verse: Jesus' power, authority, and sovereignty. Here it is important to highlight that the only verb with imperative force in the Great Commission is "make disciples" (*matheteusate*). New Testament scholars point out to the fact that the participle "having gone" (*poreuthentes*) found in the beginning of the verse should be translated as "as you go." Jesus is here clearly directing His disciples to go to all the nations with a purpose: make disciples. This is indeed a mission passage. Jesus' disciples are always commanded to go. Making disciples is "the heart of the commissioning."[28] The remainder of the verse better defines what it means "to disciple": baptizing and teaching people from all ethnic groups around the world.

The Assurance of Discipleship—Verse 20b. Matthew begins his last sentence with one final emphatic emphasis, as if to say, "No one less than I Myself am with you." Thus, the Great Commission ends with Jesus' promise of continuous presence with His followers. As Hendriksen writes: "At the beginning, in the middle, and at the end of Matthew's Gospel, Jesus Christ assures the church of his constant and comforting presence."[29]

It becomes obvious that the Great Commission was intended beyond the first disciples gathered at that particular circumstance. Obviously the first disciples of Christ could not go to the whole world by themselves to fulfill the new given mission of making disciples. Therefore, the commission is universal in its scope since every true follower of Jesus Christ should be engaged in disciple-making. Furthermore, the message to be conveyed—the eternal gospel of Jesus Christ—is intended for the whole world, with no geographical or ethnical limits.

Love One Another

"A new command I give you: Love one another. As I have loved you, so you must love one another. By this everyone will know that you are my disciples, if you love one another" (John 13:34, 35, NIV).

This passage in John's Gospel belongs to the farewell speech Christ shared with His disciples. In the context of these verses (verses 31-38) Jesus confirms one more time His soon departure and predicts Peter's denial. In the middle of these two announcements Jesus intentionally gives to His disciples "a new commandment" (verse 34, NKJV). However, the command to love one's neighbor as oneself was not a new teaching to Jesus' disciples (Leviticus 19:18; cf. Proverbs 20:22; 24:29; Matthew 5:43, 44). Yet the new aspect was Jesus' command to love one another with a new dimension: "as I have loved you." In other words, the love is to be of the same nature.[30] Köstenberger writes, "This rule of self-sacrificial, self-giving, selfless love, a unique quality of love inspired by Jesus' own love for the disciples, [would] serve as the foundational ethic for the new messianic community."[31] This was the "new" feature of it.

Christ's love to humankind in giving up His life for everyone was completely new. Obviously, on one hand, the essence of Jesus' love for His followers cannot be reproduced by or in themselves. It was an act of love that makes their salvation a reality. On the other hand, every follower of Christ can follow His example. Thus, Jesus' disciples are to love one another: they should follow His example of sacrificial service to one another. Consequently, a new model and standard was established to the followers of Jesus Christ to obey. It is not, however, something transcending the great moral law, which is "the old commandment" (Exodus 20:3-17; 1 John 2:7; Mark 12:28-33), but that law should be lived in a new and peculiar way.[32]

Jesus continues saying in John 13:35, "by this all will know" (NKJV), referring to the main characteristic of those who decide to follow Him. Christ boldly and unashamedly points out to the ultimate mark of discipleship: *if* you *love* one another. Once again, the conjunction "if" is present, indicating that this attitude is a choice—a voluntary and deliberate decision to practice, in love, the example of the Master as a disciple.

Follow Me

> *"And He was saying to them all, 'If anyone wishes to come*
> *after Me, he must deny himself, and take up his cross*
> *daily and follow Me'"* (Luke 9:23, NASB).

There are many texts in which Jesus explains in greater detail and with other descriptions the true meaning of being His disciple, but the call to follow Him is the first and probably the most basic explanation. The heart of Christ's call is to be with Him (Mark 3:14) and to know Him intimately (cf. 1 Corinthians 1:9; Philippians 3:10). It is a dynamic process that indicates a voluntary movement toward Jesus.

The invitation "follow Me" is found in a number of references in the Gospels. It first appears in the calling of the first disciples (cf. Matthew 4:19; Mark 2:14; Luke 5:1-11; John 1:43). The pattern of the calling is well defined: (1) Jesus chooses the ones He would call; (2) He summons them; and (3) the response was immediate. The same pattern is repeatedly found in the Gospels.[33]

Among the "follow Me" calls of Jesus, Luke 9:23 undoubtedly better elucidates the cost involved in following the footsteps of the Master. Bock says: "The path of following Jesus, in light of where he is going, is hard. Jesus prepares the disciples for the journey, expressing it simply in terms of wishing 'to come after him.' This remark sets the context for interpreting what follows."[34]

In the passage, discipleship includes three crucial instructions: "deny oneself," "take up daily," and "follow Me." The sequence presented in the text indicates that out of the personal and essential decisions made about the self and the bearing of the cross on a daily basis comes a transformational process—the real experience of following Jesus. In other words, real discipleship demands transformation.

It is important to emphasize that Jesus starts His call with the conjunction "if." Using this conditional word, the Gospel of Luke makes it clear that Christ is not commanding anyone to do anything, but actually He is inviting His followers into a journey, a new way of life, an experience that will bring them everlasting fulfillment. In other words, Jesus' invitation is a choice one needs to make in order to follow Him.

The ultimate aspect of the invitation is "follow Me." In the New Testament this verb occurs primarily in the Gospels (79 out of 90 occurrences). It has two literal meanings: "follow" in the sense of "go behind" and "follow" in the sense of "making company." By metaphorical extension, it also means "be a disciple of," in the sense of adhering to the teaching or instructions of a master and promoting the cause of that master.[35] It is remarkable that this figurative meaning of "follow" is found only in the four Gospels and in Revelation 14:4, when the 144,000 follow the Lamb regardless of the cost.

In Luke 9:23, as noted above, one can obviously perceive some of the most pressing elements of discipleship: obedience, repentance, submission, and commitment.[36] As we look at these and other elements of discipleship, one question yet remains: What would happen if what Jesus intentionally did to 12 men more than 2,000 years ago could be done again today, in our churches? This is the purpose of the SigaMe Forum to which we now turn.

SigaMe: CREATING A CULTURE OF DISCIPLESHIP

The *SigaMe* (FollowMe) forum started while I was still pastoring the *IASD Nova Semente* (New Seed SDA Church) in São Paulo, Brazil.[37] The main goal? To create a culture of discipleship at the local church level, in our own church, and also to inspire and motivate similar actions with other pastors and church leaders. Is this possible? In reality, this is not a matter of possibility. It is an issue that involves responsibility and a calling: the responsibility to fulfill the command that Christ has left us: "Go and make disciples of all nations"; the call to live the real experience of love and to fully accept the invitation "Follow Me."

The *SigaMe* forum is a unique annual event that has happened at Nova Semente since 2014. The first edition was a two-day event. But in the subsequent years it became a daylong gathering, usually on a Sunday, where participants can better understand and above all share true experiences on following Jesus. During *SigaMe* participants are challenged to rediscover the meaning of the Master's invitation to each of His followers and how to best develop tools to make this a reality in their own lives.

During the event, essential elements[38] of the discipleship process are explored in different sessions in which, after a brief 25-minute reflection led by an expert and/or a practitioner on the topic, participants can have a unique relational discipleship experience in discussions, exchange of experiences, and spiritual interactivity in a small group setting comprised of six to eight people around a table specifically prepared for this purpose.

The open and enriching dialogue about discipleship generated through this intentional format has created a unique learning environment at *SigaMe*. One of the first lessons we have learned is that for those who are looking for ways to improve the discipleship experience in their own churches, they must first do a self-analysis and then consider how their personal discipleship understanding and practice needs to grow. We believe this has been one of the first steps in creating a culture of discipleship at the local church level.

Second, how can we encourage and motivate other people and churches to have a real discipleship experience if we as leaders have not yet lived that experience in our own lives? In other words, any real and life-transforming discipleship experience does start with each one of us. Before we can make a disciple, we truly need to become one. Attending and participating in the FollowMe forum has provided unique opportunities to establish a new vision and practice in that direction.

Third, we have also learned that an interactive relational discipleship experience has the potential to challenge, inspire, and transform the participants' perspective on what it means to be and make disciples for Jesus.

CONCLUSIONS

Historically speaking, we can essentially find two paths for discipleship. The early Greek understanding of discipleship was, to a great extent, to sit under a teacher/master to gain knowledge. In other words, discipleship was centered more on *intellectual understanding*, more of a cognitive exchange of ideas and/or philosophical, political, and religious convictions. First-century Jewish understanding and practices of discipleship, on the other hand, were centered more on *following* the rabbi/teacher, sitting at his feet not only to gain knowledge but also to learn how to do what he did, how to live as he lived. Basically, the first-century Jewish discipleship process was focused on how to become like the master. Jewish disciples were life learners of the Torah, where this process primarily occurred in the context of community.

As we have also seen, the lack of discipleship terminology in the Old Testament does not mean the absence of its concepts and practices. Although few words are used to describe the master-disciple relationship, several practical examples found in the Old Testament express the essence and extent of the discipleship process. However, the New Testament discipleship, especially in the Gospels, is centered on the dynamics of following Jesus, learning not only from His teachings but also from His own life examples. The New Testament *mathētēs* is more than just a "student" or "learner." A true disciple of Christ is a "follower," someone who completely obeys His instructions—in theory *and* practice—making His teachings the rule of life and conduct.

Comparing the discipleship elements found in the New Testament passages analyzed in this chapter—such as obedience, transformation, and love—with the current state of discipleship within in the Seventh-day Adventist Church, I tend to come to the conclusion that, unfortunately, the church, in general terms, still places considerable emphasis on the Western, Greek-based intellectual/cognitive aspect of discipleship. This emphasis is not entirely wrong, but it is not enough. Discipleship needs to have a deeper understanding and practice. In many parts of the world the "Christian life" of Seventh-day Adventists is limited to a couple of hours, on Sabbath morning, within the limits of four walls of a church building. Most of them are good church members, but unfortunately have never understood nor lived the life of a real disciple of Christ during the ordinary days of the week.

Discipleship does not happen overnight. Through the *SigaMe* initiative in creating a culture of discipleship I have learned that real discipleship takes intentionality and time. In spite of their importance, discipleship curricula, event-based training, and resources readily made available are not enough. Planning and implementation of a discipleship process at the local church level must take into consideration the one-on-one approach as well as a community-based structure as found in the biblical examples of discipleship. This new approach to discipleship could be made on a pilot-basis level and in different cultural contexts before it is mass-distributed to the world church.

Finally, the radical nature and cost of biblical discipleship involved in the call Jesus places before us is more than just intellectually accepting doctrinal instruction. If we are to operate up to our mission statement as it reads ("The mission of the Seventh-day Adventist Church is to call all people to become disciples of Jesus Christ, to proclaim the everlasting gospel embraced by the three angels' messages [Revelation 14:6-12], and to prepare the world for Christ's soon return"), we need more than numerical growth, we need more than church members: we need real disciples who have accepted in their minds and in their hearts the call: "Follow me, and I will make you fishers of men."

KLEBER D. GONÇALVES, Ph.D.

Kleber D. Gonçalves was born in Brazil and has served the Seventh-day Adventist Church in the areas of publishing work, pastoral ministry, church planting, and teaching. Kleber serves the world church at the General Conference as the director of the Global Mission Center for Secular and Postmodern Studies. He is married to Nereida C. Gonçalves, and they have three children: Isabella, Nichollas, and Gabriella.

ENDNOTES

1 Dan Kohn, *Discipleship in the Postmodern Age: One Disciple's Journey . . . and Yours* (Bloomington, Ind.: Xlibris, 2010), p.12.
2 Kleber D. Gonçalves, "Transforming Discipleship: Opportunities in Following the Master in a Postmodern World," *Journal of Adventist Mission Studies* 12, no. 2 (2016): 278.
3 I have originally published this subsection, with minor changes, in *ibid.*, pp. 278-281.
4 Bill Hull, *The Complete Book of Discipleship: On Being and Making Followers of Christ* (Colorado Springs, Colo.: NavPress, 2006), pp. 52, 53.
5 Michael J. Wilkins, *The Concept of Disciple in Matthew's Gospel: As Reflected in the Use of the Term* "Mathētēs," Novum Testamentum supplements (Leiden, The Netherlands: E. J. Brill, 1988), vol. 59, pp. 11, 12.
6 *Ibid.*, pp. 70-73.
7 Michael J. Wilkins, "Disciples," in *Dictionary of Jesus and the Gospels,* ed. Joel B. Green, Scot McKinght, and I. Howard Marshall (Downers Grove, Ill.: InterVarsity, 1992), p. 176.
8 Everett Ferguson, *Backgrounds of Early Christianity* (Grand Rapids: Eerdmans, 2003), p. 330.
9 *Ibid.*, pp. 102, 103.
10 D. F. Watson, "Education: Jewish and Greco-Roman," in *Dictionary of New Testament Background,* ed. Craig A. Evans and Stanley E. Porter (Downers Grove, Ill.: InterVarsity, 2000), pp. 308-310.

11 Thomas P. Rausch, *Who Is Jesus? An Introduction to Christology* (Collegeville, Minn.: Liturgical Brothers, 2003), p. 71.

12 James Swanson, "Lamadh," Dictionary of Biblical Languages With Semantic Domains: Hebrew (Old Testament), electronic ed. (Oak Harbor, Wash.: Logos, 1997), p. H4340.

13 Michael J. Wilkins, *Following the Master: A Biblical Theology of Discipleship* (Grand Rapids: Zondervan, 1992), p. 55.

14 Walter C. Kaiser, "Lamadh," *Theological Wordbook of the Old Testament,* ed. R. Laird Harris, Gleason L. Archer, and Bruce K. Waltke (Chicago: Moody, 1980), p. 480.

15 Francis Brown, S. R. Driver, and Charles A. Briggs, *The Brown-Driver-Briggs Hebrew and English Lexicon* (Peabody, Mass.: Hendrickson, 1994), p. 541.

16 Wilkins, *Following the Master,* p. 56.

17 *Ibid.,* p. 64.

18 Hull, p. 58.

19 Wilkins, *Following the Master,* p. 56.

20 James L. Crenshaw, *Old Testament Wisdom* (Louisville, Ky.: John Knox Press, 2010), pp. 24, 25.

21 Ernest C. Lucas, *Exploring the Old Testament: A Guide to the Psalms and Wisdom Literature* (Downers Grove, Ill.: InterVarsity, 2008), pp. 40-43.

22 James Strong, "Μαθητής," *Strong's Exhaustive Concordance With Greek and Hebrew Dictionary,* electronic ed. (Oak Harbor, Wash.: Logos, 1980), p. G3101.

23 K. L. McKay, "The Use of Hoi De in Matthew 28:17: A Response to K. Grayson," *Journal for the Study of the New Testament* 24 (1985): 71.

24 David E. Garland, *Reading Matthew: A Literary and Theological Commentary, Reading the New Testament* (Macon, Ga.: Smyth and Helwys, 2013), pp. 271, 272.

25 John Nolland, *The Gospel of Matthew: A Commentary of the Greek Text, The New International Greek Testamentary Commentary* (Grand Rapids: Eerdmans, 2005), p. 1264.

26 William Hendriksen, *Matthew, Exposition of the Gospel According to Matthew* (Grand Rapids: Baker, 1984), p. 998.

27 James M. Boice, *Christ's Call to Discipleship* (Grand Rapids: Kregel, 1998), pp. 160-162.

28 David J. Bosch, *Transforming Mission: Paradigm Shifts in Theology of Mission* (Maryknoll, N.Y.: Orbis, 1991), p. 73.

29 Hendrikson, p. 1003.

30 Marvin R. Vincent, *Word Studies in the New Testament* (New York: Charles Scribner's Sons, 1887), p. 236.

31 Andreas J. Köstenberger, *John* (Grand Rapids: Baker, 2004), pp. 423, 424.

32 Robert Jamieson, A. R. Fausset, and David Brown, *Commentary Critical and Explanatory on the Whole Bible* (Oak Harbor, Wash.: Logos, 1997), vol. 2, p. 155.

33 Wilkins, Following the Master, p. 107.

34 Darrell L. Bock, Luke 1:1–9:50, ed. Robert W. Yarbrough and Robert H. Stein, Baker *Exegetical Commentary on the New Testament* (Grand Rapids: Baker Academic, 1994), p. 852.

35 David E. Aune, "Following the Lamb: Discipleship in the Apocalypse," in *Patterns of Discipleship in the New Testament,* ed. Richard N. Longenecher (Grand Rapids: Eerdmans, 1996), p. 275.

36 Boice, pp. 17-20.

37 For a brief story of the first steps of New Seed SDA Church, see Kleber D. Gonçalves, "The Challenge of the Postmodern Condition to Adventist Mission in South America," *Journal of Adventist Mission Studies* 5, no. 1 (2009): 14-16.

38 The first edition of the SigaMe forum (2014) was entitled "Essential Elements of Discipleship." The discipleship elements explored were: communion, intentionality, community, obedience, service, submission, and transformation. In the subsequent years discipleship elements and themes were extracted from: "The Parables of Jesus" (2015); "The Lord's Prayer" (2016); "A Church That Makes Disciples" (2017); "Mission Issues in the Contemporary Society" (2018).

Implementing a Mission Scorecard

ANTHONY WAGENERSMITH, D.Min.

DURING THE FIRST FEW YEARS of my ministry I was more effective at getting new people into the church than at retaining them. New members were immersed in water without being immersed in a clear discipling process. And unfortunately, because there was not an intentional plan before and after baptism, several of these individuals and families are no longer part of the Seventh-day Adventist Church today. I was most certainly a product of my environment, having grown up and been trained in a paradigm in which baptism is the primary metric of success. Fortunately, there was a shift in my experience. I discovered that while baptism will always be a key milestone in the journey of evangelism and discipleship, it must be placed within the larger framework of mission. Developed in the trenches, refined through study, and adaptable to your context, what follows is a simple process to implement a mission scorecard in local churches.

Specifically, this scorecard asks, What areas should our churches focus on both before and after baptism, and how might we measure it? Furthermore, how can such a process be adaptable to various contexts, contributing to a more wholistic culture around evangelism? A four-step process is recommended: start with biblical principles rather than best practices, identify what you will measure, create a functional scorecard, and celebrate culture change.

START WITH BIBLICAL PRINCIPLES, NOT BEST PRACTICES

As with any initiative, it is essential to start with biblical principles rather than best practices. What follows are a few key concepts that speak to the "why" before the "how."

We Cannot Have the Retention of All Believers Without the Ministry of All Believers

Jesus' commission in Matthew 28:18-20—the most familiar of His five Great Commission communications (Matthew 28:16-20; Mark 16:15; Luke 24:46-48; John 20:21; Acts 1:8)—applies not only to the apostles but to all believers. While the exact sequence of these communications is debated, what emerges from these 40-day, post-Resurrection interactions is the larger body of believers whom Jesus instructed (Matthew 28:7-10; Luke 24:36-49; Acts 1:15; 1 Corinthians 15:6). "The commission had been given to the twelve when Christ met with them in the upper chamber; but it was now to be given to a larger number. At the meeting on a mountain in Galilee, all the believers who could be called together [about 500] were assembled."[1] Emphasizing how all believers are ordained to carry out the Great Commission, White continues:

"The Savior's commission to the disciples included all the believers. It includes all believers in Christ to the end of time. It is a fatal mistake to suppose that the work of saving souls depends alone on the ordained minister. All to whom the heavenly inspiration has come are put in trust with the gospel. All who receive the life of Christ are ordained to work for the salvation of their fellow men."[2]

Given the role that language plays in shaping culture, how might our terms of reference become synchronized with the ministry of all believers as taught in Scripture? The late British evangelist, writer, and preacher John Stott writes about such realignment that took place in his personal life around 1950:

"We do a great disservice to the Christian cause whenever we refer to the pastorate as 'the ministry,' for by our use of the definite article we give the impression that the pastorate is the only ministry there is. . . . I repented of this view, and therefore of this language, about twenty-five years ago, and now invite my readers, if necessary, to join me in penitence."[3]

"Together, built upon Jesus Christ the chief cornerstone, all believers are living stones forming a new priesthood (1 Corinthians 3:16; 6:19; Ephesians 2:20, 21; 1 Peter 2:4-6). Shifting our focus from holy places to holy people, the New Testament expects all believers to minister in all places."[4]

The Way We Come Into the Church Shapes the Way We Continue With the Church

When new people join a church culture as consumers without contributing

DISCIPLING, NURTURING, AND RECLAIMING

in meaningful ways before baptism, expecting them to minister actively after baptism is often foreign. In the New Testament, being baptized into Christ is not simply a change of status but one of identification and participation in the ministry of Christ' suffering, death, and resurrection (Romans 6:3; Galatians 3:27; Colossians 2:12). In the same way, being baptized into the body of Christ is about engagement with the mission of Christ, not merely a change in religious self-identification. We are all baptized into "one body" (1 Corinthians 12:13, NIV), of which we all have our parts to play (verses 14-31), based upon the various giftings we have received from the Holy Spirit (Romans 12:5). Indeed, the very act of "equipping" within this "one body" can be likened to setting a broken bone in place to restore functionality (Ephesians 4:4, 11-13, NIV).[5]

What does this all mean for nurture and retention of new members? Put simply: since involvement with mission and ministry is a key predictor of member longevity, before baptism is an ideal time to begin incorporating this engagement and culture of service. If there is no pathway to such involvement before baptism, then becoming a member through baptism lacks the biblical involvement in ministry, forcing attempts to solve the problem on the back end.

Church Growth Is God's Job: Intentional
Disciple-making Is Our Job

Our belief in who grows the church has a direct effect on the retention of new believers. If we believe church growth is our job, then making members (not disciples) becomes the primary objective, rendering retention as a secondary consideration. Fortunately, Jesus clarified that the church belongs to Him and that He will grow His church (Matthew 16:18). This understanding is not only a safeguard from the adulation of human workers—only God can be praised for growth—but also creates an authentic and attractive culture, as new people are not treated as mere numbers. Our responsibility as ministers in God's church (whether administrators, pastors, teachers, elders, etc.) is to make disciples. According to the Great Commission in Matthew 28:18-20, our mission imperative is to "make disciples" through the three participles (or means of): "going" (forming deep relationships in new places and among new people groups), "baptizing them in the name of the Father, Son and Holy Spirit" (immersion in water and the character of the triune God), and "teaching them to observe all things" (active obedience to the doctrines of Jesus Christ and Holy Scripture). If we will embrace our view as intentional disciple-makers, equipping and nurturing new people both before and after baptism, God will surely grow His church. As expressed by Ellen White in the context of all members being called to mission work: "God depends upon you, the human agent, to fulfill your duty to the best of your ability, and He Himself will give the increase."[6] v.8, 189

The primacy of making disciples over making members takes on an expanded significance when placed within the context of God's end-time commandment-keeping people:

"The Adventist Church has always claimed to be God's remnant church, because it keeps all the commandments of God. Could it be that a church cannot claim to be the remnant church if it does not keep the commands of Christ as well? That would simply mean that to be God's remnant, the church must be keeping the Great Commission, which demands the making of disciples as the primary aim of the mission of the church. Any church that is not doing so cannot claim to be the remnant. Such a disobedient church needs to repent of its omission—its failure to fulfill the Great Commission."[7]

Identify What You Will Measure

Since God is responsible for the outcome, the church must develop new metrics other than outcomes. A key concept to stimulate thinking around what you will track is the difference between a lead measure and a lag measure. Lead measures are present-tense activities that are influenceable and predictive of future goals; lag measures tell us if those goals were reached, exist in the past, and cannot be changed.[8] While we will always measure outcomes, conventional church culture overemphasizes lag measures to the exclusion of lead measures. Here's a chart illustrating this needed shift in a local church or conference:

	LAG MEASURE	LEAD MEASURE
Baptisms	Number of people baptized	Number of people in baptismal class
Financial Giving	Number of tithe and offering dollars given	Percent of family units actively giving
Small Groups	Number of small groups meeting	Number of people being trained to become small group leaders

Only God can change the human heart and bring the outcomes. Our job (under His guidance and empowerment) is to make disciples as we bring clarity, priority, and accountability to the lead measures. Take time in your local church or conference to identify what lead measures you will focus on in the lives of new disciples both before and after baptism:

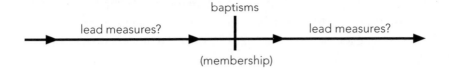

Through experience in adapting the mission scorecard to different contexts, here are three suggested lead measures for each side of the baptism experience in the lives of new people.

Recommended Lead Measures Before Baptism

- *Relationship*—What are the names of at least three members who have formed a deep and authentic friendship with the new person?
- *Ministry*—What is the name of the ministry the new person serves on?
- *Theology*—When did the new person start Bible studies and what was the date of the most recent study?

A few notes on lead measures before baptism are important here. In terms of relationship, you might decide to track the names of individual members or the names of family units—which creates a culture of families on mission and brings young children into the task of disciple-making. Second, a close relationship means sharing real life outside of Sabbath worship or other official church events. In regard to ministry, common sense is in order here. While a local church does not ask unbaptized persons to preach and teach Sabbath School, they must create ministry opportunities that are immediate and intentional for new people (these vary based upon context). In regard to theology or Bible as a lead measure, intentional and regular Bible conversation and study places new people in a position for God to transform their heart in surrender toward baptism. Some churches excel at theology but fail miserably at relationship and ministry engagement before baptism. The other extreme thrives on friendships and involvement but minimizes our prophetic message as Adventists. It doesn't have to be a sequential process; balance and a wholistic approach is key.

Recommended Lead Measures After Baptism
- *Ministry*—What is the name of the ministry the new member serves on?
- *Discipleship Path*—How is the new member being equipped to live as a disciple?
- *Relationship*—What is the name of a new person the member is relationally discipling?

A few comments on lead measures after baptism. First, the specific ministries that every member serves on should be counted toward the goal of complete member involvement. Second, while a church's discipleship path (or specific strategy for disciple-making) begins in a person's life long before baptism, the specifics of what a church does are key to produce multiplication and disciple-making disciples. Track progress through this process or steps. Third, the name of someone the new member is relationally discipling creates a full circle, with the new member now becoming one of at least three individuals or family units forming authentic and intentional relationships with a new person. Nurture and retention is impacted positively through this process as new members continue in meaningful relationship, engagement with ministry, and deepening discipleship, and a clear sense of a larger purpose or mission. While the above recommendations must obviously be contextualized, it is essential to decide what you will measure both before and after baptism. Building upon the above, here's a sample grid for the mission scorecard:

CREATE A FUNCTIONAL SCORECARD

With your key lead measures in place, it's time to create and implement a functional scorecard. To accomplish this, think through four basic questions:

What Group of Leaders Is Best Suited to Work With the Scorecard on a Regular Basis?

Since the scorecard is an internal way to intentionally make sure new people not only join but stick with the church in full engagement, what specific team in the local church is best situated to have access to and work with the scorecard? Some common examples include the elder team, Sabbath School or small group leaders, church board, ministry leaders, evangelism planning council, etc. This is the group that needs to be involved in shaping what the lead measures will be, and taking an active part in its implementation.

Who Will Be the Caretaker of the Scorecard?

Once you have a designated group, you need a specific individual to be the caretaker of the scorecard. While anyone on the team will report and can update the scorecard, the caretaker is the primary person responsible to make sure it is updated and current (including adding or removing names). A common choice is the church secretary, a role with significant mission potential. Since they already track membership transfers and adjustments, being a caretaker of the scorecard enhances their role in tracking lead measures around becoming and retaining a fully engaged membership. Some churches have also selected their personal ministries leader as a caretaker. A temporary but meaningful option would be a Bible worker for an evangelistic effort, in which their primary purpose is not simply giving biblical studies with interested persons but ensuring the new people are connected to the lead measures you have decided on in advance.

What Tool Will You Use to View and Update the Scorecard?

The scorecard combines both the traditional "interest list" (those who are not yet members) and "inactive member list" (those who are technically members but have left or are often on the verge of leaving the church), placing them within a more wholistic context of disciple-making. In order to have a functional list that is easily viewable and updatable by your designated team, decide what tool will be best for you to use. One simple and free practice is to place your prebaptism and postbaptism lead measures on a spreadsheet, and have each of your team members download it onto a free spreadsheet app (such as Google Sheets) on their phones or computers; then each person can update it in live time. To shape intentional prayer and awareness of needs, it is important that the scorecard be both accessible and confidential among team members.

How Will You Create a Healthy Rhythm of Accountability When Using the Scorecard?

Now that you have identified your lead measures, the specific group and caretaker working with it, and how you will view and update the scorecard, it's time to implement it. To create an ongoing culture (not merely one-off events) that prioritizes discipleship and retention, it is essential to create a rhythm of accountability for the team members working the scorecard. Gather your team regularly to pray over and give reports on the scorecard, either through integrating it into an existing meeting (elders, church board, small group leaders) or a scorecard-specific meeting. When you're together, review the process, pray over the names, and ask (don't tell) each team member what one thing they will do to move someone further along in the scorecard (either toward baptism or after baptism) before you meet next. Have the caretaker of the scorecard write down everyone's commitments ("who does what by when"), including the person leading out. For example, if a new person is receiving

Bible studies and has close relationships but is not yet involved in ministry, one commitment might be to introduce the new person to a ministry leader involved in an area of common interest before the next meeting. Then at the start of each meeting, ask team members to give a report on the commitments they made and how it went. This ensures a rhythm of built-in accountability in which following through becomes the norm, not the exception. While it's true that all cultures handle accountability different, the engagement of team members in whom and how they are nurturing goes a long way.

CELEBRATE CULTURE CHANGE

The future of growth and retention will be realized in placing a greater emphasis on developing an evangelistic culture than on evange-listic programming. As changes begin happening, celebrate how the Lord is changing your culture. The implementation and impact of a mission scorecard carries with it the retention of new members as a consequence of wholistic evangelism and intentional disciple-making. In light of the massive membership losses in the Seventh-day Adventist Church, it has been observed in many settings that what we are facing is fundamentally a discipleship—not a retention—issue. The scorecard is simply one of many ways to address the disease rather than the symptoms. Further opportunities to assess and address a church's culture—what people feel and experience when they connect with a church—also contribute to courageously approaching this issue in practical ways. And yet, while strategies and scorecards do indeed have their place, God's church is fundamentally a spiritual organism, not an organization. Program-driven views of the church create programmatic solutions. And unfortunately, there are ultimately no administrative solutions to the spiritual problems of how we treat others both before and after baptism. May the same Lord who promised the accompaniment of His Spirit to the "ends of the earth" (Acts 1:8, NIV) transform our hearts to honor Him in stewardship of the millions of precious souls who will join or are part of the Adventist movement.

ANTHONY WAGENERSMITH, D.Min.

Anthony WagenerSmith is associate director at the NAD Evangelism Institute and a professor of Christian Ministry at the SDA Theological Seminary at Andrews University. He pastored and planted churches in both urban and rural contexts, has a doctorate in missional church planting, and facilitates equipping experiences across North America. His wife, Liánro, is a school psychologist, and they have two children, Levi, 10, and Sage, 8).

ENDNOTES

1 Ellen G. White, *The Desire of Ages* (Mountain View, Calif.: Pacific Press Pub. Assn., 1898, 1940), p. 818.

2 Ibid., p. 822.

3 J.R.W. Stott and C.J.H. Wright, *Christian Mission in the Modern World,* updated and expanded ed. (Downers Grove, Ill.: InterVarsity Press, 2015), p. 55.

4 A. WagenerSmith, "Urban Church Planting: Three Functional Shifts From the New Testament," Journal of Adventist Mission Studies 15, no. 1 (2019): 118-133.

5 J. Strong, *Strong's Exhaustive Concordance of the Bible,* updated and expanded ed. (Peabody, Mass.: Henderson Publishers, Inc., 2007).

6 Ellen G. White, *Manuscript Releases* (Silver Spring, Md.: Ellen G. White Estate, 1990), vol. 8, p. 190.

7 R. Burrill, *Radical Disciples for Revolutionary Churches* (Fallbrook, Calif.: Hart Research Center, 1996), p. 51.

8 C. McChesney and S. Covey, *The Four Disciplines of Execution: Achieving Your Wildly Important Goals* (New York: Free Press, 2016).

What Did Jesus Do to Become the Communicational Impact of History?

MARCOS ANTONIO SALAS NÚÑEZ

INTRODUCTION

Jesus is the perfect combination between being and doing: His personality and His character were one. The great work that Jesus did was the result of the greatness of His character. And this teaches us that success in mission depends on two aspects that the Holy Spirit controls in us, a character in transformation and strategies based on inspired principles.

Matthew 4 begins by presenting Jesus alone in the desert and ends by saying that crowds went after Him. Was it a product of a miracle? the result of a strategy? both? What principles in this chapter can help the Seventh-day Adventist Church in its eschatological mission? How can we implement the success of Jesus as the key to the consolidation of the members of our church?

CHRIST, HIS CHARACTER

Most Christians intellectually believe in the power of God to work miracles. Resuscitating the dead, healing the sick, or feeding crowds must have been instruments to powerfully draw people's attention. Logically we can conclude that Jesus based His ministry on these divine acts, but it was not so. The vindication of God's character in the universe and the salvation of the fallen race required much more than momentary solutions. The success of Jesus was rooted in His character and strategies based on invincible principles. In the face of the end of the great conflict we need, as never before, to dig with prayer and determination in this chapter of Matthew and learn from Jesus how to overcome the Great Babylon, thus fulfilling what is written.

Jesus Allowed Himself to Be Led by the Holy Spirit. Matthew 4:1.

In the earthly experience of our Master we find that He understood the role of the Holy Spirit in the dosage of confrontation with evil. He knew that it is necessary for the integral development of His people because it helps us to take away our trust in us and put it in God. Matthew tells us that after His baptism Jesus was led by the Spirit into the desert to be tempted by the devil, as is the case with all Christians. In order to understand the reason God the Spirit has to do this, we need to understand what He is looking for when we decide to work with Him. As expressed by Jesus in Mark 12:29-31, 33, God seeks that we love Him above all, that we love ourselves properly and love our neighbor in the light of the plan of salvation. Most Christians have a hard time accepting this. Hence the "eternal" dispute between the concepts of salvation by faith or works. If we try to pay attention to God, we will accept that once we have been baptized, anything God allows or does in our life seeks to develop in us love. Even the confrontation with evil has this objective. The Holy Spirit had this in mind when He led Jesus into the desert. Whether He takes us to Patmos, to the desert to meet a stranger, or to visit a desperate widow in Sarepta, He is looking for us to have experiences that teach us to love, so that we have the seal or character of God and so the world can recognize us as His children.

Jesus Knows Who He Is. Matthew 4:3, 5, 6.

After His baptism, the first two temptations enticed Jesus to doubt His condition. In both, the tempter began by saying, "If You are the Son of God" (Matthew 4:3), inviting Jesus to question His personal condition. In baptism we are adopted into the family of God; we are made children of God. From then on, everything that happens to us is for our good, as the apostle Paul declares in Romans 8:28. Although this is true and legal, it does not mean that Satan will leave without fighting for what until then was his domain. He knows that our carnal nature will constantly lead us to seek our salvation in a selfish way, based on the I, not on Jesus. That is why Jesus wants us to believe not what appearances dictate, but what His Word says about what we are thanks to Him. He also warns us that in the time of the end many false christs will come, and there will be a constant attack on His Divine-human personality.

God wants us to think of ourselves as Laodiceans that, thanks to Him, become the 144,000. It is true that our church today wants to vomit God. That is why we so easily find faults that lead us to disunity. The same situation faced Jesus with the church of His time, however, He never stopped considering the church as the girl of His eyes, the object of His greatest care. He warned us with the parable of the 10 virgins that all would fall asleep, although five were ready by the time the bridegroom arrived. That is the reason to teach our new brothers to know that we are Laodiceans in the process of becoming the 144,000. Show them that God is working with us to make our life His perfect work. No defeatism or triumphalism. We are the militant church, a movement with a mission.

Jesus Combined the Scriptures With Prayer and Mission. Matthew 4: 4, 7, 10.

Whoever reads the Bible without a clear mission will soon stop doing so or will become an obstacle in the God's work. Most Christians walk through their lives without practicing the only things that give the Holy Spirit time to transform our character. Satan is interested in staying in the church, and without a vital connection with God as we will become a bad witness of the gospel. For a vital and transformative relationship with Jesus, we need God to speak to us, to listen to us, and to walk with us. He speaks to us through His Word, He listens to us through prayer, and He walks with us while we attack evil on this earth. In order to support children, young, new, and old in the faith, it is important to have at least the Bible and their Sabbath School study guide. In addition, we must help them with a personal study plan. New members need trained and experienced older members to help them search their needs in the biblical "menu." Pastors and elders must be experts in this matter.

New members find challenges when they agree to study the Bible. Some Old Testament books have "boring" portions that must be studied with a keen intention to be assimilated. In their first love the new ones in the faith read the Pentateuch, the first five books of Moses. When they begin to face some not very rosy aspects of their new lives and of the church and they have to read books like Chronicles and others that have a style that requires some "chronologies" that may jeopardize their interest in studying, they are likely to take refuge in exclusively studying the Sabbath School study guide, which may also contain confusing elements for their new faith. That is why some propose that the new in faith should first study the Gospels to get to know Jesus better before entering into the other biblical portions. Whatever the case, we need to have a group that personally takes care of the new members so that they receive the spiritual nurture they need.

This process should include teaching about prayer. How nice would it be if the new ones in the faith based their prayers on what they had read that day, in addition to other things that they want to talk to God about, such as mission. The mission challenges us, creates the need for guidance from God and to ask Him on how to solve challenges. As a consequence, we gradually come to love God and our neighbor.

Jesus' Mission Was Above His Personal Interests. Matthew 4:8-11.

As it has already been said, mission is what unites us to God and gives meaning to our devotional lives. Jesus calls us to be fishers. It includes that He wants to give us a successful life, having as its focus the work that we do with Him in the great conflict. An essential element that the new members must learn is that their secular work is given by God to sustain themselves, but the mission is what they really are. We should all come to think like fishers. Some of us have to catch small fish and others large fish, using different means. When someone asked Jesus, "Who are you?" He responded in different ways that He was the Messiah, the Savior of humanity. He never said He was a carpenter, although this profession is very honorable.

The Bible says that when Jesus was victorious, "angels came and served Him" (Matthew 4:11). When our role in the plan of salvation is our reason to be, which gives us meaning and we live for it, God is committed so that our sustenance is assured. Imagine a small group and a congregation that works in this way. The apostle to the Gentiles tells us that God established some as apostles, others as prophets, others as evangelists, and some as pastors and teachers (Ephesians 4:11). In fact, the church of Antioch worked like that at the time when the Spirit chose Paul to send to the Gentile world to preach the gospel.

In the description of Ephesians 4 the Spirit tells us that in the church there are four main divisions of fishers. Apostles are called and trained to be specialists in the search for strategies to bring children, youth, and adults to the feet of Jesus. Today we call this group biblical instructors. The prophets, the older members, are specialists in creating and developing ways to sustain new members in the faith. They use the Bible, the Spirit of Prophecy, the Church Manual, and other instruments of God to edify the new members. Evangelists, now called lay preachers, are called and adapted to evangelize crowds. Pastors or teachers are the specialists in teaching everyone. That is why today we call them lay instructors. All departments and ministries of the church must contain these main groups, from which any number of ministries and functions we need in the church are derived. The reason these are the four main general ministries is that ultimately our duty in the church is to win, consolidate, preach, and teach.

CHRIST, HIS PLAN AND EXECUTION

If the first law of heaven is order, it should be the same in the case of Jesus. Those born in the kingdom of God are born as missionaries, or fishers. That statement implies a plan and a structure for its implementation. That is why Jesus had to follow the plan devised before the foundation of the world, a plan that has a personal dimension for each one and a general one that includes all those immersed in the great conflict. In this section we will analyze the plan that made Jesus the event of His time and eternity, and, above all, we will seek our Lord in prayer to implement these principles.

Jesus Had a Plan. Matthew 4:12.

"When Jesus heard . . ." is a very interesting biblical expression. It manifests planning, to expect something planned to happen to move to a new stage. The time had come to move from near anonymity to the explosion of salvation. God and the world are waiting for the same to occur with the remnant.

As a church we have an inspired, logical, and effective structure. It is perfectible and should be reviewed, but it has been effective in leading us to be one of the fastest expanding churches. The biggest challenge is at the local church. We must take care of some concepts that confuse the Lord's flock, such as the one that places the main emphasis on baptizing and not on discipling, or the one that says we do not like to baptize, because we seek quality and not quantity. Our mission is to have disciples in whom your love for God and your neighbor grows every day thanks to the study of the Bible, prayer, and the fulfillment of your ministry. If we do not baptize, we will not have disciples; so planning must encompass discipleship.

Jesus teaches us that the challenge in mission is what makes structure and integration necessary. The unity, love, and financial investment of the church come as a result of the mission plan. God expects us to teach how to work in an organized way, and that the organizational structure will help us so that all members, including the new ones, have a personal plan to implement their ministry. Of course, this plan has everything to do with the small groups plan and that of the congregation. We are not referring only to a calendar of activities; we are talking about a five-year and annual strategic plan and an annual mission project. Our educational institutions must make pastors aware of the fundamental principles of planning and finance. The new ones in the faith must arrive at a people group that knows what it is doing, which little by little will guide them in such a way that that they will be able to fulfill their function within the mission planning and project. This is consolidation.

Jesus Sought a Strategic Location. Matthew 4:13, 14.

The first part of Jesus' strategy was to get to the right place. He chose Capernaum for several important reasons that we will analyze shortly. The location tells us what we will give most importance to, as it establishes what or whom we are looking for. We tend to work in our comfort zone, which we have already reached and which represents the least amount of effort to survive. Today Jesus encourages us again to leave Nazareth and go to Capernaum to be able to make healthy disciples.

Capernaum was the city of Peter, Andrew, James, John, and Matthew, the disciples. It was one of the three cities that Jesus cursed at the end of His earthly ministry for its lack of faith. Jesus had a prophetic reason to choose it as the center of His work, as what was said by the prophet Isaiah should be fulfilled. This characteristic is very important in planning, because it is the one that gives the passion and the reason to fulfill the mission. When the planning is based on a writing, we have all the necessary support to insist until we successfully crown our plan. Our mission is impossible to accomplish if God does not intervene. That is why we need the members to see that it is God who determines the place, which is what drives us and always keeps advancing by faith, outside our comfort zone. The new one in the faith must know that it is not by their strength or ability, it is by working with the Holy Spirit that their will successfully fulfill the mission among their family, friends, and strangers. The same must be seen in all the church estates. It must be seen that our motto as a movement is to move forward, to extend our stakes because God says in His Word that we can reach the whole world with our message. To all—rich, poor, secularized, and of all religions.

The second reason Jesus chose Capernaum was that it was located on the "sea road," because it was a "maritime city" (Matthew 4:13-15). With this description the Bible tells us that Jesus made His planning on the trade route that linked Mesopotamia with Egypt through Palestine. The first was the main area of the Asian continent, and the second that of the African continent. All those who came from Europe also passed through there. So it was a city with a privileged location so that most of the known world could understand the plan of salvation. Jesus based His planning on the lost, not on the ones already in the kingdom. That is why Jesus became the world event of history: He wanted to impact the whole world. One of the great Adventist inconsistencies is that we say things that we do not support with our facts. We educate our missionaries and pastors for people who live for a long time in "university bubbles," whose center is the one in the kingdom. Many times we invest the greatest amount of our resources to sustain what we have, and forget about the lost. Many churches make their planning with the intent of keeping their membership attending church services and giving their tithes and offerings. We are creating a defensive culture, not an offensive one. Jesus understood what many sports technicians know today is the key to success; the best defense is the attack. How many blessings are invested for our churches: great preachers, extraordinary music, master classes, and colorful and even special art manifestations. Everything within our comfort zones. Jesus today sends us to think about the places where the greatest quantity of people are. That is the best way to consolidate our new and old members, asking as the widow of the parable the blessing of God, with insistence to bring the gospel to all.

"Capernaum" today requires from us education and creativity. Let's not continue comparing ourselves with the neighboring churches, presenting beautiful programs that have as the ultimate intent the program and not the human being. Commercial companies have a fierce war among them for the conquest of consumer interest. Those who conform to what has been achieved and live on their past glories are doomed to extinction. Hence the need to educate church ministries leaders, and the need for departments or specialists in all levels to educate church members to go out as an army to meet people. As the prophecies say, the united education with a creativity directed by the Holy Spirit will make a dent in the enemy protections until their complete destruction.

The next reason Jesus chose Capernaum was that it was an important city in "Galilee of the Gentiles" (Matthew 4:15). The first reasons had to do with a strategic area; the latter has to do with people who lived in that place. After the deportation of the 10 northern Israelite tribes by the Assyrians, this land was repopulated by "Gentile" people. In Jesus' day many Jews had settled there, but they were populations with large numbers of descendants of Gentiles. It is reiterated in this way that it is the lost and not those in the faith who are the objective of the mission of Jesus and the church, so that we can become the salt and light of the world. That is why it was written, "The people living in darkness have seen a great light; on those living in the land of the shadow of death a light has dawned" (Matthew 4:16, NIV).

Jesus Had a Clear and Expansive Message. Matthew 4:17.
Jesus' message is: "Repent, for the kingdom of heaven has come near"

(NIV). Which leads us to ask ourselves, What does it mean to "repent"? And what did Jesus mean when He said that the kingdom of heaven has come near?

The message of Jesus and that of John the Baptist was one and the same (Matthew 3:2). We find that both preaching led people to be baptized and confess their sins, which was unusual in those times because being part of God's people assumed that circumcision was their "baptism," or entry into the kingdom of God and that the sanctuary system was the way to confess their sins. Of course, neither John nor Jesus were against these two sacred teachings of God's covenant with His people. Something that can shed light on the reason for this change is found on the time in which John confronted the Pharisees and Sadducees when they came to be baptized. Instead of congratulating them on their decision, he called them a "brood of vipers" (verse 7). John wanted to know who had taught them to flee from the wrath to come (verse 7) and where their "fruits worthy of repentance" (verse 8) were. Instead, they were protecting themselves, thinking they were children of Abraham. The Pharisees had not learned from anyone, because they considered themselves so good that they felt them had no need for that. Much less were they interested in changing their lives or thinking that anger was coming; they wanted to continue exactly with their positions and behavior and hope that their social and economic condition would improve with the coming of the Messiah. They wanted to be baptized to have all the necessary requirements to achieve well-being in this world.

The message of John and that of Jesus were the same of the sanctuary, humble repentance before God to be saved. That is why the veil had five colors. They represented the five main characteristics that the Messiah would have: purity (white), crimson (atoning sacrifice), purple (domain), gold (control of the Holy Spirit), and blue (divinity). They were to be taught and led by the Messiah to flee the wrath of God. They had to be "born of water and the Spirit" (John 3:5) in order to enter the kingdom of God. They should take the yoke of Jesus, an attitude of sacrifice in the face of need, to let the Holy Spirit change their lives and thus be able to bear the fruits of someone who is following the Messiah. That is why the sacrificial altar was located first, and then the lavatory. They could not be baptized, the lavatory, without first being willing to be taught and to sacrifice themselves to have a character like Jesus', as represented by the sacrificial altar.

Yesterday, today, and tomorrow, we are all like the Pharisees and Sadducees. That is why John and Jesus call for repentance and its fruits. Nothing we are or do saves us from the wrath to come. We need to repent, to say, accept, believe, and work according to what is established by Jesus. In practice this is being willing to be taught, to understand the plan of salvation as it is in the Scriptures and to accept that plan when baptized. At that moment, having been justified by becoming children of God, we have escaped the wrath to come. From there, sanctification begins. We remain open to divine guiding and to the changes He wants to generate in us. There is no condemnation, because we are in Christ; there is only constant transformation and to be filled with that love that makes our salvation possible.

At this point we must ask ourselves: How are we Adventists known? Some believe that we are not evangelical, which means we teach a way of salvation without Jesus. They say that we do not eat pork, we do not work or play on Saturdays, we do not dance, we do not use alcohol or coffee, we do not eat meat, and that we were organized by the teachings of Ellen White. We must recognize that the public in some places does not have a clear picture of our message. We do not want to discredit the importance of the things for which they know us, but perhaps we need to make a clearer presentation of the extraordinary evangelical message that we have, as Revelation 14 states. The answer could be found in the next part of Jesus' message: "the kingdom of heaven has come near" (Matthew 4:17, NIV).

So that we could all understand the gospel, Jesus, the kingdom of God, approached us. Jesus was a friend of the people, of the bad and of the "good." It related to the "vetoed" of the congregations. That is why today He sends us to approach pastors and priests of other denominations, including the pope, the presidents of the nations, nuns and homosexuals, the stinkers and others with whom it is not easy to relate. We are so worried in our congregations about the type of music, the haircut, and other things that could be important that we run out of energy to implement the method of Christ. We must be a church in which everyone can worship and feel free to be transformed by the Holy Spirit, while He gives patience to the old woman who criticizes us or us who criticize her. While this happens within, outside we must have more selfless but intentional community service. Our service of friendship must be selfless because the goal is to be friends with the sinner so that when they need Jesus we can show Him to them. We lose a lot when we approach people only because we want them to be Adventists. Some even think that we should not have some kind of relationship with the "mundane." If this were so, how could we be salt? Therefore, our friendship with the worldly must be intentional, to seek to save the sinner. That is why we pray that the Holy Spirit will lead us to find ways to present Jesus to our friends.

Regardless of whether they accept Him or not, we must be intentional at presenting Jesus. Whether they accept or not, they must remain a person who considers us in a good way. But if they do accept Jesus, then we will have one more friend in our church.

Jesus Had a Team, a Small Group. Matthew 4:18-22.

A leader without followers and a plan without people who benefit is absurd. That is why Jesus sought friends to share the gospel and the blessings that this entails. Simon Peter and Andrew, his brother, were the first disciples He encountered. Then He met the brothers James and John, who were in the boat that belonged to their father, Zebedee. From here two important points in ecclesiastical administration emerge. First, Jesus sought two adults and two young men as His first disciples. This is understood because Peter and Andrew used fishing nets that belonged to them, and the two others were working with what belonged to their father. The second aspect is that Jesus called them in pairs.

Jesus worked with adults and young people because He knew they are complementary groups. Adults have the experience, and young people have enthusiasm and new ideas. This combination is noted in the Gospels, Jesus utilizing one group to enrich the other. If the newly baptized is a child, youth, or adult, they should feel that they now belong to a small group, congregation, and other organizational strata that are wise enough to know that we not only have the same importance, but that we are all necessary. That there is room for dialogue and that opinion is respected. That participation of anyone who wants to participate is allowed, both in the planning and execution. The challenges we face as a church are so impressive that none of the generations can disregard the participation of the other under penalty of being disadvantaged.

Jesus came to establish a system that has as its fundamental nucleus a group of 12 people. God through Jethro prescribed it to Moses and there laid the success of the desert people. This is so important that when Paul was converted, he did not need any man to explain the evangelical message, but he did need to understand the role of the group as a fundamental part of the structure. Jesus established the small group into the DNA of the Christian church so that it would be possible to baptize thousands without building temples and to continue growing without structural problems. If there is a small group that takes care of its members and has a plan with which it works with other groups and with the congregation, then there is no need to fear. Members go to the congregation to receive spiritual benefits, although they receive the essential in their small group.

The other aspect that was intertwined with this axis of the structure is the missionary couple. Jesus divided the groups into pairs so that in the implementation each one had a mega friend and friends. Everyone needs someone to temper it in good times and bad. The missionary couple has functions that the small group and the congregation cannot exercise, just as they have blessings that the missionary couple lacks. That is why Jesus worked with all ages, in small groups and as a missionary couple. That is why He was so calm when He ascended. He told them to wait for the Father's promise, knowing that once they received it they would succeed, because they had learned the basis of the structure. That's how He turned them into fishers.

The church must have a worship service to train, and moments in all worship services and departments to do so. Sabbath School should serve as a platform for each small group to participate in the program and have enough time to study the Bible, to be updated with the missionary strategies to be implemented, to support missions and for fellowship. The mission segment can be used for training and as a showcase for each department to report on their missionary work. An evening worship can be a training school, and sermons must have a little more teaching to accompany the actions of the congregation.

Jesus Met the People With the Gospel Where They Were.

Jesus undertook with His disciples a very particular type of instruction, educating them with His words and with His example, inviting them to practice what they learned. He was surprised by the sun while talking to His Father and the Holy Spirit to refine the details of the new day. While they got ready and ate, He weaved His teachings with His actions while filling His friends' minds with faith. He was teaching us that all we do is evangelism. To preach of His love since we wake up in the morning, at work, in class, as fishers. Although special moments to go out to evangelize may exist, and we need them, our life is the most powerful testimony of what God wants to do with humanity. That means that Jesus traveled through "all of Galilee" to live in our territory and to expand by the fame that our testimony brings to the name of God, and by territorial progress. The disciples touched the hearts of rich and poor wherever they arrived.

An important biblical and missionary detail is the phrase "In their synagogue." As the apostle Paul did later, Jesus prayed and worked, looking for receptive people. From the moment a person is born, the Spirit of God tries to win them for His kingdom. During the rest of that life God will do what is necessary for them to accept the plan of salvation. Humans are unable to know how close someone is to accepting Jesus, but God does. When they went to the synagogues, they went to the place where there were people who had the knowledge and the desire to be with God. The Missionary Project starts by putting members to pray for people they know and want to see in the heavenly homeland. Prayer does not change God; it changes the ones who pray and awakens love for the lost, allowing God to fill them with skills and ideas to approach that person. God is the one who levels our intensity by being friendly to the people, telling us when it is time to speak to them, inviting them to the activities of the small group or the congregation and when we confront them with the decision to give their heart to Jesus. We must know that there are moments in our lives that sensitize us spiritually. So with prayer and being friendly, we will be intentional in expressing our love in times of need that the people for whom we are praying have. A death, loss of work, birth of a baby, a disease, among many other situations, can be triggers for someone to establish an eternal relationship with their Creator.

Under the direction of the Spirit we can use the three main ways to reach people's hearts: Teaching, preaching, and healing. It is good that we have several instruments to achieve this, an informal conversation, a Bible study, a special event of the small group or the congregation. That is the reason we should be intentionally evangelistic in doing the planning and calendar of the congregation. Human beings work better in cycles, so we must implement in the year activities of approach, sowing the truth, and others to harvest and consolidate. Approach activities can be: Christmas, ADRA collection, music concerts, culinary courses. Youth and children's clubs and other departments can do social, sports, and cultural activities. The objective of these activities is to show that we are a friendly, pleasant, and positive church, as our God is. The Adventist Church should be recognized for its Christ-centered and prophetic message based on the celestial sanctuary that includes the investigative judgment, for the pro-health reform message, and for being an institution that works for the family. Each of these activities should end with an invitation to other activities, and to introduce planting activities and biblical courses.

Sowing can be a Week of Emphasis on the family, or a Week of Emphasis on health. With these activities we seek that people be taught, or for them receive the preaching of the gospel, satisfying their basic needs. The intent of these activities is to get people interested in Bible studies. Then will the harvest-consolidation events come. We recommend the union of these two aspects because experience tells us that when we dedicate time exclusively to consolidation, the old part of the Lord's army can enter a dangerous territory and, above all, as Jesus did, the only way to consolidate newcomers is putting them to work for others. At this stage we find small group, ministerial, youth, and other campaigns. It would be good to divide the ecclesiastical year into two, each with its time for approach, sowing, and harvest-consolidation activities. Thus we will have the opportunity to teach, preach, and heal integrally those who decide to submit themselves to the work of the Holy Spirit.

Jesus Spread His Fame.

In conclusion, the Bible says that Jesus' fame reached Syria, Galilee, Decapolis, Jerusalem, Judea, and the other side of the Jordan. It reached those places because His goal was to teach His disciples to work with His method; after His departure they would have time to go to the whole world.

MARCOS ANTONIO SALAS NÚÑEZ

Marcos Antonio Salas Núñez has a degree in theology, having graduated from the Adventist University of Colombia in 1987. In 2005 he graduated with a master's in pastoral theology from SETAI, an educational institution of the Inter-American Division. He worked as a district pastor in the Eastern Venezuelan Union from 1988 to 2000. Then he served as the ministerial secretary in the department of personal ministries and president of the Central Venezuelan Association from 2001 to 2011. From 2011 until 2015 Núñez worked in the department of personal and communication ministries as well. Since 2016 he has directed the Hispanic district located in Saint Maarten of the North Caribbean Conference in the Caribbean Union.

* Unless otherwise noted, Bible texts in this article are from the New King James Version.

The Reclamation of Discipleship as the Primary Missional Focus in the Seventh-day Adventist Church

TIM MADDING, D.Min.

MY HOPE IS TO GIVE YOU some things to think about as you process discipleship in your sphere of influence, in your church, in your ministry context. The title of this presentation supposes that discipleship is not the primary missional focus in the Seventh-day Adventist Church. I am of the assumption that it is not, but it should be, and I'll explain what I mean by that.

The mission of the Seventh-day Adventist Church comes from the Great Commission in Matthew 28:19, 20. Here Jesus Christ says to "go . . . and make disciples" (verse 19).[1] I believe that our mission as a Seventh-day Adventist Church is to make disciples. That is our mission. That is our purpose. Everything that we do, the reason that we exist, is for the purpose of making disciples. I also believe that this is not where our focus has been, at least not recently. Over the past few decades, it has not been that focus. Our focus has been on programming and baptisms.

Let me explain . . . You measure what you value. This is demonstrated when we talk about a ministry scorecard. A scorecard is a measurement that which you value. We typically in the church (local and among the leadership) value programs and baptisms. That's what we measure. I've worked at the conference level, both on the executive committee and as a ministerial director. When we'd sit down and plan out the year, it's a lot about programming. When we evaluate the success or effectiveness of a pastor and/or church, it's baptisms. Those are the things that we like to measure to determine if we're successful.

So when we have a program in a church, and many churches will have programs throughout this Easter season, whether it's a success or not will be based on the number of people who come to the program. Did the program go well; did a lot of people come out? "That was a success; let's do it again." What made it a success? Everything went well, everybody had a good time, and there were a lot of people present. That tells us that the program is our purpose—it is our mission. Not how many people came to Christ, how many people grew in Christ, how many people grew in their relationship with God, a relationship with others, etc. Discipleship was not the value—it was the program.

Or baptisms. Throughout the North American Division and throughout the world church, baptisms are something that we measure. In fact, there are places where you cannot be ordained as a pastor unless you've had a certain number of baptisms, and pastors can be let go or fired in certain divisions in our world church if they don't acquire a certain number of baptisms. There's a whole ethical side to that issue, as to whether they're ethically getting disciples versus the number of baptisms.

So it has to be about discipleship. Discipleship is our mission. It is our purpose. A disciple is someone who is a follower of the precepts, instructions, and life of an individual. A disciple of Jesus Christ is someone who follows the teachings and life of Jesus Christ. What did Jesus teach? He taught about the kingdom of heaven, the kingdom of God. What does that mean? How does that apply to people? There is teaching involved with that.

But also the life of Jesus Christ—how He lived, how He demonstrated the character of the Father, what He did with His time, and how He treated others should be prevalent in the life of the believer. If I were to define it, I would say that a disciple is a follower of Jesus' teachings and life that is actively making disciples of others. When Jesus Christ gave the Great Commission, when He said, "Go and make disciples," He was telling the disciples to go and make disciples. A disciple is someone who believes what Jesus believes, lives what Jesus lived, and is actively making other disciples of Jesus Christ as well.

So our mission and our focus should be for people to understand what Jesus taught, how he lived. They're growing in that belief. Theology is important. They're growing in that lifestyle. They're living like Jesus. They're loving their neighbors the way Jesus loves their neighbors. They're sacrificing themselves, giving of themselves, putting themselves out for the benefit of other people. But they are also actively discipling other people in Jesus Christ. If they are not actively discipling others, then are they a true follower of Jesus? Are they living the life that Jesus lived? Are they fulfilling the mission of making disciples if they're not making disciples?

That's what we need to be pushing against. Discipleship is a journey, not a destination. And I say this because oftentimes we work so hard in our church to acquire baptisms. I do an evangelistic series almost every year. I've got one planned later this month that we're doing, so I believe in public evangelism. I believe in the three angels' messages and preach them often. I'm preaching on that in a few weeks. But we spend so much time, so much money, so much effort, to hold an event of meetings, a program of meetings, so that people become baptized, and then we're done. Our focus was on the event, the program.

OK, one more thing, and then I'll be done with this. We focus so much on the event and the planning that we miss out on what real discipleship is: people growing in Christ, developing that lifestyle of following Jesus Christ. We say, "OK, you're baptized, now you're a member of the church," and what do we do to help them continue to grow? What are we intentionally doing? Now, are we intentional about people being baptized? Absolutely. We have all the programs, all the resources available, for that, but then what? Well, we have a few things here, a few things there, but at the local church, are we as intentional about this journey of discipleship?

The second important principle to understand in discipleship is that discipleship happens through relationships, not programming. Let me illustrate this. Note Hebrews 10:23-25: "Let us hold fast the confession of our hope without wavering, for He who promised is faithful; and let us consider how to stimulate one another to love and good deeds, not forsaking our own assembling together, as is the habit of some, but encouraging one another; and all the more as you see the day drawing near."

Now, we refer to this a lot to say you need to come to church, and that's part of "assembling together." What you see in this context is a group of people that are in relationship together to help each other in their faith, to strengthen each other in their faith so that they don't fall backwards, they continue moving forward, they continue growing in their understanding of who God is, in what it means to live like Jesus lived, and to disciple other people.

This is a process of growth that is occurring happens through relationships. Everywhere in the Bible we see discipleship happening by God using one person to use another. Jesus said to Saul, "Why are you persecuting Me?" Saul had this aha moment. He had hundreds of questions. And what we do not see Jesus doing is sitting down along the curb of that street and saying, "Let Me explain it all to you." No, He sends him to a believer, because that discipleship process happens through relationships. "After these things Jesus and His disciples came into the land of Judea, and there He was spending time with them and baptizing" (John 3:22). How did Jesus disciple? He spent time with His disciples. That's how He discipled. It has to be through relationships; it has through spending time with them.

This Greek word for spending time means to rub against. When you rub against somebody, you start to rub off on them. Every once in a while I have to take my suit in and get it cleaned, because typically my shoulders get all this makeup on them, because all the nice older women in the church always have to give me their hugs on Sabbath morning. And after a while my whole shoulder is just covered in makeup. They're rubbing off on me. This is what Jesus is doing. By spending time with them, He's rubbing off on them.

So when we're talking about discipleship, it doesn't happen through programming—it happens by people being in a relationship together, intentional relationships of moving people forward. I believe that just as intentional as we are about an evangelistic series, about people coming to baptism, we need to be intentional about our discipleship path, what it means to be in discipleship. The key is to understand that we are moving people from wherever they are into a stronger relationship with Jesus Christ.

Ellen White said this: "The members of the church should give diligent attention to the Word of God, that they may understand their duty, and then labor with all their energies of mind and heart to make their church one of the most prosperous in the land."[2] Now, I don't think when she says that our church would be the most prosperous in the land that she meant it to be the biggest church, the wealthiest church, coated in gold and diamonds. I think what she means when she talks about being the most prosperous in the land is that it is the most influential, the church of the greatest Christian influence in the community.

And that happens only through focusing on discipleship. I think what Ellen White is calling us to do is fall down on our knees, to pray, to study, to research, and to ask ourselves how we can be most effective at accomplishing what Jesus Christ has called us to do: to be making disciples.

There is this spiritual receptivity scale developed by James F. Engel, often referred to as the Engel scale. This spiritual receptivity scale is a way of representing the journey from no knowledge of God to spiritual maturity as Christian believer.

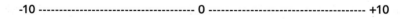

-10 ----------------------------------- 0 ----------------------------------- +10

Zero, the center of the scale, represents baptism. The far left of the scale represents those people who are not yet with Christ, and the right of the scale represents those people who are growing in Christ. So to the far extreme left at negative 10 are those people that are either hostile toward God or have absolutely no knowledge of God whatsoever, as they continue to grow from negative 9, 8, 7, 6, 5, 4, 3, 2, 1. Zero is a place a baptism, surrendering their heart, falling on their knees, and giving their lives fully into the lordship of Jesus Christ. Then they begin growing in Christ, positive 1, 2, 3, all the way up to positive 10, where we see the image of Jesus Christ fully reflected in the life of the individual.

Everything we do as a church is to move people wherever they are on this scale, up the scale one step at a time. So where are you at? Where do you see yourself on this scale? You see yourself at a positive 1, positive 2—positive 6, maybe? Do you think God is happy with you staying at positive 6, or do you think He wants you to grow to positive 7? What are we as a church doing to help you grow to a positive 7? What about your neighbors that might be down at a negative 5 or 6? What can we do to help them to move from there up the scale, one step at a time?

Everything we do as a church should be to move people wherever they are on the scale up one step at a time. That is discipleship. And we are doing it intentionally. We're not spending massive amounts of money, mass amounts of effort, to pull off a program that lasts four to six weeks. We baptize 20, 30, 40, 60 people and then say, "All right, we're done. Now we can just get back to church as normal," which is just a bunch of regular programs to entertain the members. Because then what happens is we get all these people baptized, and then they're gone. They're not staying. They're not connected. Why? Because we put so much energy into them to coming to the place of baptism but nothing after that.

So how do we do that? We need to be thinking steps versus programs. When we're thinking discipleship, we think of steps, not programs. If someone is coming to Christ, what are the steps that take place from a place of somebody who doesn't yet have a relationship with Christ toward the image of Christ being fully reflected in the life of the individual? And as a church, you need to wrestle with that. You need to take the time praying it through and saying, What are the steps that happen in the life of the individual to get from where they are to where God has called them to be? A program is a system of services, opportunities, or projects, usually designated to meet a social need. Steps, on the other hand, are a series of actions, processes, or measures taken to achieve a goal.

We're looking to move people one step at a time in their relationship with God, so what are the steps that we identify as a church? Baptism is one of those steps. Often the first step in the process of discipleship is the public proclamation and a decision that they have made in their heart. When we develop these steps, every step should be easy. Not to say surrendering your life to Jesus Christ is easy, but the opportunity for them to make that decision should be provided for them. They shouldn't have to go through a series of obstacle courses to figure out what they need to do to get baptized. What do I need to do to start Bible studies, get baptized, join the church, etc.? Every step should be obvious.

Everybody, wherever they are, should know their next step in discipleship is this—whether they are new to your church or have been a member for years. Somebody who has just started coming to your church should know, when they are ready to take their next step, what it is. They should know what those steps are. Every step should be strategic. It should be designed to help them grow in their relationship with Christ, as a disciple of Jesus Christ. We are intentionally moving people one step at a time through that process.

In order to do that, we want to begin with a clearly defined process, designate a clear entry point to the process, design ministry for each step of the process, and evaluate whether such steps create movement. So we're creating movement, helping people move in discipleship. We're looking at our process of discipleship as to whether it's accomplishing these. People know how to jump on board, like a carousel. They know where to jump on board; or if you're using a baseball analogy, they know the first step is to home plate. Do they know how to do that? And do they know where they go next? When somebody hops off the carousel, do they know where to hop on next when they want to hop on, or what those opportunities are?

"God does not generally work miracles to advance His truth. . . . He works according to great principles made known to us, and it is our part to mature wise plans, and set in operation the means whereby God shall bring about certain results."[3] We're just providing that opportunity for people to take their next step in their relationship with Christ.

Let me just share with you briefly some of the things that we're doing at the Beltsville Seventh-day Adventist Church. We're constantly evaluating and looking at how we're doing at accomplishing discipleship, so let me just share a few things for you. The first thing is that we have identified a clear discipleship process. We've outlined four steps in the process:

1. Connecting people with God.
2. Connecting people with each other.
3. Connecting people with the community.
4. Connecting people with a life of spiritual growth.

These are the four steps that we have outlined in our church. Please do not replicate them in yours. You've got to go through the work to make it happen. You've got to figure out what discipleship means for you in your context. Our church took quite a long time to work through this process to come up with this. I mean, we even spent a whole meeting discussing whether we wanted to use the word "connect."

So you've got to figure out what you want to do. Obviously, connecting with God someone's giving their life to Christ. Baptism is what that is—Bible studies, preparing for Bible studies, etc. Connecting with each other, they become part of the local church. They're using their spiritual gifts within the church. They're plugged into ministry in the church. With the community, they're actively sharing their faith in Jesus Christ with other people in their family, etc., and they're also serving the community by actively doing something to engage the social needs of the community. And a life of spiritual growth, knowing how to pray, how to study the Bible for themselves. They're not dependent upon the pastor or a Sabbath School teacher to help them grow in their relationship with God. They are actively mentoring other people in their relationship with Christ.

This is how we've identified what a discipleship process looks like for us. At Beltsville Seventh-day Adventist Church we have identified our discipleship process. We call it Next Steps. That's our Next Steps process, and we talk about Next Steps all the time, and we use that phrase because we want people to be thinking, *What is my next step?* Right now we are completely redesigning our look, so we've taken this Next Step look.

If you come to the Ammendale campus, the original campus of the Beltsville church, our welcome desk is covered with this, so that people know that's where they go to find out what their next step is if they don't know. We have banners with this on it that we've put up. We've identified these four steps in the process and are encouraging people to figure out what their next step is in their discipleship process.

As such, we have created four connect cards, one for each step in our process. These are out and available. We reference these on a regular basis, encouraging people to take their next step, whatever it is in their discipleship process.

So it's this intentionality about moving people forward in discipleship. Just about everyone who comes is beginning to think, **What's my next step?** Now, whether they choose to take it or not is up to them, but they're getting that opportunity to know what their next step in their relationship with Christ is. Thank you.

TIM MADDING, D.Min.

Tim Madding, D.Min., serves as lead pastor of the Beltsville Seventh-day Adventist Church, beginning there in October 2014. Tim, his wife, Andrea, and son Ethan live in Beltsville, Maryland, just outside our nation's capital. Tim believes that the local church is God's primary tool for the salvation of the world, and his personal mission is to prepare as many people as possible for the second coming of Jesus and is committed to resourcing the church for that purpose.

ENDNOTES

1   Bible texts in this chapter are from the New American Standard Bible.
2   Ellen G. White, in *Review and Herald,* Sept. 6, 1884.
3   Ellen G. White, *Christian Service* (Washington, D.C.: Review and Herald Pub. Assn., 1925), p. 228.
4   *Ibid.,* p. 121.

The Amazing Influence of Sabbath School for Discipleship and Growth

RAMON J. CANALS, D.Min.

CHRISTIANITY HAS BEEN EXPERIENCING a continuing decline in Bible study and prayer. According to the Pew Research Center, only one third of Christians in the United States read the Bible at least once a week. Like many Christian churches, our own church is being affected. If transformation is to happen in the church, the study of the Bible must be front and center, for without it there is no spiritual growth. Ellen G. White writes, "None but those who have fortified the mind with the truths of the Bible will stand through the last great conflict." As Seventh-day Adventists we are blessed to have a religious-education institution for members of all ages—Sabbath School! Sabbath School was designed with the purpose of helping its members grow in spiritual understanding as they get into the Word of God daily. Sabbath School has a tremendous qualitative and quantitative influence on making disciples and growing and developing the church. What changes must happen in local church Sabbath Schools to harness their potential to improve and enlarge the church? What is the secret of getting church members excited about coming to church early and staying in the church? These are questions many people are asking.

The answer to these questions might be a different kind of Sabbath School—a Sabbath School focused on worshipping God through prayer, Bible study, genuine fellowship, and uncompromising focus on mission. This is not a dead or boring Sabbath School. This is what I call "Sabbath School Alive"!

Sabbath School has been called the "heart of the church" for good reasons. If rightly conducted, Sabbath School can bring life to the church, just as the heart brings lifesaving blood to the body. In other words, Sabbath School has an amazing influence for church growth and retention of members. Calling Sabbath School the heart of the church might sound like a cliché, yet it is an undeniable truth.

Not only is Sabbath School the heart of the church, but its importance in the life of the believer cannot be underestimated. I like to define Sabbath School as an opportunity for developing relationships: relationship with God, relationships with one another, and relationships with the community. Thus, Sabbath School is about restoring relationships on the Sabbath day—a day designed by God for worship and fellowship. It is about worshipping God and making disciples—learning and growing in the knowledge of God (Colossians 1:10).

As in the days of the Colossian church, we face the danger of being deceived by the elemental spiritual forces of the world rather than growing by abiding in Christ. We face the danger of forgetting who we are and why are we here. We should never forget that we are people of the Bible and that we are called to prepare the world for the second coming of Jesus.

I was baptized into the Seventh-day Adventist Church at the age of 20 after a dramatic encounter with the Lord Jesus Christ. Although I grew up serving as an altar boy in the Catholic Church, I had never read the Bible. After my baptism as a Seventh-day Adventist I was given an assignment that I credit with helping me develop a love for the Bible and for Sabbath School. I was asked to teach the youth Sabbath School lesson.

Although I had never studied the Bible before, let alone taught it to others, I took this responsibility seriously. I began to study the Bible study guides and the Bible intensely, getting up very early every morning to study. One of the reasons I spent so much time studying the Bible was that I knew so little about it and I wanted to be sure I knew my lesson well when before the class on Sabbath. The effort of getting up early in the morning and dedicating hours to prayer and the daily study of the Bible were instrumental in cementing my faith and deepening my love for my Savior, Jesus. Reading the Bible daily helped me acquire a deeper understanding of God's will as it is outlined in the Bible, and a desire to share this knowledge with other people. I grew spiritually as I spent time with God and His Word.

The result will be the same for anyone who decides to spend time with God and the study of His Word. As we grow spiritually, we become aware of our fallen condition and are more willing to become partners with God in saving souls for the kingdom of heaven. As we continue to grow in the knowledge of the will of God, we will learn to please Him in everything we do. It is this knowledge and a love for Jesus that keeps people in the church. We can devise plans and strategies to keep people in the church. We can try to close the back door and the windows and pehaps the chimney to prevent people from leaving the church. But unless we help them develop a close relationship with Jesus thorough the study of the Bible and prayer, all efforts will fail.

Church growth has been a subject of much study in recent years. Everyone in church leadership is concerned about the empty pews. As a pastor, I hated the empty pews. And I asked myself the question "How can I reverse this trend? How can I fill the empty pews?" Several years ago I was serving as a pastor in a church that had been declining for years. As I started praying and thinking about what to do, I realized that the answer to my questions was right in front of my eyes: the Sabbath School class. Yes, the Sabbath School class! I realized that all the resources I needed to bring revival to the church were right there staring at me.

The Sabbath School class is the perfect structure for church growth because of its size. Any expert in church growth will tell you that to grow a healthy church, you need to develop small groups. Why small groups? Here are 10 reasons:

1. **Jesus' Example:** To grow His church, Jesus chose a small group of disciples. Small group ministry was Jesus' way of making disciples. "You did not choose me, but I chose you and appointed you to go and bear fruit—fruit that will last—and so that whatever you ask in my name the Father will give you" (John 15:16).[3]

2. **Ellen White's Counsel:** Ellen White encourages small groups focused on mission. The Sabbath School class is a functioning small group. "The formation of small companies as a basis of Christian effort is a plan that has been presented before me by One who cannot err."[4]

3. **Spiritual Growth:** The Sabbath School class is ideal for spiritual growth. Small groups provide a special environment for experiencing God as we worship Him through the study of the Bible, prayer, and fellowship. "For where two or three gather in my name, there am I with them" (Matthew 18:20).

4. **Encouragement:** To encourage one another in a small setting is better than in a large group. Small groups help facilitate biblical applications to your personal situation. "See to it, brothers and sisters, that none of you has a sinful, unbelieving heart that turns

away from the living God. But encourage one another daily, as long as it is called Today, so that none of you may be hardened by sin's deceitfulness" (Hebrews 3:12, 13).

5. **Fellowship:** The best way to find fellowship is in a small group. Small groups provide growth in Christian lifestyle through shared experiences, victories, and challenges, in a familiar setting. "They devoted themselves to the apostles' teaching and to fellowship, to the breaking of bread and to prayer" (Acts 2:42).

6. **Responsibility:** Sabbath School helps members become responsible for their own spiritual growth. Instead of depending on the pastor to nurture and care for them, through the small Sabbath School class they learn to care for themselves and for one another. The small-group setting can help members overcome sin through the encouragement of sharing struggles and victories. "Submit to one another out of reverence for Christ" (Ephesians 5:21).

7. **Discipleship:** A small Sabbath School class can facilitate discipleship more effectively than the large church (see Matthew 28:18-20). Small groups help fulfill the Great Commission to make disciples by offering a place to worship, pray, study the Bible, and grow.

8. **Meaning and Fulfillment:** There is nothing more powerful to help people stay in the church than a sense of belonging and meaning. The small Sabbath School class can develop projects to impact their community. Small groups offer the opportunity to serve God by helping others. "Day after day, in the temple courts and from house to house, they never stopped teaching and proclaiming the good news that Jesus is the Messiah" (Acts 5:42).

9. **Tender Loving Care:** The small Sabbath School class is effective in caring for and loving one another. Small groups are an intimate place where love and care are given and received. "Be kind and compassionate to one another, forgiving each other, just as in Christ God forgave you" (Ephesians 4:32).

10. **Success:** The small Sabbath School class focused on Bible study, prayer, and soul winning is resulting in church growth wherever it is implemented (see Acts 2:41-47). Wherever this methodology is carefully followed, it yields fruit! It is successful in making disciples!

How can Sabbath School be an influence to help you grow your church and make disciples? Here are three ways.

I. SABBATH SCHOOL HELPS YOUR CHURCH GROW SPIRITUALLY

Spiritual growth can happen only as we feed ourselves from the Word of God. Ellen G. White comments, "The beauty and riches of the word have a transforming influence on mind and character."[5] If church members depend on the 30-minute sermon from the pulpit once a week, they will become weak, dependent church members. On the contrary, if they study for themselves daily and connect with God individually, they will be strong, independent disciples growing in grace and serving their communities.

Sabbath School is a tremendous influence on growth in the Christian faith and on maturing in Christ. Ellen G. White writes, "The influence growing out of Sabbath school work should improve and enlarge the church."[6]

Influence to Improve the Church

Sabbath School is the very basis of our Christian growth; it is the daily, weekly, continuous focus on God's Word that leads an individual, and the church collective, to grow in spiritual strength. The emphasis on Sabbath School, and Sabbath School attendance, is vital if the individual and the church are to flourish in spiritual growth and biblical understanding.

The influence of Sabbath School in the growth of the church cannot be underestimated. Sabbath School, if rightly conducted, can be an agency for growth in the church by helping its members know God and develop a close relationship with Jesus. There is nothing more effective for spiritual development than the study of the Bible. Satan is aware of the power of the Bible for spiritual transformation and for keeping people connected to Jesus and active in the church. Ellen G. White asserts, "Satan well knows that all whom he can lead to neglect prayer and searching of the Scriptures, will be overcome by his attacks. Therefore he invents every possible device to engross the mind."[7] This is why we must do everything possible to help people love and study the Bible. People cannot love Jesus, who is our life, if they don't know the Bible, because it is in the Bible that Jesus is revealed.

II. SABBATH SCHOOL HELPS YOUR CHURCH GROW NUMERICALLY

Influence to Enlarge the Church

To enlarge the church means simply to make it bigger—to help it grow. Sabbath School can enlarge the church by teaching members how to give

Bible studies, how to share their faith, how to work in their communities, and how to make disciples. The importance of Sabbath School as an instrument for church growth was clearly set forth by Ellen G. White when she said, "The object of Sabbath school work should be the ingathering of souls."[8] Notice that she saw Sabbath School as an institution that could help enlarge the church through numerical growth.

Mandate to Make Disciples

The Great Commission of Jesus is a mandate to make disciples. Therefore, making disciples should be a priority for any pastor or church leader who wishes to follow in the footsteps of the Master. The Sabbath School class has the perfect structure for discipleship and disciple-making.

The Gospel of Matthew introduces the beginning of Jesus' public ministry with His preaching the arrival of the Kingdom of God (Matthew 4:17). "Follow me, and I will send you out to fish for people" (verse 19). "Go rather to the lost sheep of Israel. As you go, proclaim this message: The kingdom of heaven has come near" (Matthew 10:6, 7). After Jesus' resurrection He gave His disciples His final all-encompassing command to make disciples of all nations (see Matthew 28:19). With this command Jesus created a self-perpetuating, living organism that will never run out of human resources. Sabbath School, if done correctly, can be a powerful instrument in making disciples.

III. SABBATH SCHOOL KEEPS YOUR CHURCH UNITED THEOLOGICALLY

Sabbath School is the instrument designed by God to keep the church together theologically, because Sabbath School is the vehicle through which the universal message of the three angels of Revelation 14 is proclaimed to its members. The global perspective of the SDA Church is acquired through the Sabbath School. If Sabbath School disappeared, the church would lose its integrity as a world church. Thus, Sabbath School is the golden thread that keeps the Seventh-day Adventist Church united theologically and sociologically.

A study conducted by the General Conference Department of Archives, Statistics, and Research found two important factors regarding Sabbath School. The first factor was that Sabbath School is a powerful, positive influence in church life around the world. The study found that the adult Sabbath School lessons are well liked and regarded as spiritually beneficial by church members everywhere. So too is the overall experience of Sabbath School. The researcher, David Trim, concluded that "it is a strength on which the church should build."[9]

Another important takeaway from the study, Trimm reported, was that less than half of all Seventh-day Adventists worldwide have experienced any denominational education, and many pastors have had limited Adventist education. Although the percentage of church members who have attended Adventist educational institutions partly reflects rapid church growth rather than lack of commitment to denominational education, this means there is a growing need for education for the children of the many recent converts. There is also a need for pastors to receive a thorough and distinctively Adventist training and to have opportunities for continuing education.

CONCLUSION

As I travel and speak with church leaders around the world, one thing has become clear. They feel that people are not attending Sabbath School and church in some places because those places have lost their focus on mission. And because of the weak spiritual condition of the members.

Sabbath School was created to strengthen the spiritual lives of the members as they study the Bible and seek to share their faith with other people. It is one of the divinely appointed methods for instilling the gospel in every nation, kindred, tongue, and people. The key to church growth and Sabbath School revival is every member involved in the mission of saving souls by practicing what they have learned in Sabbath School. "The Lord desires that those who are engaged in the Sabbath school work should be missionaries, able to go forth to the towns and villages that surround the church, and give the light of life to those who sit in darkness."[10]

The writings of Ellen G. White affirm that those who engage in Sabbath School work should be men and women of faith, humility, consecration, and spiritual knowledge. They will then be able to go forth into the world to share God's amazing love for His children. The Great Commission of Jesus was not for church growth. The Great Commission was to make disciples. However, if we make disciples instead of members, the church will grow exponentially. It's worth noting that Jesus' mandate necessitates that the church train laypeople for evangelism. Encouraging Sabbath School classes to be actively involved in their community is one way people of any language or ethnic background can be motivated, trained, and equipped to fulfill Christ's mandate. Then, as the disciples grow spiritually, the church will grow numerically.

RAMON J. CANALS, D.Min.

Ramon J. Canals is the director of the Sabbath School and Personal Ministries Department of the General Conference. Previously he was vice president of the North Pacific Union Conference and also served as evangelist, evangelism coordinator, and ministerial and Hispanic ministries director. He graduated from Central American Adventist University in Costa Rica (B.A.). He also holds a Master of Divinity (M.Div.) and a Doctor of Ministry (D.Min.) from Andrews University. Canals' mission is to encourage, energize, empower, and equip the saints for the mission of saving souls. Canals enjoys racquetball, reading, music, and memorizing entire chapters and books of the Bible. He is married to Aurora, an assistant treasurer at the Chesapeake Conference who holds a Bachelor of Business Administration. They have two adult children, Jessica and Gabriel, and three beautiful grandchildren.

ENDNOTES

1   https://www.pewresearch.org/fact-tank/2017/04/14/5-facts-on-how-americans-view-the-bible-and-other-religious-texts/.
2   Ellen G. White, *The Great Controversy* (Mountain View, Calif.: Pacific Press Pub. Assn., 1911), p. 593.
3   Bible texts in this article are from the New International Version.
4   Ellen G. White, *Evangelism* (Washington, D.C.: Review and Herald Pub. Assn., 1946), p. 115.
5   Ellen G. White, *Christ's Object Lessons* (Washington, D.C.: Review and Herald Pub. Assn., 1900, 1941), p. 132.
6   Ellen G. White, *Counsels on Sabbath School Work* (Washington, D.C.: Review and Herald Pub. Assn., 1938), p. 9. (Italics supplied.)
7   E. G. White, *The Great Controversy*, p. 519.
8   E. G. White, *Counsels on Sabbath School Work,* p. 61.
9   David Trim, *Strategic Issues From Global Research* (Silver Spring, Md.: General Conference of Seventh-day Adventists, 2011-2013).
10 Ellen G. White, in *Sabbath School Worker,* Sept. 1, 1892, p. 74.

Two Sides of Sanctification

BONITA JOYNER SHIELDS

SOME PEOPLE BELIEVE THAT DISCIPLESHIP and stewardship are one and the same. As a former discipleship coordinator and now a stewardship director, I disagree. Having said that, I have, after studying both, arrived at the conclusion that they are two sides of the same coin.

The coin: sanctification.

Before I begin, let me say that this is the first time I've presented these thoughts in a formal setting. They have been germinating in my mind for several years. So, please, let's dialogue. I believe discipleship and stewardship are very important to our sanctification. In my presentation I use the terms process and *practice*. My intention is not to place these two aspects of our Christian lives into a box. However, these terms aid me in explaining my hypothesis.

Discipleship is a *process* through which believers travel as they express their faith and obedience. Through this process we grow in their connection with God, self, and others; in our understanding of Jesus and His teachings; in our service in God's mission of revelation and reconciliation; and in our living in community to help one another know, love, and serve God. (This process is explained more fully later in the presentation.)

Stewardship is a *practice* through which believers express their faith and obedience. Through this practice we grow in their faithfulness in managing the tangible and intangible resources of God that He has so graciously bestowed on us in our new life. These resources include our time, our abilities, our possessions, our relationships, even God's grace. (To understand more about the role of faithful stewardship in our lives, go to www.nadstewardship.org.)

Of course, process and practice overlap. Being a fruitful disciple and a faithful steward are both works of faith. Both require obedience. Both are essential aspects of the work of sanctification in our lives—which we all know is a work of a lifetime.

In this next section I will give a history of the process of discipleship that was identified by the General Conference and Andrews University and unpack the concept. I will also unpack the concept of stewardship.

TOGETHER GROWING FRUITFUL DISCIPLES IN CONTEXT

In 2005 a vision was cast at the General Conference session for the 2005–2010 quinquennium for the *Tell the World* initiative. Part of this initiative was Disciples Alive!—a comprehensive, integrated thrust created by Mike Ryan, GC vice president, and Marty Feldbush, director of GC Chaplaincy Ministries. The purpose of Disciples Alive! was to refocus and align the departments around a common paradigm, diminish overlap, identify gaps for more efficient and comprehensive discipling, and enable departments to focus their expertise on the common task of discipling.

In 2006 the General Conference invited Jane Thayer of the SDA Theological Seminary to present on the subject of discipleship, in which she introduced the four processes of discipleship: connecting, understanding, ministering, and equipping. From that beginning, the steering committee of the General Conference Ministries Committee (MINCOM) developed a working theology of discipleship and, the same year, MINCOM adopted the concept of discipleship as a paradigm for itself.

In 2007 MINCOM renamed the discipleship thrust Growing Disciples and an in-house management team was named: Ron Flowers, Kathy Beagles, Maria Ovando-Gibson, and Bonita Shields. The Growing Disciples concept was presented to the 2007 Annual Council.

During the years of 2007–2009, Kathy Beagles (assistant professor, Seventh-day Adventist Theological Seminary) validated the *Growing Disciples in Community* model in her dissertation using Valuegenesis 2 data, with equipping as the independent variable (or discipling aspect) and the others—connecting, understanding, and ministering—as the personal processes of personal discipleship.

During the years 2009–2010, Glynis Bradfield (CIRCLE, director, Andrews University) validated a self-assessment aligned to the Growing Disciples framework, with a sample of adolescents in three world divisions: North American, Southern Africa-Indian Ocean, and South Pacific. This confirmed the four-process model. Based on her research, an assessment tool is available online at www.growingfruitfuldisciples.com.

In 2010, because of trademark issues, *Growing Disciples* was renamed

Together Growing Fruitful Disciples (TGFD). Also, during this year Ron Flowers retired, Bonita Shields assumed leadership, and TGFD was placed in the General Conference Sabbath School and Personal Ministries Department (SSPM).

During the years of 2010–2016, the events listed below took place (not an exhaustive list):

2011

- The TGFD framework is shared with Sabbath School and Personal Ministries (SSPM) division counterparts during the SSPM advisory in Silver Spring, Maryland.
- The Greater Sydney Conference implemented the TGFD model in their conference, churches, and schools.

2012

- *In Step With Jesus,* the New Members' Bible Study Guide, based on the TGFD framework, was developed.
- The *Journal of Adventist Education (JAE)* dedicated the entire Summer issue to discipleship.
- Kathy Beagles, Glynis Bradfield, and Bonita Shields gave TGFD presentations at the NAD Teachers' Convention. The special issue of *JAE* was placed in each teacher registration bag.
- The GC Youth Ministries Department created a five-series discipleship curriculum based on the TGFD framework.

2013

- Bonita Shields met with Lawrence Burn and Dale Goodson from Adventist Frontier Mission to discuss how TGFD could inform their work. Burn and Goodson voiced their desire to have the GC develop principles/guidelines for discipleship to guide them in their work.
- Bonita Shields met with Rick McEdward from GC Adventist Mission to discuss the church's need for a discipleship model in the context of mission.
- Bonita Shields met with Paul Brantley and several NAD church pastors as a discipleship consultant in Wingdale, New York. This meeting preceded the Urban Mission Conference, for which she gave an opening address and presented a workshop on discipleship.
- Shields presented a five-lesson course on teaching for discipleship in workshops to GC and world leaders.

I share this history not to put you to sleep! I share it to show how this model has been taught to many throughout the world field and hopefully to show its potential to help the world church operate under a common understanding of the discipleship process.

WHAT IS TOGETHER GROWING FRUITFUL DISCIPLES

This model includes two primary elements:

The Framework. This framework describes the process of discipleship that I mentioned earlier: connecting with God, self, and others; understanding Jesus and His teachings; serving in God's mission of revelation and reconciliation; and living in community to help one another to know, love, and serve God.

Within this framework are listed commitments, statements of action that reveal our dedication to the process of discipleship. For example, if I am connecting with God, self, and others, one of the ways through which I commit to this is to develop a dynamic, deepening relationship with God by communing with Him regularly through His Word, prayer, and other Christian disciplines; participating with other believers in worshipping God on Sabbath and at other times; paying attention to what God is doing and praising Him for His love and faithfulness, etc.

This is *not* a checklist. It merely offers commitments that we believe growing disciples make to God and to themselves as they seek to walk in faith and obedience to Jesus, and indicators that the Spirit is working in their lives.

Spiritual Growth Inventory. A user of the website will create a free online account, then answer an 84-question survey that will give real-time feedback regarding the person's spiritual growth in relation to the TGFD discipleship model. For example, a user will answer such questions as "I am deepening my relationship with God," "I am sharing my faith through my daily activities," "I am encouraging others to spend time with God daily," etc. From these answers, a graph will be created showing in what areas a person is strong in their discipleship journey and in what areas he or she has needed growth.

This tool was created with the world church in mind: something not so specific that other contexts around the world couldn't use it, or so nebulous that no one could use it.

But questions remain:

1. How can we use this tool to bring the church together in discipleship work?

2. How can we use this tool to equip our leaders in their discipling of members?
3. How can the member use it in their personal discipleship journey?

STEWARDSHIP AS LIFE MANAGEMENT

Just as important as the *process* of discipleship to our sanctification is the **practice** of stewardship—managing the new life that God has given us as disciples of Christ—this includes tangible and intangible resources. To understand stewardship more fully, we have to go back to the beginning.

Reversal

We were created to be stewards. We were rulers of the free world—the Garden of Eden. But we believed the lie. What was the lie? The lie that Satan convinced Adam and Eve of in the Garden was this: *They didn't have enough.*

They didn't have enough trees to pick from.

They didn't have enough knowledge.

They didn't have enough respect.

God was withholding.

A relationship with God wasn't enough.

Satan created in Adam and Eve a mind-set of scarcity (it's never enough) and took away their mind-set of abundance (our Creator has given us all that we need). Satan succeeded in convincing them to focus on what they didn't have, rather than on what they had. Thus, they had neither.

Not much different from today, is it?

Most Christians live in that same mind-set of scarcity. Rather than believe that God is the owner and the source of all we need, they believe they are the owner and source of all they need. Rather than believe that God has control of the world, they try to control the world and everyone around them! Rather than believe that God's design for our lives is best, they believe their way is superior. Rather than embrace their roles as stewards/managers of God's world, they have decided to take over the world! That's a heavy burden. But the good news is that through Christ, we can be reinstated as stewards.

Redemption

First Timothy 1:3, 4: "As I urged you when I went into Macedonia, stay there in Ephesus so that you may command certain people not to teach false doctrines any longer or to devote themselves to myths and endless genealogies. Such things promote controversial speculations rather than advancing God's work—which is by faith" (NIV).

What did Paul consider "God's work"? Did he use the word *euaggeli'on,* the Greek word from which we take "evangelize"? Did he use the word **erga'zomai,** which means "work, perform, do, acquire by labor"?

No. He used the word *oikonomian.*

"What's *that*?" you ask.

That's a form of the Greek word that is directly translated as "stewardship."

"Where did *that* come from?" you ask.

My sentiments exactly.

Paul was in essence saying that *stewardship* is God's work. How could that be? Actually, stewardship is *not* an outdated concept, as many people think. Nor is it a method for pastors to fleece their flocks of their money. *Stewardship is an active, dynamic principle* for the Christian that has long been misunderstood and even ignored. *Stewardship is the means through which we learn to manage the new life God gives us as disciples in this present life, and to qualify us for the management of eternal things in the future life.*

God's work in redemption involves not only what He does *through* us, but what He does *in* us. It is so much bigger than what happens on Sabbath mornings or in evangelistic meetings. God's redemption tells us that God is the Creator and Source of Life, that we were made in His image, that He is the owner of all we have, that we were given dominion over His world, and that we are His children and have all that we need.

HOW DO DISCIPLESHIP AND STEWARDSHIP ALIGN?

To answer this question, let me tell you a story.

Otto Koning was a missionary in New Guinea. He worked among a native tribe that had known only their village ways. One of those village ways was stealing from others. When Otto and his wife arrived and moved into a hut, the natives often came by to visit. The Konings would notice that after the natives left the missionaries' home, various household items had disappeared. They saw these items again when they went to preach in the natives' village.

The only fruit Otto could grow on the island was pineapples. Otto loved pineapples, and he took pride in the pineapples he was able to grow. However, whenever the pineapples began to ripen, the natives would steal them. Otto could never keep a ripe pineapple for himself. This was a frustration, and he became angry with the natives. All during the seven-year period in which this took place, Otto preached the gospel to these natives, but never had a conversion.

The more the natives stole, the angrier Otto became. Finally, one day Otto had a German shepherd dog flown in from another missionary to protect his pineapple garden after other frustrated efforts failed. This only further alienated the natives from him.

Otto took a furlough to the United States and attended a conference on personal rights. At this conference he discovered that he was frustrated over this situation because he had taken personal ownership of his pineapple garden. After much soul searching, he gave his garden to God. Soon the natives started having problems among their tribe. They discovered that Otto was the reason for their problems because he had given his garden to his God. The natives saw a correlation between what Otto had done and their own lives being affected by calamities in their village. When Otto gave his garden to God, he no longer got angry, and was free from worry. The natives started bringing him fruit from the garden because they didn't want any more calamities to come into their village.

The light came on one day when a native said to Otto, "You must have become a Christian, Otto. You don't get angry anymore. We always wondered if we would ever meet a Christian." They had never associated Otto with the kind of person he was preaching about, because his message did not line up with his life. Otto was broken in spirit when he realized he had been such a failure.

At the end of seven years he witnessed his first conversion, and many began coming to Christ once he fully gave his garden to God. The fruit grew so abundant that Otto began exporting it and growing other types of fruit, such as bananas. His village became the most evangelized in the whole region, yet for seven years he had not one convert.

Otto realized something each of us must realize: To gain your life, you must lose it, along with your possessions. It was only when he gave all his possessions to God that he became free from them. God measured back to him manifold once He had complete ownership.

"Whoever finds his life will lose it, and whoever loses his life for my sake will find it" (Matthew 10:39, ESV).*

CHALLENGE

It wasn't until Otto became a faithful steward of what God had given him and acknowledged God as owner of all that he had did he become a fruitful disciple.

How might faithful stewardship impact your discipleship journey?
*https://coachellvalley.com/pineapple-story/

Bonita Joyner Shields was director of stewardship for the North American Division when she gave this presentation. As of November 2019 she serves the North American Division as vice president for ministries.

BONITA JOYNER SHIELDS

Prior to serving in the North American Division, Bonita Joyner Shields served for 14 years in the General Conference as an editor and assistant director for the discipleship in the Sabbath School and Personal Ministries Department and as an assistant editor of the Adventist Review/Adventist World. She began her ministry as an associate pastor of the Spencerville church in Silver Spring, Maryland. Shields received her undergraduate degree in theology at Washington Adventist University and her master's degree in pastoral ministry from Andrews University. She holds certifications in financial coaching and stewardship. Shields believes that an understanding of our identity in Christ as not only fruitful disciples but faithful stewards of our entire lives will help God's people live more gratefully, joyfully, and generously. She lives in Silver Spring, Maryland, with her husband, Roy, of almost 36 years.

---

* https://coachellavalley.com/pineapple-story/.

Nurture and Heart Retention

A reliable predictor helps to prevent dropout.

MARCOS FAIOCK BOMFIM

THE ADVENTIST CHURCH IS CURRENTLY facing a challenging average retention rate of 50 percent,[1] obviously with a corresponding evasion rate. More than a problem for the church as an institution, it may also represent an eternal life-or-death issue for those involved. A question that may be important for those in church administration—from the local church to the higher institutions—is whether there is a reliable church-evasion predictor. If identified, it may help leaders to provide priority ministerial attention (nurture) to those in greater need, which would certainly affect retention rates.

This article aims to contribute to that discussion, suggesting a church-evasion predictor, which is probably the easiest to assess. It will present some concepts and strategies from the Bible and Ellen G. White's writings, as well as some recent suggestive data, about how to encourage church members to become more fully attached to God and heaven. This article will focus on ways that generosity and spiritual financial giving,[2] or their absence, may function as apostasy predictors and impact church-retention rates.

THE "HEART RETENTION PRINCIPLE" IN THE BIBLE

Heart retention (inward adherence), instead of just body retention (outward adherence), is a foremost concern of Jesus, evidenced in His preaching (e.g., Matthew 5–7). When asked about what to do to inherit eternal life, Jesus' answer surprises the inquirers, since He presents an affection—to love God with all possible capabilities and their neighbors as themselves—as a mandate of supreme importance. The radical emphasis on how this affection should be pursued, "with all your heart, with all your soul, with all your strength, and with all your mind" (Luke 10:25-27;

see also Mark 12:29-31; Matthew 22:37-39; Deuteronomy 10:12),[3] may suggest that this "nurture" endeavor is the essence of any retention program. It is so essential that without it any religious exercises such as public worship or offering giving are considered meaningless by God (Mark 12:33; Isaiah 1; Hosea 6:6).

But in a world so full of distractions, how can Jesus' followers develop this radical affection toward God? In Matthew 6:19-21 Christ states that material possessions are carriers of affections. Therefore He warns His disciples to use them as instruments for placing the affections (the "heart") in the right place, in heaven—with God in His dwelling place— "for where your treasure is, there your heart [affections] will be also" (verse 21).

The immediate context (verses 25-31) makes it clear that by "treasure" (wealth), Jesus means material possessions, money included. But how do we transfer treasures to God and to heaven, and consequently place our affections there? In Luke 12:33, 34 Jesus mentions charity primarily as a way to place treasures in heaven (and, consequently, the heart also). This, however, involves a far broader spectrum that includes all that may be dedicated to the Lord, which is suggested by the dualism earth/heaven found in the corresponding text of Matthew 6:19-21, as well as by Ellen G. White's writings.[4]

To know that to love God is the most important choice for eternal life, and that this affection may be started and increased by spiritual financial giving, is important information for those interested in developing nurture and retention strategies. Jesus is describing here His "heart retention principle"—a divine strategy devised to keep the heart in His kingdom, and not just the body in the church.

Even though Jesus' "heart retention principle" is obviously not limited to spiritual financial giving, this activity must be included as an integral item on the list of Adventist personal piety practices, according to Rob McIver.[5] McIver proposes that those practices that connect people to God must be assessed and studied together for nurture and retention purposes, including spiritual financial giving.[6]

The reversed application of the heart retention principle establishes that professed disciples who are not directing their possessions (and, consequently, their affections) to heaven (to God) are investing them in the earth and are being distressed and deceived by them (Matthew 13:22). In this way they are increasing their affections for the wrong objects, choking God's Word, and becoming spiritually unfruitful (verse 22). This misguided affection becomes a spiritual malaise called materialism, also acknowledged by John as the love of the world, or the love of things. This produces a corresponding loss of spiritual sight and a loss of love for the Father (1 John 2:15)—a fatal outcome from the nurture and retention perspective!

Even though the Bible is not against possessing wealth in this world (God is "He who gives you power to get wealth" [Deuteronomy 8:18]), riches should not be desired or sought after (1 Timothy 6:9); otherwise, God may be hated or despised (Luke 16:13). As "you cannot serve God and mammon" at the same time (verse 13), the first attention should be given to "the kingdom of God and His righteousness," and then "all these things shall be added to you" (Matthew 6:33). This obviously includes necessary material possessions.

Paul also points to the extreme spiritual risk of materialism for retention purposes by saying that the "desire to be rich" prevents many from spiritual financial giving and drowns "men in destruction and perdition." Then he explicitly relates materialism and love of money to apostasy by saying that "the love of money is a root of all kinds of evil, for which some have strayed from the faith (1 Timothy 6:9, 10)—a clear connection between church evasion and greed.

ELLEN G. WHITE AND THE SPIRITUALITY INDICATOR

Ellen G. White agrees with Paul when she says that increased "devotion to money getting" is something that "deadens the spirituality of the church, and removes the favor of God from her."[7]

If we assume that the spiritual state of a church will affect its retention rates, then we may expect that "devotion to money getting" among members will worsen those rates. Should we just sit and wait to see what will happen next with such members? May we rightly consider a "spiritually dead" state as preceding apostasy? How can the church recognize this "devotion to money getting" and "spiritual death" condition in a church member; and, if identified, how should church members deal with that person for whom Christ died? Can we consider financial unfaithfulness toward God as evidence of "devotion to money getting" and of "dead spirituality"?

Another Ellen G. White statement suggests a clear answer to that last question. Referring to Luke 16:1-13 (the parable of the unjust steward), she presents the extended and ruinous influence of financial unfaithfulness toward God by saying that "he that will withhold from God that which He has lent him will be unfaithful in the things of God in every respect."[8]

This radical and far-reaching statement ("will be unfaithful in the things of God in every respect") connects a church member who is withholding from God with the gradual development of all kinds of imaginable unfaithfulness. This leads to a "dead spirituality" stage, and finally to apostasy and church evasion.

How the "love of money" and the consequent financial unfaithfulness may also relate to apostasy and church evasion may be explained by research conducted by the South American Division (SAD) secretariat,[9] which involved the tithe and offering giving patterns of all 1,054,367 members who were removed from membership in their territory from 2015 to 2017.[10] The study findings showed that an average of 86 percent of those who had their names removed from membership during this period did not have any tithing record for at least 36 months prior to officially leaving the church, and 91 percent of them had no offering record during the same period.[11] What can we do to motivate church members to secure their hearts in the cause of the present truth, in heaven, and in God?

Ellen G. White says that the more contributors invest in the Lord's treasury, the "more wedded to the cause of present truth" they will be,[12] making church evasion far less likely. Not to leave any doubt, God's messenger explains that "spiritual prosperity is closely bound up with Christian liberality."[13] This is why Christian liberality must be emphasized, practiced, and studied whenever spiritual prosperity and higher retention rates are expected. Ellen White goes even further by saying that the "churches who are the most systematic and liberal in sustaining the cause of God are the most prosperous spiritually,"[14] and that the work of imparting the heavenly gifts (through tithes, offerings, and charity) "is the life and growth of the church."[15]

It seems clear that spiritual financial giving is strongly related to church growth and spiritual prosperity of churches, making apostasy less probable. But more than that, it is evaluated by God (2 Corinthians 9:7)[16] and therefore has definite spiritual and moral implications (Malachi 3:8-10). A broader investigation is still needed to verify data regarding the relationship between spiritual financial giving and church-retention patterns. But at least from a biblical and Spirit of Prophecy perspective, it seems evident that spiritual financial giving is closely related to church growth and spiritual prosperity and is expected to increase church retention rates. For that reason, spiritual financial giving must be encouraged, practiced, assessed, and studied, as its absence can be considered a predictor of apostasy. Members' financial records should also be studied by a select group of church leaders as a vital tool, helping them to recognize and possibly prevent apostasy by giving priority attention to those members at higher risk. A subsequent essay will be presented to address strategies and programs intended either to strengthen systematic giving and/or to establish appropriate interventions when it is absent.

Marcos F. Bomfim is the director of Stewardship Ministries at the General Conference of Seventh-day Adventists, Silver Spring, Maryland, United States.

MARCOS BOMFIM

Born in a ministerial family, Marcos Bomfim began his ministry as a pastor in Brazil, serving for nine years in five different districts in the city of São Paulo. After that, he served in the SAD territory for 16 years in different conferences, one union, and in the division, in stewardship ministries and other capacities, including the SAD Ministerial Association. Since 2015 he has been the GC Stewardship Ministries director, and his main goal is to motivate church members around the world to put God First in their lives and to be prepared for life in heaven.

ENDNOTES

1 Considering 2012-2017, according to GC online statistics reports (http://documents. adventistarchives.org/Statistics/Forms/AllItems, retrieved on Feb. 19, 2019).
2 We will consider "spiritual financial giving" as all that is given to God as a way for His stewards to worship Him, or to recognize Him as the owner of all things. It may include tithes, offerings, and charity.
3 Texts in this article are from the New King James Version.
4 One example: "There are only two places in the universe where we can place our treasures—in God's storehouse or in Satan's; and all that is not devoted to God's service is counted on Satan's side, and goes to strengthen his cause" (Ellen G. White, *Counsels on Stewardship* [Washington, D.C.: Review and Herald Pub. Assn., 1940], p. 35).
5 Robert K. McIver, *Tithing Practices Among Seventh-day Adventists: A Study of Tithe Demographics and Motives in Australia, Brazil, England, Kenya, and the United States* (Avondale Academic Press and Office of Archives, Statistics, and Research, General Conference of Seventh-day Adventists), p. 153.
6 After studying Adventist giving patterns in five conferences on five continents, McIver identifies five "practices of personal piety positively correlated to tithing," which are to "[1] attend Sabbath school, [2] open and close Sabbath, [3] study the Sabbath school quarterly, [4] read and reflect on the Bible each day, and [5] pray often during the day." For that reason, he suggests that tithing should be included "as part of the practices that make up personal piety for Seventh-day Adventists" *(ibid.).*
7 E. G. White, *Counsels on Stewardship*, p. 20.
8 Ellen G. White, *Testimonies for the Church* (Mountain View, Calif.: Pacific Press Pub. Assn., 1948), vol. 1, p. 198.
9 PowerPoint presented by Edward Heidinger, South American Division secretary, on August 4, 2018, to the SAD executive committee, with data obtained from the ACSM (Adventist Church Management System).
10 An average of 351,455 by year: 313,473 in 2015; 368,123 in 2016; 372,771 in 2017.

11 Even though the study may not be considered conclusive, it does suggest a trend that will require additional research.

12 E. G. White, *Counsels on Stewardship*, p. 73.

13 *Ibid.,* p. 49.

14 E. G. White, *Testimonies for the Church,* vol. 3, p. 405.

15 *Ibid.,* vol. 6, p. 448.

16 John C. Peckham, *The Love of God: A Canonical Model* (Downers Grove, Ill.: IVP Academic, an imprint of InterVarsity Press, 2015), p. 123.

Discipleship—Woman to Woman

GENERAL CONFERENCE WOMEN'S MINISTRIES

INTRODUCTION

BRINGING PEOPLE TO JESUS IS something everyone can do—men, women, and children. The purpose of this seminar is to teach women how to disciple new believers. This seminar was originally written by Jean Sequira in 2003 and was updated by Bonita Shields in 2018. This seminar is part of Level 2 of the General Conference Women's Ministries Leadership Certification program. The program was designed to train women globally in areas of leadership and has four levels to the program.

The seminar materials include:

- The presenter's outline
- The PowerPoint presentation
- Handout
- Activity sheets (for participants to use in the discipling process)

This seminar is somewhat unique in that, unlike other women's ministries seminars, it has an outline format rather than a manuscript format. Please personalize it with your own life experiences and illustrations to help make it more meaningful for you and the participants.

The PowerPoint presentation and handouts are related to the seminar. However, the activity sheets are for the participants' use in the actual discipling process. You should briefly review these activity sheets with the participants when presenting the seminar. The important thing is to ensure that the participants understand their role in the discipling process, and how to use the activity sheets.

For a fuller understanding of the discipling model referenced in this seminar, visit www.growingfruitfuldisciples.com.

This seminar was presented during the Nurture and Retention Summit in 2019 and submitted for this publication as a resource material by Heather-Dawn Small, the director of the General Conference Women's Ministries Department.

DISCIPLING NEW MEMBERS

The following is included as the introduction to the handouts for this seminar.

> **Say:** The purpose of this seminar is to help you learn how to disciple a new member. Included is a handout for use during the seminar, as well as activity sheets to use during the discipling process.
>
> Discipling a new Christian is both a privilege and a responsibility that should be taken quite seriously. Dedicating your time and energy to help a new believer understand the "how" and "why" of being a Christian is a task that will take much time and prayer. Yet it is a labor of love that will be immensely rewarding to you and the recipient.

Opening Activity: "Yeshiva Experience" (20 minutes)

Intro: "Today I will be your rabbi, as best I can, and you will be my disciples, as best you can. As a first-century rabbi, I will give you no answers. I will only ask you questions."

Scenario: "Someone you know quite well has just come to you and asked, 'Will you disciple me for the next 18 months? I will go anywhere you say, do anything you suggest, and experience whatever you think would benefit me. Time and money are not constraints. Will you please be my spiritual mentor/discipler/guardian for the next 18 months?'"

Tell the class to assume there is a discipling compatibility between the two of them, and that, for this class assignment, they **must** respond with an enthusiastic "YES" to this person!

Ask: "Now what?"

- If someone suggests they start by praying about it, ask, "For what do you think you need to pray?" If they respond, "Wisdom," then ask, "What kind of wisdom do you think you need?"
- If someone suggests they first get to know the person, ask, "What do you think you need to know about this person? What would you be looking for in their background?"
- If someone suggests they would teach the person how to study the

Bible, ask, "How do you intend to accomplish that?"
- If someone suggests they teach the person how to pray, ask, "Why do we pray? What is the purpose of prayer? Why do so many of our prayers not even rise to the ceiling, let alone the heavens?"

> **Say**: While most of us truly want to disciple another believer, unfortunately we don't know how to go about it. As Doug Greenwold, author of the book *Making Disciples Jesus' Way*, discovered when he took his Sunday School class through this exercise, few had any idea of how to go about it, and did not know how to address a person's understanding of God, their habits, sins, etc., that they might still be carrying around from his or her past.
>
> This doesn't mean we have to know all the answers before we can disciple someone. Actually, it's quite the opposite. Knowing what questions to ask is just as important as knowing the answers. But ultimately the most important aspect of discipling someone is walking alongside them to help them know, love, and serve God.
>
> This seminar shares with you a discipling framework that shows processes we all go through in our growth as disciples and disciplers. It includes several objectives for each process, and offers resources to help you grow as a disciple and spiritual mentor. The Together Growing Fruitful Disciples framework and the Growing Disciples Inventory (GDI) at www.growingfruitful-disciples.com will be valuable to you in your discipling of others.
>
> Let's begin!

I. CONNECTING WITH GOD

Objectives
- A. Develop a daily, dynamic, deepening relationship with Christ.
- B. Develop an identity that is complete in Christ.
- C. Develop habits for intentional spiritual growth.

Christian discipleship occurs in relationships. The number-one goal for a Christian is to abide in Him so that he or she can become more like Him—the source of life.

"The strongest argument in favor of the gospel is a loving and lovable Christian."[1]

"There is no limit to the usefulness of one who, by putting self aside, makes room for the working of the Holy Spirit upon his heart, and lives a life wholly consecrated to God."[2]

1. PRAYER

"Pray in the Spirit at all times and on every occasion. Stay alert and be persistent in your prayers for all believers everywhere" (Ephesians 6:18, NLT).

Resource: "The Privilege of Prayer," *Steps to Christ*, pp. 93-104.

"Consecrate yourself to God in the morning; make this your very first work. Let your prayer be, 'Take me, O Lord, as wholly Thine. I lay all my plans at Thy feet. Use me today in Thy service. Abide with me, and let all my work be wrought in Thee.'"[3]

2. BIBLE STUDY

"All Scripture is God-breathed and is useful for teaching, rebuking, correcting and training in righteousness" (2 Timothy 3:16, NIV).

Resource: *In Step With Jesus* (New Members Bible Study Guide), www.instepwithjesus.org.

"Fill the whole heart with the words of God. They are the living water, quenching your burning thirst. They are the living bread from heaven. . . . 'The words that I speak unto you, they are spirit, and they are life.' John 6:63."[4]

3. WRITINGS OF ELLEN G. WHITE

"During her lifetime she wrote more than 5,000 periodical articles and 40 books; but today, including compilations from her thousands of pages of manuscripts, more than 100 titles are available in English. . . . Her life-changing masterpiece on successful Christian living, *Steps to Christ,* has been published in more than 140 languages. . . . Seventh-day Adventists believe that Mrs. White was more than a gifted writer; they believe she was appointed by God as a special messenger to draw the world's attention to the Holy Scriptures and help prepare people for Christ's second advent"[5]

"The Lord has given a lesser light to lead men and women to the greater light. Oh, how much good would be accomplished if the books containing this light were read with a determination to carry out the principles they contain!"[6]

Resource: George R. Knight, *Meeting Ellen White.*

II. UNDERSTANDING GOD'S PLAN

Objectives

A. Understand the consequences of the human fall from God's original plan.

B. Understand that God forgives sin and heals brokenness.

C. Understand that Christ redeemed us from sin and now lives to restore us to physical, mental, and spiritual wholeness.

We learn from God—through His Word and other revelations of His character—what He intends us to be and do.

"And do not be conformed to this world, but be transformed by the renewing of your mind, that you may prove what is that good and acceptable and perfect will of God" (Romans 12:2, NKJV).

1. PURPOSE OF THE CHRISTIAN LIFESTYLE

The purpose of the Christian lifestyle is

- to understand more fully God's character as revealed in Jesus (John 10:30).
- to embrace the forgiveness of God (1 John 1:9).
- to experience the abundant life that Christ came to give/restore (John 10:10).
- to be Christ's ambassadors, participating in His work of reconciliation (2 Corinthians 5:19, 20).
- to prepare God's people for works of service (Romans 12:1).
- to build up the body of Christ (Ephesians 4:11-13).
- to reach unity in faith and knowledge (Ephesians 4:11-13).
- to become mature Christians (Ephesians 4:11-13).

READING: It might be good to allow the women to read a few selected Scripture passages from this section for the group.

Throughout Scripture—especially the New Testament—preaching the gospel, forgiveness, and physical healing went hand in hand (see Matthew 4:23; 8:16; 9:1-8 for a few examples). This is an example of the wholistic nature of our being: our minds and spirits affect our bodies, and our bodies impact our minds and our spirits. When Jesus healed people, He didn't just heal one element of their condition. For wholeness to take place, all elements of our being must be addressed.

"Who forgives all your iniquities, who heals all your diseases" (Psalm 103:3, NKJV).

"Don't you realize that your body is the temple of the Holy Spirit, who lives in you and was given to you by God? You do not belong to yourself, for God bought you with a high price. So you must honor God with your body" (1 Corinthians 6:19, 20, NLT; see also 2 Corinthinas 6:16).

How we care for our bodies affects our ability to think clearly, work effectively, and relate to others in the most loving manner; it reflects the value we place on ourselves as temples of the Holy Spirit.

The Eight Laws of Life and Health
1. **Nutrition:** I will eat the right food at the right time in the right amount.
2. **Exercise:** I will work and exercise.
3. **Water:** I will be clean and will drink pure water.
4. **Sunshine:** I will enjoy sunshine.
5. **Temperance:** I will not take anything harmful into my body.
6. **Air:** I will breathe deeply and stand erect.
7. **Rest:** I will rest and get enough sleep.
8. **Trust:** I will trust and obey God for strength and health.

Being the temple of the Holy Spirit informs us not only what we put into our bodies, but what we do with our time, talents, possessions, money, and health, which are all gifts from God.

Resource: Ellen G. White, *The Ministry of Healing Vibrant Life*, www.vibrantlife.com

III. SERVING IN GOD'S MISSION

Objectives
A. Look for physical, mental, social, and spiritual needs in the local community.
B. Serve in one or more ministries in the local church.
C. Share your story of your personal relationship with Jesus with community members, family, friends, and coworkers.

In response to God's love, His followers minister to others by participating in His mission of revelation, reconciliation, and restoration.

"God might have committed the message of the gospel, and all the work of loving ministry, to the heavenly angels. . . . But in His infinite love He chose to make us co-workers with Himself, with Christ and the angels, that we might share the blessing, the joy, the spiritual uplifting, which results from this unselfish ministry."[7]

In Matthew 5 Jesus told His followers:

"YOU are the *salt* of the earth" (verse 13, NKJV)

ATTRIBUTE:	SPIRITUAL APPLICATION:
Makes thirsty	Needs Living Water
Preserves	Keep until Christ comes
Flavors	"Taste and see that the Lord is good (Psalm 34:8, NKJV)

"YOU are the *light* of the world" (verse 14, NKJV)

ATTRIBUTE:	SPIRITUAL APPLICATION:
Shines brightly	"Keep your lamps burning, like servants waiting for their Master" (Luke 12:35, NIV).
Attracts	"Shine. . . , that they may see your good deeds and glorify your Father in heaven" (Matthew 5:16, NIV).
Guides	"I have made you a light for the Gentiles. . . . Bring salvation to the ends of the earth" (Acts 13:47, NIV).

Discussion: Ask the participants to share other attributes or spiritual applications that they may have thought of.

Resource: Go to www.sabbathschoolpersonalministries.org/acs-resources to request the Adventist Community Services leaflet/handbook, which is an introductory tool for creating an organized response to the needs in your community.

"And let us not neglect our meeting together, as some people do, but encourage one another, especially now that the day of his return is drawing near" (Hebrews 10:25, NLT).

"Now concerning spiritual gifts, brethren, I do not want you to be ignorant. . . . There are diversities of gifts, but the same Spirit. There are differences of ministries, but the same Lord. . . . But one and the same Spirit works all these things, distributing to each one individually as He wills" (1 Corinthians 12:1-11, NKJV).

By using your spiritual gifts in ministry in the local church, you will:

- involve others in ministry.
- bring members into fellowship.
- help the Christian community grow.
- strengthen the body of Christ.

Resource: *Connections* (Implementing Spiritual Gifts in the Church)

"If you are Christ's follower, He sends in you a letter to the family, the village, the street, where you live. Jesus, dwelling in you, desires to speak to the hearts of those who are not acquainted with Him."[8]

Small Group Activity: Divide participants into groups of no more than three or four. Give each person the "Sharing My Story" activity sheet. Give them a few minutes to look it over. Then ask each person to share with their small group (if they feel comfortable doing so) their answer to any one question from any section on the sheet.

Just like the woman at the well in John 4, we are called to share with others our encounter with Jesus. Though we all have the same God, no two stories are the same. Every individual has a life distinct from all others. What may touch someone from your life may not touch a person from my story, and vice versa. And our confession of His faithfulness is heaven's chosen agency for revealing Christ to the world.

Resource: "Sharing My Story" activity sheet

IV. LIVING IN COMMUNITY

It is within the body of Christ that we are discipled and equipped to disciple others.

"Dear brothers and sisters, I close my letter with these last words: Be joyful. Grow to maturity. Encourage each other. Live in harmony and peace. Then the God of love and peace will be with you" (2 Corinthians 13:11, NLT).

New members may *join* our church, but unless they are cared for, fed, and nurtured, they will not *stay* in the church.

Caring about our congregation is an important aspect of evangelism. We do not want to bring in new members by the front door only to have them leave by the back door.

Why do members not become active when they join a church? (See the resource below for current statistics on the reasons people leave the church.)

- Perceived hypocrisy in other church members
- Conflict within their local church and with other members
- Marital difficulties (including an unbelieving spouse)
- Lack of friends
- Burnout from activity in a former church

We must walk alongside other new members to support, nurture, and strengthen them in love. Assimilation and spiritual growth do not happen automatically. They must be *intentional*.

Resource: "Nurture and Retention Summit," www.adventistarchives.com.

Help One Another Know, Love, and Serve God

1. Establish a process/program to help new members understand what it means to be part of your community. (Some churches have developed new member orientations.)
   a. Explain the structure of your church.
   b. Discuss the importance of giving our time for service.
   c. Explain the privilege and responsibility of tithes and offerings.
   d. Express the need for new members to choose a small group of their preference within the first three months of their arrival. Groups can be formed according to:
      i. Bible study
      ii. Place in life (single, married, collegiate, etc.)
      iii. Service tasks, such as beautifying the church grounds, hospitality for a new member class, repair and maintenance of church property, etc.
2. Allow new members to give a testimony during church time, so the congregation can get to know them.
3. Align each new member with a spiritual mentor/discipler/guardian. Baptism is an ideal time for this relationship to commence. These spiritual companions will:
   a. meet regularly with the new member to pray for and with each other, celebrate each other's joys and sorrows, assist each other through challenging times, and help them retain relationships even when conflict occurs.
   b. help the new member to study God's Word, apply biblical principles to their lives, and discern spiritual truth in a balanced manner.
   c. hold each other accountable to one another for growth toward wholeness in Christ, which involves:
      i. acknowledging our brokenness and coming to God for healing.
      ii. confessing our faults to trusted believers for the purpose of healing.
      iii. being open to caring questions and suggestions when our behaviors are damaging to us and/or to others.
   d. help each other discern where God is working in his/her life. support each other in the use of our spiritual gifts to fulfill God's mission.
4. Share ways for them to disciple within their families.
   a. Encourage the father in his role as priest of the family.

b.   Have family worship in the morning and/or in the evening.

c.   Share a bedtime prayer with your children, assuring them that angels are watching over them.

d.   Choose a ministry in which the entire family can work together in a spirit of servanthood.

e.   Prepare an agape feast on a Friday evening, eating fresh fruits and whole-grain bread. Wash each other's feet in a spirit of forgiveness and humility.

"All the believers devoted themselves to the apostles' teaching, and to fellowship, and to sharing in meals (including the Lord's Supper), and to prayer.

"A deep sense of awe came over them all, and the apostles performed many miraculous signs and wonders. And all the believers met together in one place and shared everything they had. They sold their property and possessions and shared the money with those in need. They worshiped together at the Temple each day, met in homes for the Lord's Supper, and shared their meals with great joy and generosity—all the while praising God and enjoying the goodwill of all the people. And each day the Lord added to their fellowship those who were being saved" (Acts 2:42-47, NLT).

Resources:

- "Spiritual Mentor Commitment" activity sheet
- Together Growing Fruitful Disciples Framework and Spiritual Growth Inventory, www.growingfruitfuldisciples.com
- www.indisciple.org (to access free materials for parents to mentor their children)

ENDNOTES

1   Ellen G. White, *The Ministry of Healing* (Mountain View, Calif.: Pacific Press Pub. Assn., 1905), p. 470.

2   Ellen G. White, *The Desire of Ages* (Mountain View, Calif.: Pacific Press Pub. Assn., 1898, 1940), pp. 250, 251.

3   Ellen G. White, *Steps to Christ* (Mountain View, Calif.: Pacific Press Pub. Assn., 1956), p. 70.

4   *Ibid.*, p. 80.

5   http://www.whiteestate.org/about/egwbio.asp.

6   Ellen G. White, *The Colporteur Ministry* (Mountain View, Calif.: Pacific Press Pub. Assn., 1953), p. 125.

7   E. G. White, *Steps to Christ*, p. 79.

8   *Ibid.*, p. 115.

Nurture and Retention Through Service

Creating Opportunities that Strengthen Faith Communities

FYLVIA FOWLER KLINE

WHEN DETERMINING THE WORLD'S SADDEST countries, the Annual Misery Index[1] uses unemployment as a primary predictor of misery. When the employment rate creeps toward 7 percent, a country panics[2]— crime increases, health declines, divorce is on the rise, and even life expectancy is shortened. It is a time of crisis because less money and fewer people are attempting to fund the ongoing needs of a country. More alarming, the negative consequences of unemployment often linger for decades, long after employment picks up.

The rate of unemployment reflects the number of "uninvolved" people—those not participating in a country's economy. If a country panics when 7 percent or more of its population are unemployed, should not the church panic when an average of 80 percent of church members are uninvolved in the life of their local church?[3] In the average church only 20 percent of worshippers[4] are "active"—these are the people who have a church office or who pitch in when there is a need. These active participants are ambassadors of their faith. The other 80 percent are pew warmers, worshippers who check in for worship on Sabbath and check out of church life for the rest of week.

Similar to how unemployment has a debilitating effect on a country, the higher the percentage of noninvolvement and disengagement within a church, the greater the risk of a church becoming stagnant, losing members, or worse, shutting down—"By some estimates, every day in the United States nine churches shut their doors forever."[5] According to one study in 2014, of the approximately 300,000 churches in the United States, 177,000 had less than 100 members.[6] A lifestyle of service, on the other hand, is a key performance indicator of a healthy, vibrant, growing church. The measure of a church is not in its attendance but in the transformational effect it has on its community. It's about the lifestyle of service that exists within the church family.

SERVANTHOOD—THE MARK OF EVERY CHRISTIAN

If the current service projects in your church are not making a significant impact on the health and growth of your church, it may be because (1) only a small percentage of worshippers are involved in service while the rest are passive supporters, (2) the service initiatives are perceived needs and not the true needs and desires of the community, or (3) the acts of service are happening void of close relationships, and therefore are perceived as handouts or charity rather than love and support.

Connecting with the community is not solely the responsibility of the pastor.

"Ministers should not do the work which belongs to the church, thus wearying themselves, and preventing others from performing their duty. They should teach the members how to labor in the church and in the community. There is work for all to do in their own borders, to build up the church, to make the social meetings interesting, and to train the youth of ability to become missionaries. . . . They should cooperate actively with the minister in his labors, making the section of country around them their field of missionary effort. . . .

"This work has been neglected. Is it any marvel that God does not visit the churches with greater manifestations of his power, when so large a number are shut in to themselves, engrossed in their own interests?"[7]

Servanthood—helping others in love—is not a spiritual gift. It is the mark of every Christian. Christians serve others just as Jesus did. It's as simple as that. How we serve and how we use our spiritual gifts and talents are an assorted variety, but the call to serve is the common call of all worshippers. To experience maximum impact in your church, service opportunities need to be strategic, intentional, and occur at all of these three levels:

1. The church as a whole—service projects that the corporate church does as one large body (e.g., adopt a nursing home and visit the residents regularly with church worshippers on a rotating schedule).
2. Small groups—service projects that come out of relationships created between worshippers and their friends and neighbors in

the community (e.g., two families from church who live in the same neighborhood and who have children or the same age begin a book and babysitting club with two other families in the neighborhood, taking turns meeting in one of the four homes each month; after a brief study of the book, all the children are babysat by the host of the month in their home while the other three couples go on a date).[8]

3. **Families/Individuals**—service projects that individuals and families choose to participate in that make service an integral component of their Christian lifestyle (e.g., a musically gifted family offers their services once a month to a neighboring Sundaykeeping church, providing the family with opportunities to make friends outside of their own church and to partner with another church in community projects, etc.). "It is no small matter for a family to stand as representatives of Jesus, keeping God's law in an unbelieving community. We are required to be living epistles known and read of all men. This position involves fearful responsibilities."[9]

When service opportunities are supported by strong relationships and spiritual nurture, churches can result these positive outcomes:[10]
- increase in giving and in church attendance and involvement
- increase in spiritual growth
- increase in efforts to share one's faith

An example of this is a church in Groesbeck, Texas, a small town of about 4,000 people and 20 churches. When John Carabin stepped into this church as its new pastor, the building was falling apart and its membership was at just nine faithful worshippers. First they changed their name to "Living Proof." Then they began living their new name by proving God's love to their town through meaningful service that met specific needs. Two and a half years later, in 2016, their membership was 90. By 2019 it had grown to 200.[11] "In every land and in every community there are many opportunities for helpful service. . . . Look these ones up. Use your talent, your ability, by helping them. First give yourself to the Master; then He will work with you. To every man He gives his work."[12]

SERVICE—THE SHARED SPACE

"A company of believers may be poor, uneducated, and unknown; yet in Christ they may do a work in the home, in the community, and even in 'the regions beyond,' whose results shall be as far-reaching as eternity."[13] In their analysis of community-centered, externally focused churches, Rick Rusaw and Eric Swanson emphasize that "the power of service requires a deep understanding of three intersecting circles that form a visual construct for the externally focused church. Wherever churches are engaged in community transformation, the avenue they've chosen lies at the intersection of the needs and dreams of the city or community, the mandates and desires of God, and the calling and capacity of the church."[14] This section is a summary of their three-circle concept that describes the connections between the local church, its community, and God's desire for both.

The first circle represents the needs and dreams of the community. Rather than assume, learn what the true needs are. Being connected to people who work in key areas such as city government, law enforcement, and schools is an easy way to be tuned in to the needs of the community. One church, for example, hosts a monthly lunch for a few leaders and business-people. The guest list is created with strategy and intention to encourage brainstorming and networking among one another, making the church a great community liaison.

The second circle is the mandates and desires of God. "From Isaiah 65:17-25, Dr. Raymond Bakke, speaking of a future city, outlines six char-acteristics of a healthy community from the heart of God—public celebrations and happiness (verses 17–25), public health for children and the aged (verse 20), housing for all (verse 21), food for all (verse 22), family support systems (verse 23), absence of violence (verse 25). To this list we would add meaningful work (verses 22, 23)."[15] This is what God wants for people everywhere.

The third circle is the calling and capacity of the local church. "The capacity of each local church determines the part it will play as an agent of community transformation. No church can do it all, but every church has the capacity to serve the city and the people of the community in a meaningful way that represents the love, mercy, and power of God."[16]

When these three circles come together, intersecting spaces are

DISCIPLING, NURTURING, AND RECLAIMING

formed that define what happens between these circles and how they are connected. Rusaw and Swanson use John Calvin's term, *common grace*, to describe the space where the city's needs and desires of a city meet the mandates and desires of God—"Common grace is God's beneficence toward everyone as reflected in Luke 6:35: '[God] is kind to the ungrateful and wicked' and Matthew 5:45: 'He causes his sun to rise on the evil and the good, and sends rain on the righteous and the unrighteous.' God desires for all people to live in safety and with justice. The city wall that provides protection for believer and unbeliever is an expression of common grace. . . . Common grace is part of the reason we 'give to Caesar what is Caesar's' (from Mark 12:17)."[17]

Control takes up the space shared by the city and the church. There are often limitations, boundaries, and laws a relationship between the church and the city.

Salvation takes up the shared space between what God wants and what the church is called to do. "God 'wants all men to be saved and to come to a knowledge of the truth' (1 Timothy 2:4). God's words to the exiles who were carried off to Babylon are also relevant here: 'Seek the peace and prosperity of the city to which I have carried you into exile. Pray to the Lord for it, because if it prospers, you too will prosper' (Jeremiah 29:7)."[18]

The circles and the intersecting spaces point out that "as much as God wants the city to be saved and the task of saving the people of the city is the calling of the church, salvation is really outside of what the city desires."[19] If you were to ask city leaders to list their needs and desires, salvation would most likely not be on that list. Service, on the other hand, is the space that is shared by all three circles.

"Service is something that the community needs, God desires, and the church has the capacity to do. The community may not care much about salvation, but it does have needs. It is in meeting those needs through service that meaningful relationships develop, and out of relationships come endless opportunities to share the love of Christ and the gospel of salvation. The early church grew because its people loved and served. We believe servants can go anywhere. Service gives us access not only to places of need but also to places of influence. . . . Barriers to the gospel melt away when people are served and blessed. It's been said, 'There is only one way to God and that is through Jesus. But there are a thousand ways to Jesus.' By creating a thousand entry points into the community, we create a thousand ways to show the love and share the good news with the city."[20]

THE COMMUNITY—AN EXTENSION OF THE CHURCH

When you view the church's immediate community as an extension of itself, it becomes easier to find ways to integrate the church into the life of the community, to "meet people where they are, and take them where Jesus wants them to go. . . . Leading people on a personal level must involve hearing their individual story, understanding their worldview, and engaging persuasively through building bridges to a gospel-centered, word-centered way of life."[21] The strategy is simple—weave a fabric of friendship and relationships within the church's immediate community.

One way to do this is to become a part of community events, initiatives, and organizations such as the chamber of commerce, Lions, Rotary, etc. This provides unparalleled opportunities to connect. Here is how one particular church takes advantage of its membership at the local chamber of commerce.[22]

1. **They show up and make friends**—Whether it is the casual weekly meeting for small businesses or the formal monthly luncheon, they are there. But they don't just attend to be seen; they show up early to greet and connect and stay back to help clean up. This extra 15 minutes makes a huge difference in not only how they were perceived but also gives them opportunities to mingle and get to know others. It is not just the pastor who attends—church officers and worshippers, be they members or not, take turns, ensuring the church is always represented.

2. **They connect through service**—Organized and intentional, worshippers form teams based on interest and relevance. For example, church families with children that attend the local public high school make up a team and work together to find ways to connect and build relationships with other parents in the school. This "team" represents the church by meeting needs specific to the school community. During the basketball season, for example, they provide bottles of water for the team and help out at school events.

3. **They are always available**—The church always keeps up with local news. When there is a news story about a need, they are the first to show up with a plan, ready to serve, and to rally other businesses to get the job done.

4. **They take the church to the community**—Rather than hold events at the church to lure the community, they go into the community, where the people are. In the middle of town, during

DISCIPLING, NURTURING, AND RECLAIMING

the week, they run a community center that offers a variety of programs such as after-school care and tutoring, various trade classes, and community service credits for teens on probation. And on their day of worship the church has a parallel worship service right there in their community center. Because a majority of worshippers are active participants and not pew warmers, they have enough volunteers to do all of this.

Ellen G. White points out that "in almost every community there are large numbers who do not attend any religious service. If they are reached by the gospel, it must be carried to their homes."[23] While she was specifically referring to the work of missionary nurses, the premise is applicable in other situations. "It takes between 12 and 20 positive bumps (refreshing encounters with the church) before people come to Christ. Our presence in the public square through service gives us opportunities to provide these refreshing encounters."[24] Take a look at the current programs in your church and determine which ones can be repurposed for your community. Here are a few examples:

- If you have a Sabbath designated for children's church, repurpose it as free day care to the first 10 who sign up.
- Consider having the Pathfinders and Adventurers meet somewhere in the community and marketing it as a kids club for the neighborhood families.
- Partner with a local organization and take movie night from the church gym to a public space.
- Move your smaller Bible study groups from the church to a local coffee shop. The chances of random strangers joining your Bible study at Starbucks are slim, but the probability of strangers considering God and prayer during a bleak moment in life because of what they saw in Starbucks is a possibility.

WORSHIPPERS—NOT VISITORS

Within these relationships spiritual seeds will be sown. "Let us not grow weary of doing good" (Galatians 6:9, ESV). We must serve without any agenda but to reflect the life of Jesus on earth. If and when they come to church is the work of the Holy Spirit. Jesus served with no expectations. He healed 10 lepers knowing only one would say thank you. In His last act of service of washing the feet of His disciples, He had no agenda or expectation in return. Had He expected faith in return, he would have skipped Thomas. Had He expected loyalty, Peter's feet would have remained caked in dirt. He didn't even expect honesty, for He washed Judas' feet.

When the church is connected in its community and worshippers are plugged into their neighborhood, people from these relationships may visit your church. And as a church we must welcome them as if we have been expecting them. From the moment someone new steps into our church, they become a worshipper—one of us. Calling them visitors implies a temporary connection.

Like meeting for the first time the family of the one you've been dating, first-time worshippers are often apprehension. But just as how one is slowly but intentionally drawn into a new family, it is important to build and nurture relationships from the moment they first walk into the church. The power of service can play a very important role in your strategy: Just as one gets comfortable with a new family through trivial yet significant tasks such as helping with the dishes, the church needs a plan that takes a first-time worshipper from "Welcome" to "Here's the broom," from "Good to meet you" to "You're family."

SERVICE PROJECTS—NOT JUST FOR MEMBERS

New members who are not plugged into the life of the church either leave or become nonparticipants. Don't wait until you're sure they are there to stay. Be ready with ways to be inclusive. Don't wait for baptism before you integrate a worshipper into church life. Have ready a strategy of friend-making and a list of ways they can be involved that don't require membership. Here are some practical ways to be ready for and connect with new worshippers:

- Groom people with the gift of social skills to be pew ambassadors. Have them in the same spot at church every week and look for first-time worshippers in the pews closest to them. Their primary task is to befriend first-time worshippers by following a plan which the church may need to be periodically tweaked, depending on feedback and what doesn't work.
- When they begin frequenting the church and at the appropriate time, pew ambassadors connect the new worshippers with others in the church who share a common interest, are of the same age, are from the same neighborhood, etc.
- Plug them in to the life of the church by matching their interest with the church's needs. Find ways to connect them to Christ, to their calling, to others in the church, and to their community.

- Most important, grow your relationship with the now not-so-new worshipper.

SERVICE—WOVEN INTO LIFE EVENTS AND RELATIONSHIPS

Plugging people into service opportunities is not just giving them a chore to do or an event in which to participate. It's about discipling them, strengthening their spiritual health so they are comfortable sharing their story of Jesus. A nurturing plan that runs parallel to service opportunities addresses this need. Acts of service need to be combined with social connections and spiritual nurture. To begin, the group needs to have something in common that they can self-identify with—say they are empty nesters, moms, men, or young families. Then they need to add a social element as well as a service-focused assignment. For example, three empty-nester couples who meet for a Bible study every week [spiritual nurture] also volunteer together at a local shelter once a month [service] and take an annual trip together [social connection].

A legitimate barrier to any service initiative is the lack of time in people's everyday lives. One way to combat this is to integrate service into events already on people's calendar. Take, for example, two women at church who belong to a quilting group that meets at the community craft store. Since this is an activity they have already made time for and is one that brings them in contact with others in the community, this becomes their community connection, one where they intentionally, and together, befriend others and build relationships. This is an example of missional living, in which you "take your everyday, ordinary life—your sleeping, eating, going-to-work, and walking-around life—and place it before God as an offering" (Romans 12:1, 2, Message). Alan Hirsch puts it well: "We are *designed* and *destined* to be a missional-incarnational people. . . . There is no such thing as an unsent Christian! We are *all* missionaries. It is not a profession; it's the calling of every disciple."[25]

Just as important as it is to build new relationships is the need to repair broken ones. Reaching out to those who no longer worship with you is like making up after a bad breakup. It's hard work to woo a person back into your life. You must be willing to admit when you're wrong, forgive, make some positive changes, and most important, nurture a hurt relationship back to good health. You have a better chance of success if (1) you really knew the person in the first place and (2) if you make them feel loved and needed and again.

Service opportunities can bridge paths back to the church. People are more inclined to engage with a community project connected to the church before they consider returning to church. Following private, honest conversations geared toward reconciliation and renewed relationships, connect them to one of the church's community projects. For example, if the person has audiovisual skills, ask if they'd be willing to help with a community concert. Then continue involving them in projects while rebuilding the relationship. Prayerfully and patiently wait to invite them to church at a time that feels appropriate. If you're turned down, preserve the relationship and continue connecting them with community events and service projects.

SERVANTHOOD—WITHOUT AN AGENDA

"Long has God waited for the spirit of service to take possession of the whole church so that everyone shall be working for Him according to his ability. When the members of the church of God do their appointed work in the needy fields at home and abroad, in fulfillment of the gospel commission, the whole world will soon be warned and the Lord Jesus will return to this earth with power and great glory."[26]

But even when energized by our call to service and to share God's love, we must remember that we can control only plans and projects,[27] not people and hearts. That's the business of the Holy Spirit. When you've done all you can within the space where your gifts and calling intersect with God's plans, shake off your frustration but continue in grace and service, love and prayer—and always strengthen your relationships. We must merely be "willing to step outside the safety net of our church pews and cross the street into real-life, real world acts of service in order to share the truth of Jesus Christ."[28] Let your life speak the truth louder than your words.

NURTURE THROUGH SERVICE
Implementation Ideas
By Fylvia Fowler Kline

Note: Some of these are my ideas, and others are what I've seen work in churches. With every plan: 1. Add a spiritual element to your services without creating a sense of expectation or requirement. For example, provide a short devotional after an English class only for those interested. 2. Whatever the project, be regular, consistent, and dependable.

1. Small groups studying God's Word in groups of four to six to

allow the addition of another four to six of new worshippers. Meet in the community and add a social element to it.

2. "Kind" bags for worshippers to take on their way out to give to the homeless. Content suggestions: juice box, granola bar, encouraging thought or Bible text, a dollar bill. Place these by the door for worshippers to pick up on their way out after worship. It's an easy way to engage with first-time guests.

3. Friendship ambassadors assigned to pews to sit at the same place every week in order to engage with new worshipers and connect them with members who may have things in common with them.

4. Host families—regular worshippers ready to take new worshippers home for a meal.

5. Babysitting Club—A small group of families with children in the same age group who meet once a month, rotating homes. They have devotional time or read a book together (as a book club), after which all the couples go on a date—except the ones hosting, who watch the kids. The longer the tradition, the closer the ties.

6. Host a family movie night in the community. The church can do this in a community center—In most small towns there is an organized movie-in-the-park event; partner with another business. Families can do this for their neighborhood (project the movie on a garage door and invite neighbors to bring lawn chairs).

7. Super Bowl party with another community business.

8. Quarterly block party on church grounds or somewhere public for the neighbors within a block/walking distance.

9. Partner with a business to start a community garden.

10. Adopt an apartment building—better yet, rent an apartment in the building you adopt. Have a strong disciple live there to minister to the people, to hold small group meetings, etc.

11. Repurpose current events into community services—Pathfinders, VBS, Sabbath School (take all of these to the community, outside your walls. Be intentional about including children from the community).

12. Begin various craft clubs that meet in public places (there's a knitting club in the Panera near my home; tutors help kids at the eatery in Wegman's).

13. Offer cooking classes in other churches right after their Sunday service (include a free meal).

14. Offer report card rewards to local schools.

15. Offer language classes in a community space (e.g., library).

16. Read the local newspaper to identify immediate needs and for long-term planning. Follow up and help!
17. Offer free rides to the airport (stick to a schedule, be dependable—offer this in airport advertising).
18. Welcome basket for people who buy homes in the neighborhood (home sales are public information).
19. Begin Bible studies at the local university.
20. Begin a travel club (worshippers traveling with nonworshippers provide many opportunities to share their faith).
21. Partner with a local hospital to provide a free gift to babies born there (beginner's quarterly, a pair of booties, book for parents).
22. Join local community groups such as the chamber of commerce, Lions Club, etc. Encourage members to join as well.
23. Plan for a permanent presence in the middle of the community.
24. Have offsite worship services in your community center or in a public space.
25. Families and individuals find ways to connect with others in things you already do: e.g., young parents from the church having play dates at the same time, same place, same playground to connect with other parents in the community.
26. Join trivia night at the local bar (e.g., many bars in the U.S. that serve meals as well designate one evening as family night and host family-friendly activities).
27. Worshippers gifted in music offer their services to churches of other denominations (most churches pay for special music and pianists).
28. Mini concerts in parks.
29. Monthly lunch with community leaders (six possible areas to target: business, government, education, health and social services, media, religion)
30. Social media ads, ads on buses (of your services and not what you are).
31. Identify businesses that will allow literature and handouts. Keep these stocked, ensuring the material is appropriate and includes the church's name. E.g., stack of healthy recipes at the local grocery store; health DVDs at the Health and Human Services office; notes on positive living at the yoga studio; free women's health magazines at the hair salon; packets of seeds at the craft store.
32. Post on community boards a list of the month's services and events the church provides. Keep these current :)

DISCIPLING, NURTURING, AND RECLAIMING

33. Create a detailed database of your worshippers—their profession, hobbies, fears, names of children, hours of work, favorite food, spiritual gifts, etc.
34. Have a plan that ensures someone of the leadership team has a one-on-one with every worshipper outside of sickness and death.
35. Assign a got-to personal church liaison to every worshipper. The liaison contacts everyone on his list at least once a month.
36. Solicit service ideas from worshippers and provide new and more opportunities to serve.

FYLVIA FOWLER KLINE

Fylvia Fowler Kline, manager of VividFaith, has expertise in nonprofit administration, marketing, and communication. Her insights relevant to this topic are from her time as vice president of one of the largest chambers of commerce in the United States and from the six years her family served as missionaries in Nepal when only 0.1 percent of the population was Christian. Finding creative ways to share the Christian faith has been especially important to her since her stay in Nepal.

ENDNOTES

1 Johns Hopkins economist Steve Hanke's misery index is the sum of unemployment, inflation, and bank lending rates, minus the change in real GDP per capita. For the 2018 misery index, see Katie Jones, "The Most Miserable Countries in the World," *Visual Capitalist,* Oct. 4, 2019, https://www.visualcapitalist.com/the-most-miserable-countries-in-the-world, accessed Nov. 3, 2019.

2 See, e.g., these news stories: "Greek Unemployment Rate Fell to 18 Pct in December 2018," *The National Herald,* Mar. 2, 2019, https://www.thenationalherald.com/233755/greek-unemployment-rate-fell-to-18-pct-in-december-2018, accessed Apr. 2, 2019; "India unemployment rate highest in 45 years," *Aljazeera,* Jan. 31, 2019, https://www.aljazeera.com/news/2019/01/india-unemployment-rate-highest-45-years-report-190131144720377.html, accessed Apr. 2, 2019; and "South Africa's economic growth stutters," *Financial Times,* March 5, 2019, https://www.ft.com/content/1688aa70-3f53-11e9-b896-fe36ec32aece, accessed Apr. 2, 2019.

3 According to several research studies, e.g., Scott Thumma and Warren Bird, *The Other 80 Percent: Turning Your Church's Spectators into Active Participants* (San Francisco: Jossey-Bass, 2011).

4 The author uses the term worshippers instead of church members to be inclusive of all who attend church, be they members or nonmembers, and because a lifestyle of service has the same effect on both members and nonmembers.

5 Angie Mabr-Nauta, "Mourning the Death of a Church," *Christianity Today,* Mar. 11, 2014, https://www.christianitytoday.com/ct/2014/march-web-only/mourning-death-of-church.html, accessed April 2, 2019.

6 *Ibid.*

7 Ellen G. White, *Historical Sketches of the Foreign Missions of the Seventh-day Adventists* (Basle, Switz.: Imprimerie Polyglotte, 1886), p. 291.

8 Children in this group also benefit from this practice and often remain friends into their college years and adulthood, continuing the tradition of spiritual nurture and social connection.

9 Ellen G. White, *The Adventist Home* (Nashville: Southern Pub. Assn., 1952), pp. 31, 32.

10 Based on a study of more than 7,000 people and 35 churches, these findings are from Diana Garland, Dennis Myers, and Terry Wolfer, *The Impact of Volunteering on Christian Faith and Congregational Life: The Service and Faith Project* (Waco, Tex.: Center for Family and Community Ministries School of Social Work, Baylor University, 2006), https://www.baylor.edu/content/services/document.php/22980.pdf, accessed Apr. 2, 2019.

11 "A Living Proof of Love—How a Dying Church Was Transformed Through Service," *Outreach,* May/June 2016, p. 34. The author confirmed 2019 membership with Pastor Carabin, phone call, Jan. 6, 2020.

12 Ellen G. White, *Selected Messages* (Washington, D.C.: Review and Herald Pub. Assn., 1958, 1980), vol.1, p. 103.

13 Ellen G. White, *The Ministry of Healing* (Mountain View, Calf.: Pacific Press Pub. Assn., 1905), p. 106.

14 Rick Rusaw and Eric Swanson, *Externally Focused Church* (Loveland, Colo.: Group, 2004), pp. 562-564.

15 *Ibid.,* pp. 581-583.

16 *Ibid.,* p. 594.

17 *Ibid.,* pp. 599, 600. Bible texts within this and the following citation are from the Holy Bible, New International Version. Copyright © 1973, 1978, 1984, International Bible Society. Used by permission of Zondervan Bible Publishers.

18 *Ibid.,* p. 609.

19 *Ibid.,* p. 611.

20 *Ibid.,* pp. 616-620.

21 Todd Engstrom, "Meeting People Where They Are," toddengstrom.com, Nov. 19, 2013, http://toddengstrom.com/2013/11/18/meeting-people-where-they-are, accessed Apr. 2, 2019.

22 This was a non-Adventist church that the author observed during her time as vice president of a chamber of commerce.

23 Ellen G. White, *Counsels for the Church* (Nampa, Idaho: Pacific Press Pub. Assn., 1991), p. 311.

24 Dave Workman, pastor, Vineyard Community Church, quoted in Eric Swanson, "Changing Evangelism in Campus Ministry," ericjswanson.com, http://www.eric-jswanson.com/2010/09/changing-evangelism-in-campus-ministry, accessed April 2, 2019.

25 Alan Hirsch and Dave Ferguson, *On the Verge: A Journey Into the Apostolic Future of the Church* (Grand Rapids: Zondervan, 2011).

26 Ellen G. White, *The Acts of the Apostles* (Mountain View, Calif.: Pacific Press Pub. Assn., 1911), p. 111.

27 See the list of 36 service ideas entitled Nurture Through Service: Implementation Ideas, which follows this chapter.

28 Kirsta Petty, "Connecting Your Church to Your Community—First Steps to Externally Focused Ministry," http://www.faithformation2020.net/uploads/5/1/6/4/5164069/five_steps_to_an_externally_focused_church.pdf, accessed April 2, 2019.

Cross-cultural Disciple-making

GORDEN R. DOSS, Ph.D.

TODAY I AM AWARE THAT I am "preaching to the choir," because we all agree on the need to enhance the nurture and retention of new church members. David Trim has spoken powerfully about the grief he feels over the high attrition rate of our members. Cheryl Doss, Oscar Osindo, and others have added very helpful insights. Some have offered complete packages describing new approaches. My approach will be to offer a few "bricks," or concepts, that can be built into "house" of Adventist mission.*

Possibly the first and most important step in decreasing membership attrition and enhancing nurture is to clarify the goal or measure of success in mission. Car dealers define success as selling cars and mountain climbers define it as reaching the top of the mountain, but what does it mean to succeed in mission? In Christ's method, making disciples is the goal. His Great Commission makes that clear (Matthew 28:19, 20).

Jesus mingled, built relationships, attracted people to follow Him, and then invested His entire energies in disciple-making. People did not become mature disciples at the moment they decided to follow Jesus. There is no record that Jesus baptized converts. Aside from Pentecost, the New Testament records a surprisingly small number of baptismal events. Neither Jesus, nor Paul, nor the other apostles emphasized baptism as the main goal of their work. Without question, baptism is a moment of deepest theological and experiential significance on the journey of discipleship (see Romans 6). But even at Pentecost, with its unprecedented revelation of the Holy Spirit's power, much disciple-making work remained to be done among the converts after the large baptisms.

Adventists have tended to define success in mission as baptism. We feel that we have achieved success when the candidate emerges from the waters of baptism to become a church member. The fact is that new church members have a long way to grow to become mature disciples. Some members, new and old, never really become disciples in a meaningful way. We have disciple-making structures in place, such as Sabbath School, Pathfinders, and other departments. However, these structures may not fulfill their full potential, because of our unarticulated confidence that the "job is done" at the baptistry.

There may be some good reasons for this perspective that are rooted in Adventist history. The Adventist pioneers and their early converts were often deeply committed Christians who were already quite mature disciples. For them, the Adventist message was a "value added" or "finishing truth" message, set in the perspective of biblical prophecy. They felt that they became more complete Christians by becoming Adventists.

In the twenty-first century biblical literacy has declined among many self-identified Christians, secularism has become prominent, and people of the non-Christian world religions have yet to be reached effectively. Against this background the Adventist message needs to be seen not as a "finishing truth" for Christians but as a "starting truth" for almost everyone because so many need the most rudimentary gospel teaching. To understand the Second Coming, people must first understand the first coming of Christ. The spiritual journey toward baptism and the ongoing path to mature discipleship is very much longer for nominal Christians and non-Christians than for biblically literate, committed, discipled Christians of other denominations. To illustrate, leading a Buddhist to mature discipleship is a much more challenging task than guiding a mature Baptist Christian to be a mature Adventist disciple.

A disciple is one who experiences continual transformation toward the fullness of Christ in a biblically faithful way, in a culturally appropriate way, at the worldview level, in personal spirituality, in emotional wholeness, in personal lifestyle, in family relationships, as a member of the body of Christ, and as a disciple-making disciple. Christ's method includes all of these factors in a prebaptism, baptism, and postbaptism process wrapped into a package called discipleship.

Let us note two things about Christ's method of making disciples. First, He placed major emphasis on inner transformation. Passages like the Sermon on the Mount and the parables were aimed at making deep inner change. Without inner transformation, the work His disciples would do would not be effective. The "mission trip" of Matthew 10 was a valuable lesson for the Twelve, but it did not stand alone as a disciple-making method. He wanted the Twelve to become fishers of men, but His curriculum emphasized changing their hearts.

Perhaps Christ's method should be a helpful corrective for Adventists. We may rely too heavily on getting new members involved in soul-winning activity as the key to making them true disciples. Without a doubt, soul winning is a blessing that facilitates some of the inner transformation

DISCIPLING, NURTURING, AND RECLAIMING

disciples need to experience. However, soul winning should not be seen as a "silver bullet" for making disciples. Spiritual growth does not happen on autopilot. Inner transformation into the likeness of Christ needs to be addressed directly and intentionally. The Bible is the primary text for spiritual transformation, and such books as *Steps to Christ* and *The Desire of Ages* are outstanding supplemental resources.

Second, Jesus used culturally available and appropriate methods and modes of instruction. He could have created modern-style books, smartphones, radio, television, or public-address systems, but these methods were not culturally available. Instead, He stood to read the synagogue scroll and sat down to teach, as was customary. He used natural settings and events from which to draw lessons. The world's greatest Teacher left no known documents written by Himself. His example demonstrates that the Adventist message is not to be identified with or limited by a single methodology. Christ's whole methodology was receptor-oriented. He always considered where His audience was coming from culturally and spiritually, and used the best available methods to lead them into discipleship.

Some of the most effective methods used by Christ span the centuries because of their universal appeal. Stories, proverbs, parables, and drama are modes of communication that penetrate deeply into peoples' hearts. Stories are not merely valuable for child entertainment. Rather, stories are used in the Bible, and notably in the Gospels, as primary vehicles of truth. Propositional statements of truth have their place, but the stories of the Bible carry life-changing power. Human life is not lived as a series of propositions, but as a series of dramatic scenes. Truth-filled Bible stories intersect with the human story to make the deepest impact, whether among Muslims, Hindus, Buddhists, Christians, or nonreligious people.

GORDEN R. DOSS, Ph.D.

Gorden R. Doss was born in the U.S.A. and grew up in Malawi. His time in service has been divided between Malawi and the United States. Since 1998 he has taught world mission at Andrews University. He earned a Doctor of Ministry from Andrews University and a Doctor of Philosophy from Trinity Evangelical Divinity School. His wife, Cheryl, is director of the Institute of World Mission at the General Conference. They have two married children and four grandchildren.

ENDNOTES

* This written version of the presentation includes some material omitted from the spoken presentation because the scheduled time was shortened. My book, Introduction to Adventist Mission, discusses what follows and much more. See chapter 14, "A Model for Strategic Adventist Mission," especially

The Importance of
Contextual Discipleship

BRUCE L. BAUER, D.Miss.

In addition to good biblical teaching concerning the 28 fundamental beliefs, recent research highlights a disconnect between what people say they believe and their application of those beliefs to cultural and contextual issues. More emphasis must be given in helping people apply the Word of God to everyday issues of life.

THIS CHAPTER EXPLORES THE IMPORTANCE of discipleship, which is an ongoing process that lasts the entire lifetime for the people of God and answers two questions. What is a disciple? What is contextual discipleship? I begin by looking at the question of what it means to be a disciple of Jesus Christ.

Jesus said, "Students are not greater than their teacher. But the student who is fully trained will become like the teacher" (Luke 6:40, NLT); therefore, a fully trained disciple is like his teacher. In first-century Palestine, rabbis accepted students who were willing to imitate them in all aspects of life. The goal was really to "create little rabbis who can become just like" their rabbi.[1] Those who have traveled internationally will often encounter Jewish men who dress in black slacks, a white shirt, black hat, black overcoat, and with curls hanging below their ears. They are trying to imitate in all aspects their deceased rabbi. The meaning of what Jesus was asking of those who became His disciples was for them to imitate Him, thinking and doing what Rabbi Jesus would do in all situations.

Contextual discipleship recognizes the need for Jesus' disciples to wrestle with how the Word of God applies to every cultural and contextual issue faced in life. It is not enough to know and keep the 28 fundamental beliefs of Adventism. A true disciple applies the Word of

God to all types of cultural issues that are out of step with what Jesus would do if faced with similar situations.

This seems to be a weak point in the Seventh-day Adventist Church. Our church is very good at making clear, easy-to-understand presentations on the 28 fundamental beliefs in our evangelistic series. I agree that this is an important step; however, when people just give assent to the important Adventist belief statements without also learning how to apply those statements and other biblical principles to real-life challenges in their cultural context, too often what happens is that when they are confronted with cultural or contextual issues, they flounder.

In 2013 the General Conference commissioned a Global Church Member Survey and received responses from 26,343 people in nine divisions. In 2018 a follow-up survey had 63,756 responses from all 13 divisions, with a margin of error of less than 1 percent.[2] Some of the findings are troubling, to say the least, and again perhaps indicate that Adventists have done a good job of teaching doctrinal beliefs but not so well at helping people apply those beliefs to their specific situation. Below are just a few statements and responses from that survey.

One of the items on the survey stated, "When people die, their bodily remains decay and they have no consciousness or activity until they are resurrected." This is good Adventist teaching. Among respondents from all divisions, 89.6 percent agreed or strongly agreed. However, in a subsequent statement that said, "The soul is a separate part of a person and lives on after death" 8.3 percent of the respondents said they were not sure and an additional 32.5 percent agreed or strongly agreed with that statement. It is interesting that a large majority answered the belief question correctly, but when it came to applying that statement to cultural concepts and assumptions, a large percentage continued to believe in an immortal soul. Perhaps we should not be surprised, for many new Adventist members share a cultural and religious heritage with strong Catholic and Protestant teachings concerning an immortal soul or come from cultures in which most people believe that the ancestors and spirit beings interact with the living.

This ingrained assumption is an important part of many people's worldview. Most Christians believe that when they die they immediately go to heaven. Brief discussions during an evangelistic meeting or talking about this topic in one Bible study usually will not change this deeply held belief. Worldview change takes time, and usually needs multiple stories and experiences to affect deeply held values.

Notice one more statement from the survey. "People who have died believing in Christ are in heaven right now." Among all 13 divisions, 8.2 percent were not sure and an additional 19.5 percent agreed or strongly agreed with that statement. This means that 27.7 percent of Adventists were not sure or confused on this issue and seem to reveal deeply held cultural and religious values and assumptions that continue to inter-mingle with their Adventist belief system.

These examples illustrate that in all regions of the world there is still much work to be done in discipling people to help them become biblically shaped disciples. One concern is that in our haste to add *members* we have spent too little time in making *disciples*. Even though new Adventists may agree with the 28 fundamental beliefs of our church, too often they do not know how to apply the Word of God to cultural and contextual issues. In those parts of the world in which secularism, Islam, Hinduism, animism, and Buddhism predominate, a two- to-three week evangelistic meeting will never be able to change deeply held assumptions and values that are not representative of biblical Christianity.

DANGERS LURKING IN PRESENT ADVENTIST EVANGELISTIC AND DISCIPLING METHODS

What is creating this discord between doctrinal belief statements people say they accept and contradictory values and assumptions that lurk beneath the surface? It seems that during the past 35 to 40 years the very character of Adventism has changed with an eroding of com-mitment to biblical beliefs and values. Adventists used to be known as people of the Book because of their deep understanding to God's Word. Fifty years ago interests often attended six to eight weeks of evangelistic meetings followed by a year or more of Bible study. This is no longer the practice.

At the risk of offending some, I believe that part of the responsibility for this discord between beliefs and the application of those beliefs to cultural issues can be attributed to widespread evangelism methods that have become the norm in the Seventh-day Adventist Church. Too often baptism marks the end of any intentional discipling of new believers, and this is especially true when foreign evangelists are invited to do a two- or three-week evangelistic series. When they return home, often no one is present to disciple the new baby Christians.

In addition, many of the world divisions have histories of extensive use of short evangelistic meetings during which after two or three weeks with between 10 and 20 presentations, people are introduced to the dis-tinctive Adventist beliefs and then baptized. It may be possible for some to make a commitment to Christ after such a short time; but it is questionable whether they can internalize the message, sort out all the implications of their new commitment, and have a truly converted worldview in just a few weeks' time.

Another contributing factor is that in two of the divisions mentioned there has been extensive use of foreign evangelists. Unless the visiting evangelists spend time studying the cultural issues, they are unable to apply their messages to the specific challenges new Christians face when they start their new life in Christ. The local people who attend the meetings hear powerful and logical presentations dealing with truths that are important to Seventh-day Adventists, but most series of meetings spend little if any time dealing with how belief in Jesus Christ affects cultural issues. If in the conversion process belief in an immortal soul, the intercession of saints, the strongly held fear about ancestral spirits, and a host of other cultural issues are not explicitly dealt with, then it is little wonder that there is a disconnect between belief statements and the application of those beliefs to the local issues of life.

Another danger of discipleship that is not contextual is dual allegiance. This is a worldwide problem and is present in every one of the world divisions. Many Adventists in the Western world follow their culture more closely rather than following biblical principles in areas such as dating habits, divorce and remarriage, or issues of modesty. In other parts of the world, issues of dual allegiance are found in such areas as how women are treated, the continued visits to diviners and shaman, or the fear of curses and witchcraft that cause members to continue to seek protection from witchdoctors.

In 1994 the world was shocked by the horrors of genocide in Rwanda. More than 90 percent of the population claimed to be followers of Jesus Christ.[3] Adventists were the third-largest denomination in the country after Anglicans and Catholics.[4] Yet Catholics killed Catholics and Adventists killed Adventists. I believe there are lessons to be learned from that tragedy—all discipleship must be contextual. Muslims and Mennonites were not involved in the killings. Those two groups had taught and emphasized brotherhood, peace, and community. Adventists did not disciple in those areas, with the result that our members killed those who were not from their tribal group. Adventists taught the importance of Sabbath observance; unfortunately, that resulted in a group waiting until sundown on Sabbath evening before throwing grenades into the local Adventist church where Tutsi refugees had sought safety. Contextual discipleship could have focused on the tribal tensions in

Rwanda while emphasizing the oneness that we have in Christ and the importance of living in peace with all people.

Dual allegiance can also allow one's primary allegiance to be focused on something or someone other than God. Consumerism, materialism, and individualism have captured the primary allegiance of many in the West, and when Seventh-day Adventists have a higher commitment to someone or something other than God, harmful things often occur. Dual allegiance also results in syncretism that allows the blending of non-Christian beliefs and worldview assumptions with the teaching of Scripture. Contextual discipleship should involve conversations about the cultural topics that are out of sync with biblical principles.

DISCIPLESHIP FOR A GLOBAL CHURCH

When we look at discipleship from the perspective of a global church, five lessons come into focus: Discipleship must be intentional, it must be formational, it must be built on community, it must address all areas of life, and it must be contextual.[5]

Discipleship Must Be Intentional

Discipleship in any context is never automatic. Knowing belief statements does not automatically translate into a lived reality where the implications of those beliefs are translated into everyday responses to cultural issues. Discipleship must be intentional, systematic, and planned in a way to teach people how to apply the Word of God to everyday life and how to imitate Jesus in everything that is done in life. It is not enough to assume that Sabbath School and church attendance will disciple new believers so they act, speak, and think in biblically appropriate ways. Discipleship must be intentional.

Discipleship Must Be Formational

When Bible study is mentioned in Adventist circles, there is usually a sense that it will involve doctrinal study. The main purpose of most Adventist Bible studies is to share biblical information with people so that they will have a correct view of the 28 fundamental beliefs, which are important to the Seventh-day Adventist Church. Again, this is not bad in and of itself; however, if this is the only type of Bible study that Adventists engage in, then there is a weakness that contributes to some of the problems mentioned above. This is especially true of new believers. Learning abstract biblical truth without encouraging discipleship can lead to weak forms of Christianity.

There must be two types of Bible study: informational study and formational study.[6] A very simple form of formational Bible study is to focus on one of the 700-plus stories in the Bible while asking three simple questions. What does this story teach about God? What does this story teach about people? What kingdom principles are there in this story that I need to incorporate into my life if I want to be a committed disciple of Jesus Christ? Adventists do very little of this type of Bible study. Even pastors spend most of their Bible study time preparing biblical information for their sermons and Bible studies. This lack of spiritual formation creates weak disciples and allows people to know Adventist doctrines while never learning to apply biblical principles to the cultural and societal issues.

Discipleship Must be Built Around a Community

Discipleship must be built around a community, a family, or a small group. Relational discipleship allows for accountability and the opportunity for group discussions on issues one faces in society. Jesus surrounded Himself with 12 disciples who were with Him for three and a half years. They had the opportunity to ask questions and to receive corrections and further insights into what being a disciple meant. Few new converts experience this type of community, which allows for accountability and spiritual growth in caring small groups. Western societies are especially weak in this area. Too many never experience community, and some are allergic to the intimacy and accountability associated with small discipleship groups.

Discipleship Must Address All Areas of Life

Discipleship must also address all areas of life. Unfortunately, many Seventh-day Adventists do not look or act much different from the rest of the people in their cultural setting. A disciple of Jesus Christ does not live a compartmentalized life, acting and looking a certain way on Sabbath, but living like the rest of society Sunday through Friday. It is not enough to know the 28 faith statements and agree with them but never learn how to apply those statements to the contextual and cultural issues. Being disciples of Jesus Christ means people want to imitate Jesus in all areas of what they do and what they think.

Discipleship Must Be Contextual

Discipleship must also address the specific cultural issues faced in each specific culture. The "so what" of each of the 28 fundamental beliefs will be different in different contexts. If people live in cultures in which same-sex marriage and cohabitation are accepted lifestyles, discipleship must seek to address those issues. If fear of witchcraft and ancestral spirits are the issues, then discipleship must address those issues. In North America 40 percent of Christians "strongly agreed that Satan is not a living being but is a symbol of evil, [and] an additional . . . 19 percent said they agree somewhat" with that statement.[7] Thus, 59 percent of Christians plus a large percentage of the unchurched population do not believe in a real devil. In such a setting, teaching on the great controversy theme and on the existence and activity of the devil is needed. I worked in Cambodia for several years. The people there had no doubts about the existence of devils, evil spirits, and evil forces. In that context their discipleship needed to emphasize how God protects and cares for those who trust him. The idea of angels watching and protecting God's people (Psalm 34:7) and the power of the Holy Spirit actually living in God's people (1 John 4:4) were important points in the discipling process.

THE GOAL: CONTEXTUAL DISCIPLESHIP

The goal of Adventist mission and ministry is a disciple who imitates what Jesus Christ would say and do if He lived in their cultural context. The Seventh-day Adventist Church needs members who have biblically shaped behavior, biblically shaped beliefs, but also biblically-shaped values and deep worldview assumptions. In other words, the Adventist Church needs to make sure that those they call to be Christ's disciples apply the Word of God to the everyday challenges and issues of life. People can begin their walk with Christ just as they are, with their old values and assumptions—their old worldviews—but if they remain in those old worldviews, they will be stunted in their Christian walk and will continue to live with conflict and syncretism.[8] What is needed, especially when working with non-Christian peoples, is a much broader evangelistic approach than just a two- or three-week evangelistic series. Extended periods of Bible study, discipleship in small groups, and nurture that is contextual should be part of every person's journey both before and after baptism.

In addition, I would recommend that much more emphasis should focus on topics that apply biblical principles to the people's cultural issues. If Adventists continue the practice of having only short series of evangelistic meetings with poor or nonexistent after-baptism nurture and discipleship, the church will continue to bring people into membership who say they agree with the belief statements of our church, but who also continue to hold on to the cultural and contextual views of their old way of life.

In North America, if the Adventist Church continues to emphasize only the 28 fundamental beliefs as it prepares people for baptism, it will also find that Adventists are drifting further and further from having a biblically shaped view of cultural issues such as same-sex marriages, Halloween, the occult, cohabitation, divorce, and what appropriate behavior is when dating. If these topics are not included when preparing people for baptism, the Seventh-day Adventist Church will also discover that a growing number of people are joining the church with schizophrenic and conflicting views that will sooner or later stunt their Christian growth and development.

BRUCE L. BAUER, D.Miss.

Bruce L. Bauer is professor of World Mission at the Seventh-day Adventist Theological Seminary, holds a B.A. in Theology and an M.A. in Religion from Andrews University and an M.A. in Missiology and a Doctor of Missiology from Fuller Theological Seminary. The Bauers spent 23 years as missionaries in Japan, Guam Micronesia, and Cambodia. Bruce has taught in the Theological Seminary at Andrews University for 25 years and is currently the director of the Doctor of Missiology program and the editor of Journal of Adventist Mission Studies.

ENDNOTES

1 Doug Greenwold,. "Being a First-Century Disciple" (2013), http://preservingbibletimes. org/wp-content/uploads/2014/03/Reflection-DRIP-5.pdf.

2 David Trim, "The Global Church Member Survey" (2018), http://www.adventistresearch. org/sites/default/files/files/AC2018%20-%20Global%20Church%20Member%20 Survey%20Data%20Report.pdf; Duane McBride, "The Global Church Member Survey: Encouragement and Challenges," *Focus: The Andrews University Magazine* 55, no. 1 (winter, 2018): 9.

3 Peter Dunn, "4 Discipleship Lessons from a Global Perspective" (2014), https://ethics-daily.com/4-discipleship-lessons-from-a-global-perspective-cms-21906/.

4 Patrice Johnstone, *Operation World: The Day-by-Day Guide for Praying for the World* (Grand Rapids: Zondervan, 1993), p. 472.

5 Dunn; Jane Thayer, *Teaching for Discipleship: Strategies for Transformational Learning.* (Berrien Springs, Michigan: LithoTech, 2015), pp. 137-140.

6 Thayer, pp. 137-140.

7 Barna Group, "Most American Christians Do Not Believe that Satan or the Holy Spirit Exist" (2009), https://www.barna.com/research/most-american-christians-do-not-believe -that-satan-or-the-holy-spirit-exist/.

8 Paul G. Hiebert, Transforming Worldviews: An Anthropological Understanding of How People Change. (Grand Rapids: Baker Academic, 2008), p. 11.

What's Missing: CH– –CH?

PAUL TOMPKINS, D.Min.

I FIRST SAW THE TITLE question posed on a wayside pulpit outside a church in the south of England. The missing letters, of course, are UR. The church in question was highlighting that it would love to see more people attending.

There is a bigger picture also. It can also be said that what is missing are people that you and I know and whom we hold dear. The loss of young people through the back door is a real issue for the church today. It is imperative that we take steps to make sure that as many as possible of those growing up in the church will remain active members.

They are our family, friends, and loved ones. "The church can have no higher priority than stemming the loss of young adults and winning back those who have left its ranks."[1]

As a church we have been holding global summits focusing on Seventh-day Adventist Church membership retention since 2013. As a reminder, the headline from the first summit was "1 in 3 Leave Over the Past 50 Years."[2]

While speaking at a Youth Week of Prayer at a junior college in Scandinavia, I asked the question "Do you think you'll still be an Adventist at age 40?" One young woman, in the top class, answered, "I hope I'll still be an Adventist at age 40, but I'm not so sure about next year." This illustrates that for young people the future whispers, but the present shouts!

Following the 2013 Nurture and Retention Summit the *Adventist Review* published a report that included three affirmation statements. The first two involved a commitment to intentionally discipleship new members, whereas, the third of these stated, "Responsibility for ensuring that every church member remains part of the body of Christ, and for reconnecting and reconciling with those who do not, is mutually shared by the church at large, each congregation, and every church member."[3]

The challenge has not gone away, for earlier this year, in the first quarter of 2019, the No 1 risk evaluation for the trustees of my home Union was "Children and Young Adults not buying into Adventism."[4]

These are usually second-generation Adventist youth, and the question must be asked, What can be done to stop the hemorrhaging of one of our most valuable assets? These youth are leaving for all sorts of reasons, and some they find hard to articulate. Could it be that many just don't feel the church of their childhood faith is the same as that of their adult faith?

PERSONAL RESEARCH

A personal research project[5] among young people who have left the church has brought the following convictions:

1. As a church we need to place in operation throughout the world church a plan that allows for every youth growing up in an SDA home to receive access to a basic youth-related Bible study course by the time they reach their fourteenth birthday.
2. This should be backed up by a youth first program targeting the key transition ages between 14 and 17. Widespread public campus ministry programs, including discipleship groups, are needed for the 18-25 age group.
3. We also need effective discipleship and spiritual growth for the 30s and 40s age group based at the local church. If we lose them, the fact is that we also lose their children.

Adventist young people tell us that the church matters, not only in theory or as something to believe in, but also regarding their own faith experience.[6] It seems clear to me, from both personal research and extensive reading on the matter, that young people want to see the following attributes in their local church:

- A spiritual home for all generations.
- A spiritual home in which Christian values can be lived together.
- Today's youth crave participation and challenge.
- They want to know whether there is a place for them in their church.
- Service and mission are high on their agenda.
- Intergenerational family warmth and support is valued.

There are also many former or lapsed church members who want the same thing. In my research one or two respondents indicated that they did not feel that they had left—they were simply not attending at the time. They were taking a break from active participation, but that did not necessarily mean that they did not still see themselves as Seventh-day Adventists. From my research, 50 percent felt they would one day return, 99 percent still called themselves Christians, and 100 percent still had a family network in the church. These figures highlight a great amount of hope for the family and friends who remain, praying daily for their loved ones to return.

Allied to this, we should never underestimate the power of warm memories, roots, and a search for past identity. One of the respondents to the pilot survey I conducted answered, "I still carry with me and remember a lot of what I was taught. I get my children to pray every evening, but need to learn more so I can answer their questions." Another stated, "My departure from the church was a gradual one. If there is going to be a return, it'll also be a gradual one."

ROOTS AND IDENTITY

So what will bring those forces into play to help precipitate a return? Roger Standing, in his book *The Re-Emerging Church*, looked at baby boomers[7] and posits that "the search is about roots and identity, and a certain degree of familiarity will be helpful."[8] He feels that almost on a whim many will try at least once to reconnect with church, and most probably with the denomination of their youth.[9]

This was certainly found to be true in another study of returning former Adventists who clearly stated that they still had warm memories from their childhood. "Eight out of ten persons interviewed expressed memories of early Adventism that reminded them of happy times in the church."[10]

The search for identity is not static. Just as "it is part of finding one's own identity that pushes young people to challenge to challenge the values of the parents and seek to incorporate a value system of their own."[11] So too the reverse search for identity may well bring them back one day to their roots. "It is clear, however, that many youth who question their parents' values and beliefs ultimately accept them as their own."[12] Roots and identity are, therefore, a powerful combination.

Allied to this, no matter how long or short someone has been away from the church, returning is always a possibility. I cannot stress this point too much. In the course of my ministry it has become very evident

DISCIPLING, NURTURING, AND RECLAIMING

that some members who have left the church most certainly do return sometime later. It cannot be claimed that all do, but those returning have included those who later become very active leaders at the highest levels in the church.

On one very notable occasion I met a young woman who had drifted away from the church at a young age. She had attended a church primary school and remembered making a decision as a young girl to give her heart to Jesus—it was specifically when a moving hymn was played in a school worship period. For some reason this was never followed up on, and she left the school, moved to a far city, and drifted away from the church. Many years later I was with a group doing a street mission in the city, and we were inviting people to come to a gospel concert. One of our group was still in contact and invited the young woman to attend. We had testimonies and songs being shared, and the young woman attended the church for the first time in years. When the last hymn was sung, tears began to come down her face—without knowing, we had chosen the selfsame hymn from her youth. She remembered this well and knew that Jesus was calling her home. Here we definitely see the outcome of both God's providence and the prompting of the Holy Spirit.

When conducting my personal study, I formed some pilot study and focus groups, and these groups identified key life stages when a person may be influenced again to think of spiritual matters. These include times when things go wrong (financial, relationships, health, etc.) and when things are going well (marriage and the birth of children). Such occurrences are not respecters of age and can occur at any time, and then the same issues of roots, identity, and familiarity will most likely play a significant role in helping people set out for home.

As people set out for home, it must be recognized that both they and the church will have a number of issues to face at this time. Not all who return, for instance, will be part of a traditional family structure, and issues regarding marriage, divorce, and relationships outside of marriage will need to be faced.

Also, just as youth left at different times and for different reasons, in reality they will also come back in different ways and at different times. Put simply, not all people leave for the same reason and not all returning youth (or adults) will come back in the same way.

Members of local churches will need to have a heart for returning youth and be committed to helping them to reconnect and stay connected. We may have only one chance to get it right; otherwise, they may leave again and this time never to return.

INTERGENERATIONAL CHURCHES OF REFUGE (ICOR)

There is no one right way to position a church, but at this point I would like to introduce the Church of Refuge program. The roots of the program came from the Center of Youth Evangelism in North America, and I have been personally involved since its inception in Europe and know that it has been developed with the needs of young people and the church family in mind. The latest generation of Church of Refuge material is the excellent iCOR[13] package, which offers a wholistic discipleship program that highlights relationships, spiritual growth, and mission, and empowers people for ministry. iCOR "has been developed by the Inter-European Division (EUD) and the Trans-European Division (TED) and is an instrument of the Seventh-day Adventist Church for value-orientated growth."[14] It has 10 iCOR values that slot into these four areas. It should be noted that "the ten iCOR values are not programs that need to be run. They are life-changing, faith-nurturing values that are vital to true discipleship and Christ's mission. They are indispensable in meeting the spiritual needs of young and old alike."[15]

> **Relationships**—connecting, caring and participating.
> **Spiritual Growth**—worshipping and teaching.
> *Empowerment*—mentoring, training, and leading.
> *Mission*—serving and reconciling.

It is important to note that iCOR takes place locally, and when it comes to remaining an Adventist, the local church congregational climate is crucial. Young people need to feel warmth and have a place where their questions can be examined. These were known as the church warmth and thinking climates in the Valuegenesis studies that were conducted by the church in North America, Australasia, and Europe.[16]

A key area to the question at the head of this article is whether the church is ready for our missing young people to return. As I've noted from my personal research, it is very significant that 50 percent of my sample group indicated that they wished to return. This is not a definitive figure, but it goes without saying that the church would welcome back with open arms those who have been away. Here a caveat may need to be raised from the parable of the prodigal son (Luke 15). The caveat is this: What would have happened if the prodigal had met the older son first?

Recognizing this perhaps the question needs to be asked as to What is "Church"? "Church means a lot of things. Church—above all, that means you and your 'brother' or 'sister' in faith. Church—ultimately, that

DISCIPLING, NURTURING, AND RECLAIMING

means us, a community of those for whom Jesus is Saviour, Lord, and Friend. Church—that is how and what we live together in faith."[17] I think we would all agree that the church should be made up of father figures rather than elder sons.

For some, returning is easy and may indeed be to a local church. Others, however, have tangled lives and will need the ongoing understanding and support from perhaps a halfway house support group as well as their local church family. In looking to the needs of those who have left church, and may wish to return, there is no such thing as one size fits all.

As a church we need to affirm our ongoing commitment to all those who wish to reconnect with the church of their youth. There is now plenty of material to help a church make this step, and includes an *iCOR Information Brochure*, an *iCOR Study Guide,* and an *iCOR Church Board Guide.* More iCOR resources are also in the process of being produced.

What's in a name? It may be that your church or mine will forge its own identity—iCOR is simply a means to an end. What is more important is that we are there and waiting for when the Holy Spirit impresses people to take that step toward reconnecting. You see, those who are out there are family. My family, your family, our loved ones. We must do everything we can to help them return.

LOST AND FOUND

Looking further at Luke 15, we have three very powerful stories of the lost. We know them as the lost sheep, the lost coin, and the lost (or prodigal) son. We tend to concentrate on the first and the last parable of the lost sheep and the prodigal son, but the middle and shortest parable, of the lost coin, is there for a reason. The coin doesn't know it is lost, and undeniably the owner is the one who has lost it. She sweeps the whole house, however, to find it once more and then calls in her friends and neighbors to rejoice with her. This gives rise to the great statement "I tell you, there is rejoicing in the presence of the angels of God over one sinner who repents" (Luke 15:10, NIV).

The aspect of rejoicing is an important refrain from the parable of the lost sheep (verse 7). It also finds an echo in the last parable when the father calls for a celebration and states, "But we had to celebrate and be glad, because this brother of yours was dead and is alive again: he was lost and is found" (verse 32, NIV). The theme of lost and found is how the trilogy ends.

The overwhelming thought in each parable is that absolutely everything was done to find the lost, or, in the case of the prodigal son, to be there when he returned. The times are different, but the principle remains the same. It necessitates someone to go out looking.

It must be recognized that just as there are many links in a chain, Churches of Refuge may well only be one link in the reclamation process. It is not important whether they are the first, middle, or last chain, but rather that they provide a strong link to making returning home possible.

The desired outcome is that returning prodigals have the chance to return to a church home that is ready and waiting to greet them. A church that greets modern-day prodigals in the same way as the father greeted the prodigal son in the parable of Luke 15.

In his book *Christ's Way of Reaching People* Philip Samaan makes the statement "The church ought to be a refuge where hurt persons find healing and restoration in Christ and His people."[18] It can be!

We began with a question. What's missing: CH——CH? In closing, I would like to reflect that the way that the question is asked, and the way that the church approaches the question, gives the answer meaning. If we slightly reframe the question to read "Who's There, CH——CH?" The answer, by God's grace, is UR. With all of our church family, young and old, safely gathered in.

PAUL TOMPKINS, D.Min.
Paul Tompkins (D.Min.) was the youth director of the Trans-European Division for 15 years, starting in 2000. In 2015 he served as senior pastor of Newbold College church. He currently serves as president of the Scottish Mission, since 2016.

ENDNOTES

1 Roger Dudley, *Why Our Teenagers Leave the Church* (Hagerstown, Md.: Review and Herald Pub. Assn., 2000), p. 37.

2 Ansel Oliver, "At First Retention Summit, Leaders Look at Reality of Church Departures," *Adventist Review Online*, Nov. 21, 2013, p. 7.

3 *Ibid.*

4 *British Union Conference Trustees Risk Analysis*, March 2019.

5 Paul Tompkins, "Bringing Home Our Adventist Prodigals: A Strategic Plan to Reclaim Youth in the Trans-European Division" (D.Min. diss., Andrews University, 2009).

6 Stephan Sigg, "A Spiritual Home for Young People? The Adventist Youth and Their Church Seen From the Valuegenesis Europe Data, Part III," *Spes Christiana* 24 (2013): 180.

7 Baby boomers are the generation born between 1946 and 1964. This group reaches retirement from 2011 onward, and Standing feels that when faced with issues of their own mortality, they will seek to reconnect with the church of their youth.

8 *Roger Standing*, Re-Emerging Church: Strategies for Reaching a Returning Generation (Abingdon, UK: The Bible Reading Fellowship, 2008), p. 10.

9   Roger Standing sees in particular the baby boom generation searching for their roots when they hit retirement age (from 2011) and when they will inevitably be faced with the big questions of life. They are the generation that still has a biblical background, and as such he feels they will turn back to the denomination of their youth.

10 Tim Lale and Pat Habada, *Ten Who Came Back* (Nampa, Idaho: Pacific Press Pub. Assn., 1998), p. 157.

11 A. Barry Gane, "Reclaiming Our Youth," *Youth Ministry Accent,* January-March 2006, p. 17.

12 *Ibid.*

13 iCOR Information Brochure: *Building Spiritual Homes: Living Our Values Together.*

14 *Ibid.*

15 iCOR Church Board Guide: *Building Spiritual Homes: Living Our Values Together,* p. 8.

16 The Valuegenesis surveys have involved a major study of adolescence and youth of the Seventh-day Adventist Church. These studies have been carried out separately in the North American, Australasian, and European divisions. The European Valuegenesis study was a collaborative project of the Inter-European and Tans-European divisions in 2007.

17 Stephan Sigg, in iCOR Study Guide: *Building Spiritual Homes: Living Our Values Together,* p. 12.

18 Philip G. Samaan, *Christ's Way of Reaching People* (Hagerstown, Md.: Review and Herald Pub. Assn., 1990), p. 30.

Cure for Hezekitis

How to Reach and Retain the Younger Generation

GARY BLANCHARD

HOW DO WE REACH AND RETAIN the younger generation? Without a doubt this is one of the biggest questions being asked by parents, youth leaders, teachers, and church administrators around the world. Especially as we hear reports that between 60 and 70 percent of our youth disappear from active church life in their 20s and never return. Interestingly, but not shockingly, the reason for this crisis is clearly spelled out for us in the Word of God. Go figure!

In Isaiah 38 we learn about the God-fearing King Hezekiah, who was diagnosed with a terminal illness but by the grace of God was healed and given 15 more years of life (verse 5). However, in the next chapter we learn that visitors from Babylon came to "congratulate" him on his recovery, and in an act of complete stupidity King Hezekiah showed them all the treasures of the kingdom (Isaiah 39:1, 2). When the delegation left, Isaiah the prophet confronted the king, prophesying that the Babylonians would return, take the treasures for themselves, and kidnap and castrate their kids, making them slaves in Babylon.

Now, notice Kings Hezekiah's shocking response to this terrible news! "'This message you have given me from the Lord is good.' For the king was thinking, 'At least there will be peace and security during my lifetime'" (Isaiah 39:8, NLT).

Why are we losing so many young people today? Why are they being dragged away from the church and assimilated into the world? Because this kind of attitude, we will call it Hezekitis, is also coming from the older generation! Notice that King Hezekiah was a godly man and was one of the greatest kings Israel ever had, but like many godly church leaders today, he was more concerned about the present, about his generation, and gave little thought to the future and those who would one day lead!

Sadly, it was during the extra 15 years of life God had granted him that Hezekiah and his wife had a child that would become one of the most wicked kings in Israel's history! He was godless, lawless, and heartless, and the Bible testifies that he became a leader who "led them [Israel] to do even more evil than the pagan nations that the Lord had destroyed when the people of Israel entered the land" (2 Kings 21:9, NLT).

Currently in the United States everything from guns to drugs is being blamed for the state of affairs among our nation's youth. Violence is high, and you can't watch the news without another school shooting or violent act being committed by the younger generation. Of course, this reality is reflected in other countries as well, but few are aware of the real systemic problem behind the moral free fall among the younger generation. It is the conviction of this writer that Hezekitis is the problem—like King Hezekiah, we are either preoccupied with our own generation or unconscious of the desperate need of the younger generation for our proactive attention. Among this generation is a deep need realized or not for spiritual fathers—an older generation who cares for the lives and souls of the up-and-coming Manassehs (millennials and Generation Z).

But there is great news! God has a cure for Hezekitis and real hope for a Manasseh generation! God's Word predicts that just before His return, He will send "Elijah the prophet," who will "turn the hearts of the fathers to the children, and the hearts of the children to their fathers" (Malachi 4:5, 6, NKJV). Interestingly. Ellen White compares Elijah to those living at the end of time. She writes, "Elijah was a type of the saints who will be living on the earth at the time of the second advent of Christ and who will be 'changed, in a moment, in the twinkling of an eye, at the last trump,' without tasting of death."[1] So just before the return of Christ, God will raise up a generation that will cure His church of Hezekitis as they wholeheartedly pursue intergenerational youth ministry.

Elijah the prophet was without question one of the greatest youth leaders in the Old Testament. He was a godly man like Hezekiah, but one who cared for the younger generation and did more than just preach "total youth involvement." Elijah "rolled up his sleeves" and invested compassionately into the younger generation as if the future of the church depended upon it! Elijah understood that effective youth ministry is intergenerational, and he did three profound but simple things to cure Hezekitis!

CARE

First, he cared for them. You will remember when the widow of Zarephath's son died, it was Elijah that carried the boy's body upstairs, stretched himself over him three times, and cried out to God to bring him to life. Intergenerational ministry follows a simple formula—proximity + prayer = revival. When the older generation builds close relationships with the younger generation (proximity) and cries out earnestly for their spiritual revival (prayer), supernatural things happen! You will remember, in Ezekiel 37, that it was only after Ezekiel prayed for the Spirit to revive the dry bones that the army of God came to life (verse 10). I believe this prophesy applies specifically to our army of youth, but that's another article. Caring for this generation is about praying earnestly for their spiritual revival as we pursue close relationships with them.

I love how Ellen White herself appeals for more proximity and prayer in regard to intergenerational youth ministry: *"The youth are the objects of Satan's special attacks; but kindness, courtesy, and the sympathy which flows from a heart filled with love to Jesus will gain their confidence, and save them from many a snare of the enemy. . . . There must be more study given to the problem of how to deal with the youth, more earnest prayer for the wisdom that is needed in dealing with minds. . . . We should seek to enter into the feelings of the youth, sympathizing with them in their joys and sorrows, their conflicts and victories. . . . We must meet them where they are, if we would help them. . . . Let us remember the claim of God upon us to make the path to heaven bright and attractive."* [2]

Helpful Resources

The General Conference Youth Department has an excellent resource that will help you, your church, conference, union, and division become more effective and intentional about caring for the younger generation and curing the Hezekitis among us. The resource is called Intergenerational Churches of Refuge, or iCOR. It is a resource that church leaders can study preferable with their leadership teams in order to care intentionally and effectively for the younger generation. You can download the resource for free at youth.adventist.org. Also stay tuned for training opportunities at @gcyouthministries and youth.adventist.org.

CHALLENGE

Second, Elijah challenged them. On Mount Carmel he did not preach smooth and comfortable messages. Instead he shook the younger generation up by challenging them to get off the fence and follow the Lord wholeheartedly. "If the Lord is God, follow him! But if Baal is God, then follow him," he declared (1 Kings 18:21, NLT).

Once a young man was sitting on the fence and Jesus approached him, challenging him to get off the fence and follow Him wholeheartedly. The young man said, "No, thank You, Jesus; I want to remain on the fence." Jesus went away sad. Next the devil appeared to the young man and invited him to follow him wholeheartedly as well. The young man replied in the same way, "No, thank you, I am going to remain on the fence." The devil smiled and said, "That's OK, young man, you can remain on the fence. After all, I own the fence!"

Yes, the younger generation needs to know that Jesus loves them, that His grace covers their sins, and that justification is theirs by faith alone and not by works. But where are the challenging messages today? Where are the messages calling young people to live holy lives for God, to keep His Sabbath, to live pure, to grow in grace, to be Spirit-filled and sanctified? Where is the challenge to live counterculture for Jesus even when it's dangerous? Where are the messages calling for health reform, mission service, tithing responsibility, and respect for religious and political authority? Maybe you've noticed that we feature tons of David testimonies but few Joseph and Daniel stories of God's grace. Moreover, where are the warning messages that the end is near and that faith as well as repentance is required of those who wish to be saved?

Ellen White writes: *"The smooth sermons so often preached make no lasting impression: the trumpet does not give a certain sound. Men are not cut to the heart by the plain, sharp truths of God's Word. . . . When will the voice of faithful rebuke be heard once more in the church? . . . If they were not so rare, we should see more of the power of God revealed among men. . . . It is not from love for their neighbor that they smooth down the message entrusted to them, but because they are self-indulgent and ease-loving. True love seeks first the honor of God and the salvation of souls. . . . God calls for men like Elijah, Nathan, and John the Baptist—men who will bear His message with faithfulness, regardless of the consequences; men who will speak the truth bravely, though it call for the sacrifice of all they have."*3

I believe it was the great Charles Spurgeon that warned, "A time will come when instead of shepherds feeding the sheep the church will have clowns entertaining the goats." Oh, Lord, how we need church leaders who will courageously challenge the younger generation the way Elijah did!

Helpful Resources

There is no better resource for this than Scripture and Spirit of Prophecy. We encourage leaders around the world to learn from credible Christian authors, but always prioritizing Scripture and Spirit of Prophecy! We challenge Adventist youth leaders to make young disciples for Christ, teaching them to "obey all" that Jesus taught, even the counter-cultural and dangerous truths (Matthew 28:19, 20).

CALL

Third, Elijah called young people. In the eyes of most, Elijah was an example of ministry success. After all, he was well loved and respected by the church, but apparently in the eyes of God his ministry was incomplete. In 1 Kings 19:16 God "commands" him to pass on leadership to the younger generation! Someone once said, "No success without a successor," and apparently God agrees. Ellen White writes, "As Elijah, divinely directed in seeking a successor, passed the field in which Elisha was plowing, he cast upon the young man's shoulders the mantle of consecration."[4]

Like many of us, Elijah seems to have obeyed God's command here halfheartedly. I may be wrong with this assumption, but you will remember that when he found Elisha, he threw the mantle over him and kept walking (1 Kings 19:19). This seems to be the common way we mentor young people today. Instead of training them for ministry and giving them responsibilities they can handle, we throw the mantle over them and shout, "Sink or swim, kid. Don't let us down; after all, you are the church of today!" But calling the younger generation into ministry and leadership is about passing it on, not dumping it on them! Jesus took the young people on His ministry team through a process that took three years. He began with observation (watch Me do it), then participation (help Me do it), and finally activation (you do it). Elijah did the same thing over a period of several years. Sister White writes, "Ministry comprehends far more than preaching the Word. It means training young men as Elijah trained Elisha, taking them from their ordinary duties, and giving them responsibilities to bear in God's work—small responsibilities at first, and larger ones as they gain strength and experience."[5]

Thankfully, Elijah grew to be an amazing mentor to Elisha. Some might even argue that he was so good at it that his young successor exceeded him! Ellen White seems to affirm this when she wrote, "When the Lord in His providence sees fit to remove from His work those to whom He has given wisdom, He helps and strengthens their successors, if they will look to Him for aid and will walk in His ways. They may be even wiser than their predecessors; for they may profit by their experience and learn wisdom from their mistakes. Henceforth Elisha stood in Elijah's place. He who had been faithful in that which was least was to prove himself faithful also in much."[6]

The greatest compliment to the older generation is the younger generation, whom they have cared for, challenged, and called into ministry, becoming even wiser than they! Unlike King Saul, who grew jealous of his young successor and even worked to sabotage him, Elijah encouraged and equipped Elisha and became a spiritual "father" to him. You will remember that as he ascended in a fiery chariot Elisha shouted, "My father! My father! I see the chariots and charioteers of Israel" (2 Kings 2:12, NLT). What a compliment to the older generation when the younger generation responds to their fatherly love expressed through caring, challenging, and calling! So, leader, never forget, if the ones you are mentoring grow to be better speakers, teachers, administrators, and even leaders than you, then praise God—you're in good company, with such empowering leaders as Elijah, Barnabas, and yes, even Jesus, who empowered His followers to even greater things. Jesus said, "Very truly I tell you, whoever believes in me will do the works I have been doing, and they will do even greater things than these, because I am going to the Father" (John 14:12, NIV). Think on that!

Resources

The General Conference Youth Department has some wonderful resources for those who want to grow as youth leaders who care, challenge, and call the younger generation to ministry for the Master. Senior Youth Leadership (SYL) is one of these training resources. We also have the new *Adventist Youth Leader Magazine,* designed to equip leaders around the world to pass on leadership to the younger generation more effectively. Both of these resources are free for download at youth.adventist.org. Why not make sure all the youth leaders in your area of influence have these resources in hand?

THANK YOU!

My deepest respects and appreciation go out to the parents, youth leaders, teachers, club directors, pastors, and administrators around the world who are investing their time, talents, and treasures into the generation coming behind them. You are the fulfillment of Malachi's promise!

On behalf of the General Conference Youth Department, we thank you! Only in the future will we know how much we owe to your vigilance, dedication, and hard work.

Hopefully this article has stimulated your thinking and strengthened your resolve to intentionally lead God's church in caring, challenging, and calling the younger generation. I believe this article contains the key to reaching and retaining the younger generation. The cure for Hezekitis is simple but not easy. We as church leaders must act intentionally now!

What matters most in these last days is that we pour into the younger generation and resist the urge to care only for ourselves and our generation. Now is the time for the Elijah leaders to step up and stand out in behalf of the younger generation. It's time to intentionally care, challenge, and call them! As mentioned above, Hezekiah was a godly king, and no doubt he cared deeply for his son Manasseh, but life has a way of forcing priorities, and if we are not careful, it is highly likely that our priority will be for ourselves and will naturally lead to neglecting the needs of the younger generation. But Jesus will help us; He prioritized children, and He can put this same desire within each of us.

Why not take some time in the next few days or weeks to come up with a written and intentional plan to "turn the hearts of the fathers to the children" in your area of influence?

Never forget that Malachi 4:5, 6 is not just a promise—it's a warning! "Look, I am sending you the prophet Elijah before the great and dreadful day of the Lord arrives. His preaching will turn the hearts of the fathers to their children, and the hearts of the children to their fathers. Otherwise I will come and strike the land with a curse" (NLT).

GARY BLANCHARD

Gary Blanchard is the General Conference Youth Director and has worked as a District Pastor, Bible Teacher, Academy Chaplain, Youth Pastor and most recently as the Texas Conference Youth Director. He is married to his best friend Erica and is the proud father of Gary, Ben and Sierra. Gary loves long walks in the woods and raising dogs. Gary's life mission is to help young people experience the grace of The Lord and become active in taking the Three Angels message to the world.

Pass it on! Identity, mission, leadership

ENDNOTES

1 Ellen G. White, *Prophets and Kings* (Mountain View, Calif.: Pacific Press Pub. Assn., 1917), p. 227.
2 Ellen G. White, *Gospel Workers* (Washington, D.C.: Review and Herald Pub. Assn., 1915), pp. 207-212.
3 E. G. White, *Prophets and Kings*, pp. 140-142.
4 *Ibid.*, pp. 219, 220.
5 *Ibid.*, p. 222.
6 *Ibid.*, p. 228.

Rethink Church

STEPHAN SIGG, D.Min.

"IN CHURCH I ALWAYS FEEL as if I do not comply." This is what my daughter said when we had a rather random chat about her local church experience. Back then she was about 15 years old. Interestingly, she couldn't specify and identify directly the things that nurtured her impression. "It is everywhere." Although a teenager is almost by nature vulnerable to feelings of inferiority, her summary struck me. I was a conference youth director at that time, and my daughter's feelings echoed many other similar talks I had with young people about church. Program-driven as I was, my immediate reaction has been to ask: "What can we do?" "What are the things we need to change?" It took me some time to realize that it is less about the things we do than about the people we are.

Those teenage feelings come from deep within and are mainly triggered by the spiritual-social environment we create as a church. *We* make them feel this way because we are the church, and it reflects who we are and what God we follow. Finally, the church is God's society in this world, a reflection of His kingdom and a living expression of the transforming power of His love. The church "is a social reality that is called to embody the gospel"[1] and as such the church is inherently both, a spiritual and social entity. We cannot have the one without the other. Spiritual growth, therefore, goes hand in hand with social growth. Growing in our relation to God implies growing in our relation to each other, thus forming a new community that follows the way of Jesus in all aspects of life. Biblically speaking, this interdependency is a simple truth: you cannot love God but hate your brother (1 John 4:20, 21). Serving God implies serving my neighbor. Yet in discussions about church we are repeatedly confronted with the assertion that church is about God, not about people. Such an understanding reduces the church to a place we go to worship and individually ponder and adore God. The notion "I'm in worship" usually informs us that I am sitting in the pew attending or participating in a religious program. But church, the *ecclesia*, is first and foremost a people, not a worship program or a set of spiritual traditions and practices we need to uphold and defend. Although it is hurtful, maybe the current wave of church dropouts can serve as a wake-up call for us to rethink what church is all about and to reconnect with our New Testament roots.

CHURCH IS RELATIONAL

Despite the fact that the phenomenon of deconversion, especially among young people today, is complex and multifarious, there is a common consent in studies about and among dropouts that meaningful relationships and the experience of community are crucial factors regarding church affiliation and faith identification. Whether a faith or believe system is seen as coherent and plausible relies not only on the facts (the truths) and individual experiences but also, and maybe even more so, on belonging to a loving community that authentically reflects as well as relevantly imparts and embodies this faith.

We learn this also from families of faith. The nucleus family is, idealistically speaking, the basic loving human community we are born into. Cross-generational studies regarding the transmission of faith now confirm that "the quality of the relationship between parent and child is a crucial component of the degree to which transmission of religion occurs. When children perceive their relationship with parents as close, affirming, and accepting, they are more likely to identify with their parents' religious practices and beliefs, while relationships marked by coldness, ambivalence, or preoccupation are likely to result in religious differences."[2]

This linkage between successful faith transmission and loving relationship is not only a central feature of the nucleus family—it also applies to the church as an extended family. These are the two social entities God directly constituted, the family and the church. This is where life (and faith) is protected, nurtured, cared for, fostered, and equipped for further expansion. "If formation in faith does not happen there, it will—with rare exceptions—not happen anywhere."[3] Empirical research in the field of youth retention widely demonstrated "that spiritual and religious communities and role models represent an enormously significant resource for the value formation and development of religiousness in emerging adults."[4] And yet, too many young people are leaving.

However, the vast "majority of young dropouts are not walking away from faith, they are putting involvement in church on hold."[5] In his longitudinal study among young Adventists from 15 to 25 years of age Roger Dudley has already pointed to this fact by summarizing: "The reason for leaving and staying away from the church is not doctrinal but relational."[6] In this light, the current dropout rates among young people can be understood like the temperature on a thermometer telling us as a church that we have a sick patient—and we are the patient. The young people do not just leave the church, they leave what we made the church to be. Therefore, before asking What we can do to stem the loss of young people? we should ask What is God's idea of His church? If we ask Jesus, it is all about being God's family.

THE FAMILY OF JESUS

It happened as Jesus was teaching in a house packed with people that, all of a sudden, the crowed got uneasy, and the information was passed to Jesus: "Your mother and brothers are outside looking for you" (Mark 3:32, NIV). What happened next must have been quite a shocking moment for Jesus' disciples and compatriots. Everyone would have understood if Jesus had stopped His lesson and paused for a moment to meet His family, since family at that time was everything.[7] Culturally it would have been the appropriate reaction to give everyone a break and to follow the call of His mother and brothers. But that is not what Jesus did. Rather He used the situation for a very profound teaching. He was even ready to embarrass His mother. "Who are my mother and my brothers?" (verse 33, NIV). In the course of His argument Jesus refers to those sitting at His feet and who are ready to follow God's will as His mother, sisters, and brothers. True family is not a question of blood relationship but of "Jesus relationship." We, the *ecclesia*, are family, and that means a hundred times more than any natural kinship."

See, we have left all and followed You" (Mark 10:28, NKJV), Peter said, so "What about us?" What Peter means with "we have left all" refers to their families and their life script in the context of their kinship. Jesus took up that line of thought and responded: "Assuredly, I say to you, there is no one who has left house or brothers or sisters or father or mother or wife or children or lands, for My sake and the gospel's, who shall not receive a hundredfold now in this time—houses and brothers and sisters and mothers and children and lands, with persecutions—and in the age to come, eternal life" (verses 29, 30, NKJV). Despite the fact that as followers of Christ we might even face persecution, what we gain by following

Jesus is true family. We will have a hundred times more fellow sisters and brothers, mothers and spiritual mentors, role models and spiritual "children" (Philemon 10; 1 John 2:1). What Jesus promised His disciples was not just the eternal life in the age to come but already in the here and now, the relational and social capital of His church, us—*God's* family.

There is in fact no other biblical metaphor in the New Testament that is as profound and fundamental for the understanding of the nature of the church as the family. Family language permeates the paulinic and pastoral letters, and it defines the very nature of our relationship to God, our Father. Yes, there is also the body of Christ (1 Corinthians 12:12-27; Ephesians 4:4), but this metaphor just underlines the relational nature of the church and the connectedness and interdependency of its members under the authority of Christ. Yes, there is also the association with the Temple *building* (not with its cultus!), which is understood as the ultimate dwelling place of God and that is built up by God's people who are united and who do live together, Jews and Gentiles, in love and peace (Ephesians 2:11-22; see also Revelation 21:3). The guiding theme when it comes to the church in the New Testament is relationship. As our God *is* love and a relational being (three but one), by His very nature His church is a relational entity in its very nature, and the family metaphor best encompasses the many facets of such a human and divine community. In this light the church is characterized as an intergenerational faith community of Christ followers where people matter more than programs or buildings. In fact, church is less about sacred buildings we are going to contemplate or spiritual programs we are organizing or attending and more about communities of faith we are living and belonging to and where the gospel is alive. The spiritual nature of the church as God's family inherently encompasses the idea that the church is social, communal, and relational. It is about people, because family is about people and our heavenly father is about people. Just note how Ellen G. White describes God's vision for His church: *"The church of Christ, enfeebled, defective as she may appear, is the one object on earth upon which He bestows in a special sense His love and His regard. The church is the theater of His grace, in which He delights in making experiments of mercy on human hearts. The Holy Spirit is his representative, and it works to effect transformations so wonderful that angels look upon them with astonishment and joy. Heaven is full of rejoicing when the members of the human family are seen to be full of compassion for one another, loving one another as Christ has loved them. The church is God's fortress, His city of refuge, which He holds in a revolted world. Any betrayal of her sacred trust is treachery to Him who has bought her with the precious blood of His only begotten Son."*[8]

THE CHURCH AS GOD'S FAMILY IS MISSION

As God's family we are called to be an open testimony to the world (John 13:34, 35), as well as to the heavenly realm for the transforming power of God's truth, which is seen in the life of Christ and expressed by the Spirit in grace and love. In fact, "the church remembers and tells and embodies the story of Jesus Christ. It shows the world what God calls the world to be."[9] Through the church the gospel of Jesus Christ does not only become visible but also tangible in this world and among the people.

Faced with high dropout rates of young people who struggle with their church experience and an increasing suspicion toward organized religion in society, we are somehow forced to rediscover the high communal and relational value of being a Jesus family, God's church. I believe that the growing realities of a post-Christian era and secular culture, especially in the Western world, are forcing us to rethink church and to reconnect with our roots in the faith communities of the early Christians. Finally, that is where we come from. It actually turns out that one of the main factors that the church grew exponentially in the first three centuries was their way to live their family-of-God identity as an open testimony of the gospel in their society.

In line with the New Testament understanding of the church, the early Christians were coined by the idea of being an extended family. It was not just because of the pressures from a pagan culture that the early church communities met in private homes and followed the common social formula of sharing commensality (*deipnon*), followed by the *symposion,* where everyone, not just the men (as generally the custom in society), participated and contributed (see Colossians 3:12-17). It corresponded with their understanding of church. "For the early Christians, the church was a family—in word and deed."[10] The impressive growth of the early church cannot be explained solely by the individual testimony of Christians or the liberating power of the message of Jesus (in contrast to all the pagan gods). Indeed, one of the most convincing reasons was the symbiotic community of believers—people with different social and ethnical backgrounds, ages, and genders.

"Against all odds the early Christians won thousands to the Savior and ultimately triumphed completely over competing religious options in the Roman Empire. And we can trace much of the vitality of the Christian movement to the surrogate family values and behaviors that characterized local church life."[11]

In view of the early Christian church growth and based on Jesus' statement that "all will know that you are My disciples, if you have love for one another" (John 13:35, NKJV) Bryan Stone is certainly right to say that "the most evangelistic thing the church can do . . . is to be the church, not merely in public but as a new and alternative public; not merely in society but as a new and distinct society, a new and unprecedented social existence. On this view, any evangelism for which the church is irrelevant, an afterthought, or instrumental cannot be Christian evangelism."[12] The relational and communal nature of the church is not in conflict with a mission focus but rather builds its fundament.

Building intergenerational faith communities that embody the gospel of Jesus and thus the "truth," therefore, must be at the top of our missional agenda. This is a biblical mandate not only because times are changing, and people are much more asking for authentic communities and good ways to live than just true doctrines, but also because it is rooted in the very nature of the God we follow.

The "family of Jesus" must be a living reality, and if we truly understand ourselves as God's family, we are not just committed to uphold the truth in this world, but to live it. Finally, we have decided to follow Jesus. Therefore, we need to be more than being right, since "the purpose of the commandment is love from a pure heart, from a good conscience, and from sincere faith" (1 Timothy 1:5, NKJV). Regardless of our personal piety "in Christ Jesus neither circumcision nor uncircumcision avails anything, but faith working through love" (Galatians 5:6, NKJV). As God's people and the family of Jesus, we are called to reflect God's character of love to the world. This happens through the works of love and in service to the people. In this context "the church doesn't have a social strategy, the church *is* a social strategy."[13] Ellen G. White has expressed it this way: "*The church is God's appointed agency for the salvation of men. It was organized for service, and its mission is to carry the gospel to the world. From the beginning it has been God's plan that through His church shall be reflected to the world His fullness and His sufficiency. The members of the church, those whom He has called out of darkness into His marvelous light, are to show forth His glory. The church is the repository of the riches of the grace of Christ; and through the church will eventually be made manifest, even to 'the principalities and powers in heavenly places,' the final and full display of the love of God.*"[14]

In this light and understanding of being church, it can never be our primal task in our thinking about nurture and retention just to come up with running better worship services and better spiritual programs, but rather to better be and provide a spiritual home for people of all ages. As God's family the church is a loving, caring, and nurturing community that empowers and supports its members to connect with each other, and live up to their full potential in Christ. Just like a family, the church has to be intergenerational, with young and old working together for God's glory. That Jesus identifies with us as His siblings is pure grace and a privilege that is hard to grasp. However, it also marks the fact that as our ultimate Brother, Jesus is our model we follow, and in Him we learn to understand what family we belong to.

STEPHAN SIGG, D.Min.

Stephan Sigg (D.Min., M.A.) is an ordained Pastor and President of the Swiss German Conference and the Swiss Union of the Seventh-day Adventist Church. He served ten years as a Conference Youth Ministries Director in Switzerland and seven years as Youth Ministries Director of the Inter-European Division. In addition, Dr. Sigg was a full-time lecturer at the Friedensau Adventist University in Germany in the field of Applied Theology. He received his Doctor of Ministry at Andrews University with a special focus on youth evangelism in a postmodern context. He was the speaker of the satellite based youth evangelism Link2Life in 2002 and 2004 which has been broadcasted in the German speaking fields of Europe. Dr. Sigg is the initiator and author of iCOR (Intergenerational Church of Refuge, icor.church). iCOR is a value based church development initiative to support local congregations to reconnect with the New Testament vision of being God's Family and a living expression of the Gospel. He is married since more than 30 years to Gabriela and proud father of two adult children. Stephan Sigg loves the mountains and all kinds of outdoor activities.

ENDNOTES

1 Alan Kreider, "They Alone Know the Right Way to Live," in Mark Husbands and Jeffrey P. Greenman, eds., *Ancient Faith for the Church's Future* (Downers Grove, Ill.: InterVarsity Press, 2008), p. 184.

2 Vern L. Bengtson, Norella M. Putney and Susan Harris, *Families and Faith: How Religion Is Passed Down Across Generations* (New York: Oxford University Press, 2013), p. 98.

3 Christian Smith and Patricia Snell, *Souls in Transition: The Religious and Spiritual Lives of Emerging Adults* (New York: Oxford University Press, 2009), p. 286.

4 Gina Magyar-Russell, Paul J. Deal, and Iain Tucker Brown, "Potential Benefits and Detriments of Religiousness and Spirituality to Emerging Adults," in Carolyn McNamara Barry and Mona M. Abo-Zena, eds., *Emerging Adults' Religiousness and Spirituality: Meaning Making in an Age of Transition* (Oxford: Oxford University Press, 2014), p. 49.

5 David Kinnaman, *You Lost Me: Why Young Christians Are Leaving Church . . . And Rethinking Faith* (Grand Rapids: Baker Books, 2011), p. 27.

6 Roger L. Dudley, *Why Our Teenagers Leave the Church: Personal Stories From a 10-Year Study* (Hagerstown, Md.: Review and Herald Pub. Assn., 2000), p. 99. See also p. 39.

7 Unlike our individualistic culture today, in Jesus' time one's identity, life script, and future were determined by the family and the kinship you belonged to. A son stepped into the footsteps of his father and was usually referred to as the "son of" so and so. In fact,

there was no stronger relational bond than that to your parents, siblings, and relatives. The loyalty to your family was even more important than the loyalty to your spouse.

8 Ellen G. White to S. N. Haskell, May 30, 1896.

9 Graham Hill, Salt, *Light, and a City: Ecclesiology for the Global Missional Community,* Volume 1, Western Voices, 2nd ed. (Eugene, Oreg.: Cascade Books, 2017), p. 156.

10 Joseph H. Hellerman, *When the Church Was a Family: Recapturing Jesus' Vision for Authentic Christian Community* (Nashville: B&H Academic, 2009), p. 117.

11 *Ibid.,* p. 214.

12 Bryan Stone, *Evangelism After Christendom: The Theology and Practice of Christian Witness* (Grand Rapids: Brazos Press, 2007), pp. 15, 16.

13 Stanley Hauerwas and William H. Willimon, *Resident Aliens: Life in the Christian Colony,* 25th anniv. ed. (Nashville: Abingdon Press, 2014), p. 43. (Italics original.)

14 Ellen G. White, *The Acts of the Apostles* (Mountain View, Calif.: Pacific Press Pub. Assn., 1911), p. 9.

Feeding the Core, Not Entertaining the Fringe

PAUL TOMPKINS, D.Min.

THE SEVENTH-DAY ADVENTIST CHURCH is losing far too many of its young people. The trend is hurting the worldwide church, the local congregation, and individual families. The church has prioritized discipleship as a key factor in reversing this decline, but the method to achieve this remains unclear and often falls into the category of "one size fits all."

We know that we must focus on children and youth as an immediate priority, and this is a critical issue for all church leaders. This paper was first presented at the 2019 General Conference Nurture and Retention Summit as a workshop presentation, and will propose that young people wish to be challenged and additionally that they want to be part of a church that inspires them to act. To do this, we need to work inside out rather than outside in. That's also how Adventist youth ministry began.

From my own context, and reflecting on the findings from the European Valuegenesis survey (2006/2007), the comment was made that "we need to feed the core, not default to entertaining the fringe."[1] In other words, our emphasis should be on strengthening and nurturing the faith of our committed young people, as they are the ones that are ready and willing to move forward.

This may well mean that we need rethink our strategy for reaching and keeping our youth. A recent book states that young people face three ultimate questions as they grow and develop: Who am I? Where do I fit? and What difference do I make?[2] These questions are best answered through a faith community modeling "God's grace, love, and mission."[3] It is an urban myth that to reach young people we need a watered-down teaching style.[4] Sometimes it is assumed that we have to make Christianity seem less radical in order to appeal to teenagers or young adults. Quite the opposite is true! It is also a myth that the church needs to adopt an entertaining ministry program. The church needs to offer something different to popular culture.

In this sense we can look back to the future. The principle of youth action and involvement has been long set, and looking back, this is the guidance that was given at the inception of Seventh-day Adventist youth ministry. Ellen White shared the following counsel:[5]

- As a church we must take our work for youth far more seriously.
- The salvation of our youth must be a priority.
- Companies of young people who truly love the Lord should be organized.
- The purpose of these groups is to organize young people for service.
- These groups should provide both training and opportunities for service.

Breaking these statements down gives a message that is timeless until this day. The purpose of Adventist youth ministry is still to organize young people for service. "Salvation and Service" has long been the call for youth ministry and is something that needs redefining with each generation.

Young people being involved and moving forward is in Adventist DNA. The Adventist Church was formed largely by young people who in their generation felt inspired by God to do something significant. Ellen and James White, John Loughborough, J. N. Andrews, and others were all young when they stepped out in faith with their zeal and God-given commitment.

At first the church held no age delineation, but later came the perceived need to emphasize a special work with and for our young people. As time progressed, Ellen White observed the work of a group called the Christian Endeavor Society,[6] which had been organized in the 1880s by Frances Clark. This society revolutionized youth ministry by encouraging youth to put their faith into action.

Seeing what was happening, Ellen White stated: "Let there be a company formed somewhat after the order of the Christian Endeavor Society, and see what can be done by each accountable human agent in watching for improving opportunities to do work for the Master. He has a vineyard in which everyone can perform good work. Suffering humanity needs help everywhere."[7]

The story of the start of the Adventist youth work is well known. In 1879 two young boys, Luther Warren and Harry Fenner, ages 14 and 17, knelt down by the roadside to pray for their unconverted friends. They were troubled by the needs of the young people of the church, and developed the idea of having a boys' society. They then went home to start youth meetings. Thus started the first Seventh-day Adventist youth society on record.[8]

Apparently, it consisted of five or six boys, and anecdotally I have been told that they first met in their bedrooms, but soon the parents allowed them to meet in the lounge, so girls could also be present. Be that as it may, the activities emphasized were missionary work and the improvement of personal conduct and healthful living. Other societies followed, and soon messages began coming from Ellen White urging the young people to organize for service.

Missionary work and activity to help others was always high on the agenda. Very soon others such as Meade MacGuire in 1891 started meetings and Sunshine Bands to involve young people in reaching out to help others. He too felt a need to do something similar to the Christian Endeavor and Epworth League. Interestingly a report in the *Pacific Union Recorder*[9] indicates that in Antigo, Wisconsin, this at first met with almost universal disapproval, except from an "elder, a saintly man, who said, 'My boy, you go right ahead. You may have the church for your meetings, and I will stand by you.'" Apparently 30 members held the meetings on Saturday nights.

Sunshine Bands were started by MacGuire, and also Warren in South Dakota, directing the young people toward missionary work. I understand that names such as "Caleb and Joshua" were given to some groups, which echo a more recent missionary endeavor in certain fields. The point is that young people have always wanted to be active and involved in missionary work and have been met with some opposition, but also, as in the case of the aforementioned elder, support by the church. All this, of course, before the official commencement of the Missionary Volunteer Society.

And so, to today's generation. Within the church we have seen in the past decade the inception and growth of the Global Youth Day,[10] where the focus has been on "being the sermon" for the day. Youth have been encouraged to go out from the church and help those in need. Recently, themes for the day, such as "Adopt" and "I Care,"[11] have been emphasized to give focus to these activities. This has grown into a worldwide movement within the church, with 24-hour news reports flooding in. The desire within our young people for active involvement is undeniably still there, and the challenge remains to turn this from a one-day event into a lifestyle for our youth.

This is happening, and the Youth Ministries Department is currently emphasizing the One Year in Mission program. "OYiM is a global youth initiative designed to give teams of young professional (18+) an opportunity to magnify Jesus in the cities of the world through the three angels messages!"[12] This is a growing movement that will also be a part of the Impact Indianapolis outreach, running alongside the 2020 General Conference session.

In other areas the influence of young people has also been noted. I work and minister in Scotland, and the Barna Research Organization has recently published their research on the state of the church under the title *Transforming Scotland*. An overall decline in membership was seen in the participating churches (not SDA), as with many countries in Western Europe. However, an unexpected spike was observed in the faith of young people. The millennial age group was attracted by the following: meaningful and authentic relationships, deep understanding of faith, and opportunities to serve others.[13]

This research, allied to the current emphasis on youth outreach and practical Christian effort in the church, shows that there is a window of hope and opportunity still before us today. Young people at heart are still the same, and they want to be part of a church that stands for something definite and in which they can be involved in sharing this message in practical ways.

The Fuller Youth Institute conducted nearly 1,500 hourlong interviews and analyzed more than 10,000 pages of research data, and discovered that much of what is often thought to engage teenagers and young people isn't so essential after all. Young people responded that they wanted challenge and opportunities to act and to make a difference.[14]

We must take hold of this and recognize that challenge is not something to avoid. In fact, young people appreciate challenging and well-presented Bible-based teaching in their church. "Contrary to popular thinking that young people today want it easy, many told us that they love their church because their church inspires them to act."[15] In short, teenagers and emerging adults in churches aren't running from a gospel that requires hard things of them. "They are running toward it."[16]

I believe that is a profoundly defining statement that finds practical application at the local church level. We need to think globally but act locally. The church has recognized this, and as one example the General Conference Youth Department theme for 2019 was "The Year of the Local Church." They set a slogan of "Give Them the Keys"[17] to involve young people in church life. Putting some flesh on this recent research by the

Office of Archives, Statistics, and Research[18] has shown that youth would appreciate the following:

- more engagement on Friday evening/Sabbath p.m. (89 percent)
- allow young adults to take more church leadership positions (83 percent)
- more days when youth lead out in Sabbath worship (81 percent)
- allowing young adults to establish and run their own ministries (71 percent)

Our church members, especially young people, want to be involved. One of our church districts in Scotland has established a series of Discipleship and Life groups. These groups act as church access points for both members and their friends of all ages. The groups take part in homes, usually consisting of approximately 12 to 14 persons per home, and run for 12 to 15 weeks in length. Members who attend the discipleship groups for two cycles or seasons (four to nine months a year) are seen to spiritually grow and through participation have a higher likelihood in leading or supporting other groups in the future. This is a pattern that could easily be replicated in other areas.

In summary, could it be that our best days are still ahead if we recognize that young people wish to be challenged and actively involved in the mission of the church? I believe so! Working from the inside out rather than from the outside in means making it a priority to nurture and support our committed core group of young people. These are the ones that we can and must influence the most.

Young people are not the church of tomorrow—they are the church of today! This can become a reality through a sustained emphasis on salvation, discipleship, and service. In so doing, the enthusiasm, passion, and positive influence of these young people will also more than likely attract others. It happened that way for me, and I believe it will for the present generation, too.

PAUL TOMPKINS, D.Min.
Paul Tompkins (D.Min.) was the youth director of the Trans-European Division for 15 years, starting in 2000. In 2015 he served as senior pastor of Newbold College church. He currently serves as president of the Scottish Mission, since 2016.

ENDNOTES

1 Manuela Casti and Stephen Currow, "European Valuegenesis Survey Report" (report presented at a Trans-European Division executive meeting, DeBron, Holland, September 2007).

2 Kara Powell, Jake Mulder, and Brad Griffin, *Growing Young* (Grand Rapids: Baker Books, 2016), p. 95.

3 *Ibid.*, p. 116.

4 *Ibid.*, p. 27.

5 See Malcolm Allen, *Divine Guidance or Worldly Pressure?* (Silver Spring, Md.: General Conference of Seventh-day Adventists, 1995), p. 50.

6 The Young People's Society of Christian Endeavor was a nondenominational evangelical society founded Portland, Maine, in 1881. Its professed object was to promote the Christian life and to make young people more useful in the service to God.

7 Ellen G. White, *Counsels on Health* (Mountain View, Calif.: Pacific Press Pub. Assn., 1923), p. 537.

8 *The Story of Our Church* (Mountain View, Calif.: Pacific Press Pub. Assn., 1956), p. 444-446.

9 *Pacific Union Recorder*, Aug. 5, 1926, p. 1.

10 Held on the third Sabbath in March during the annual Youth Week of Prayer.

11 Theme for the 2020 Global Youth Day.

12 General Conference Youth Ministries website.

13 *Transforming Scotland* (Barna Research, 2015), Part III, "Millennials Study," pp. 69-75.

14 Jake Mulder, "What Do Young People Want in Church?" (2016), p. 2, Fuller Youth Institute.org/blog young-people-want-in church.

15 Powell, Mulder, and Griffin, p. 143.

16 *Ibid.*

17 *Pass It On* (Seventh-day Adventist Youth Ministries, Strategic Planning, 2016-2020), p. 6.

18 Galina Steele, presentation at TED Nurture and Retention Summit, Montenegro, November 2017.

What Does the 2017-2018 Global Research Reveal About Adventist Young People?

GALINA STELE, D.Min.

IT IS NOT EASY TO BE a young person in the contemporary world. It probably has never been easy. However, the demand for being successful, able to adapt to rapidly changing expectations of social and professional networks, is higher than ever before. This creates a lot of pressure on the young generation. Additionally, with the transition from modernity to post and multiple modernities, traditional values and priorities of people have changed. These changes have made their impact on the religious life of young people, especially adolescents. According to the statistics of the General Conference (GC) Youth Ministries Department for the past few years, of the different categories of Adventist young people, the Ambassador Club (ages 16-21) has the lowest membership[1] *(see Figure 1).*

Figure 1. Youth Ministries

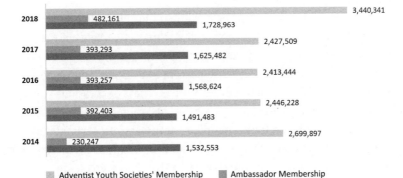

2018	3,440,341 / 482,161 / 1,728,963
2017	2,427,509 / 393,293 / 1,625,482
2016	2,413,444 / 393,257 / 1,568,624
2015	2,446,228 / 392,403 / 1,491,483
2014	2,699,897 / 230,247 / 1,532,553

Adventist Youth Societies' Membership   Ambassador Membership
Pathfinder Membership

Why do the numbers drop so drastically after Pathfinder age? What happens with our adolescents? And how spiritually alive are our young adults? Does Adventist research show in what areas we should help our young people? This article will present some recent data on young people collected in 2017 and 2018 when the Adventist Church conducted the Global Church Member Survey (GCMS) commissioned by the GC for the 2015-2020 strategic planning. This research was supervised by the GC Office of Archives, Statistics, and Research (ASTR).[2]

GLOBAL CHURCH MEMBER SURVEY: SUBSAMPLES OF YOUNG PEOPLE

The 2017-2018 GCMS became the largest survey of its kind. It was conducted in all divisions with total N=63,756. Many young people (25,460 participants) also took part in it. They comprised 40 percent of the total sample: 12 percent (7,490) were adolescents up to 20 years of age (Generation Z), and 28 percent (17,970) were millennials or young adults aged 21-35. Who are these survey participants?

Almost all respondents (96 percent average) identified themselves as Adventists (87 percent of adolescents and 91 percent of young adults had been baptized). This is important to remember when we look at research data of their beliefs and practices, because these young people consider themselves Seventh-day Adventists and thus represent young Adventists in our churches. Most of them represent lay members who are not connected in everyday life with organized religion. Only 11 percent of adolescents and 28 percent of young adults are or have been working for an Adventist organization or church.

Both genders were well represented, with almost equal division in the young adults sample and with 12 percent more females in the adolescents' group.

Their family history with the Adventist Church varied. More than a quarter (26 percent) of adolescents and a third (33 percent) of the young people were first-generation Adventists. This means they need additional care from the church. Moreover, 26 percent and 22 percent, respectively, are fourth- and fifth+-generation Adventists. These generations can have tendencies to nominal religion if their parents' religion has become just a tradition and not their faith. Combined numbers of first-, fourth-, and fifth+-generations comprise more than half in each sample. Will they make it or break it? Do their local churches recognize their spiritual needs?

Young people in our churches are busy people. While the adolescents were mostly single, half of the young adults were married (47 percent) or living together with their partner (3 percent); 42 percent of them had children, with at least one child or teenager living at home. Additionally, to complete the picture of challenges young people face in their private life, about 2 percent of the adolescents and 3 percent of the young adults have been already divorced; 2 percent of the young adults were separated, and 1 percent of them were widowed. Another small percent of the adolescents (about 2 percent) were also living together. So the picture is not homogeneous, and is more complicated than one can imagine.

Interestingly, a majority of the young adults (64 percent) had the whole household celebrating the Sabbath, while only slightly more than half (53 percent) of those up to 20 had the same favorable situation. This means that another half of the adolescents live in a household in which not all members celebrate the Sabbath. This can be challenging for the faith of a young person.

So what can we learn about devotional practices, church attendance, involvement in church life, and beliefs of these young Adventists?

FAMILY WORSHIPS AND DEVOTIONAL PRACTICES

Unfortunately, the business of everyday life prevents many young people from regular family worship and daily personal devotions. Only 29 percent of the adolescents and 32 percent of the young adults have family worships daily. It seems very important to restore an Adventist tradition of regular family worships, especially in families with children.

The situation with daily devotional practices could also be better *(see Figure 2)*. A majority of young people don't have daily personal devotions, don't read the Bible or writings of Ellen G. White (EGW) daily, and don't study the Sabbath School lesson. In each of these categories, the adolescents scored lower. The largest gap (12 percent) is in personal devotions. What is

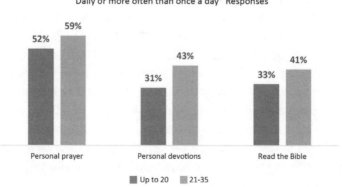

Figure 2. How Often Do You Engage in These Activities?
"Daily or more often than once a day" Responses

Personal prayer: 52% / 59%
Personal devotions: 31% / 43%
Read the Bible: 33% / 41%

■ Up to 20   ■ 21-35

even more sobering—almost half of the adolescents (48 percent) and two in five young adults (41 percent) don't have daily personal prayers at times other than meals. How can they survive in this world of constant struggle between good and evil if they are not equipped and protected by personal prayers?

Although a majority of young people do not read EGW's writings or study the Sabbath School lessons on a daily basis, it is encouraging that on a weekly basis more of them do this *(see Figure 3)*.

Figure 3. Sabbath School Lessons and EGW's Writings

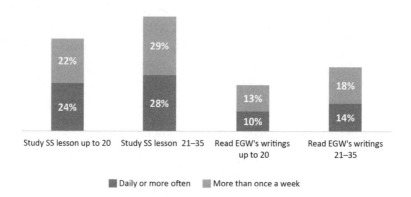

To increase these scores, we can inform them about available apps, audio, and video versions of the Sabbath School lessons, EGW's writings, different Bible translations, and devotional materials. The findings show that about 48 percent of young adults and 36 percent of adolescents use their mobile devices for Bible study or personal devotions on a daily or weekly basis.

It is hard to overestimate the long-term value of daily personal devotions in the life of a young Christian. Let's be intentional in our efforts to help them organize their life in such a way that they have regular time for their personal spiritual growth. EGW writes: *"The reason why the youth, and even those of mature years, are so easily led into temptation and sin is that they do not study the Word of God and meditate upon it as they should."*[3]

Interestingly, one of the conclusions of the "Twenty-first Century Seventh-day Adventist Connection Study," by Douglas Jacobs and his team from Southern Adventist University, was that there is a correlation between regular devotional life and commitment to Adventist lifestyle and Adventist doctrines.[4]

We need to help our young people strengthen their devotional life and grasp the importance of family worship in transmitting religious values to their children.

DISCIPLING, NURTURING, AND RECLAIMING

CHURCH ATTENDANCE, LOCATIONS, AND CLIMATE

In the modern world young people are not regular churchgoers. The GCMS asked participants about church attendance, sizes, and locations of their churches. Young people answered that perceived attendance in their congregations varied. About 74 percent of the adolescents most likely attend small (attendance of 50 or less) or medium-sized churches (attendance 51-400), 37 percent in each category. Only slightly more than a quarter (26 percent) attend large churches (attendance of 401 or more). As for the young adults, 29 percent attend small churches, while a majority (38 percent) attend medium-sized or large churches (33 percent).

Overall, about 60 percent of the young adults and 51 percent of the adolescents attend churches that are located in large cities, or suburbs, or smaller cities. They moved to urban settings to receive their education and/or to find jobs or schools for their children. However, speaking about youth retention, we need to remember that half of the adolescents still attend churches in rural areas, villages, or small towns. What can be done for young people in smaller churches?

About two thirds of Adventist young people can be called active churchgoers *(see Figure 4),* which is a very good although not perfect result. A majority (but less than 70 percent) attend church services and Sabbath School weekly or more often. Other church gatherings attract fewer people. We can keep in mind that many of them are married, are raising their kids, and many are involved in studies. Because of these or other reasons, about one third of the adolescents and half of the young adults don't attend meetings provided by the Youth Ministries Department.

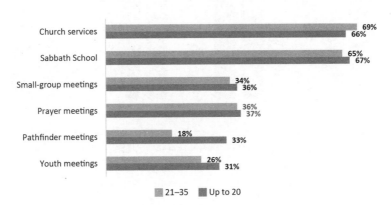

Figure 4. Attendance of Church Services and Meetings
in the Past 12 Months
"Every week" or "More than once a week" Responses

Category	21–35	Up to 20
Church services	69%	66%
Sabbath School	65%	67%
Small-group meetings	34%	36%
Prayer meetings	36%	37%
Pathfinder meetings	18%	33%
Youth meetings	26%	31%

But how do they feel in the churches they attend? The Valuegenesis studies conducted in the United States and Europe consistently showed that the atmosphere in the congregation plays an important role in young people's retention. The Valuegenesis Europe research concluded that young people experience the presence of God during worship more and grow in their understanding of God more when the church's intellectual and warm climates are high.[5]

The GCMS results show that about half of the adolescents, when at church, feel free to be who they are, feel loved and cared and able to use their spiritual gifts *(see Figure 5)*. But what about the other half? Additionally, a majority of the adolescents do not feel closeness and unity in their congregations and cannot voice their opinion. The older group of young adults has slightly different results but the same trend. These feelings could influence their response to the question about their satisfaction with their local church: only half of the adolescents and even fewer of the young adults were very satisfied with their local congregations *(see Figure 6)*. Research also showed that there is a correlation between satisfaction with the local church and programs provided for all family members. This can be an important issue for young families with children. Nevertheless, 73 percent of the adolescents and 80 percent of the young adults said it is very likely that they will be attending a Seventh-day Adventist church for the rest of their life.

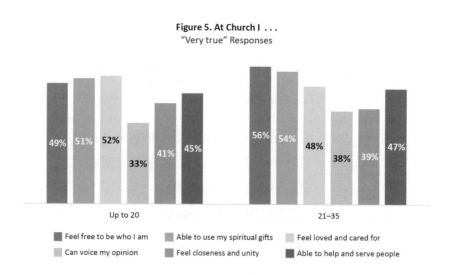

Figure 5. At Church I . . .
"Very true" Responses

Up to 20: 49% Feel free to be who I am, 51% Able to use my spiritual gifts, 52% Feel loved and cared for, 33% Can voice my opinion, 41% Feel closeness and unity, 45% Able to help and serve people

21–35: 56% Feel free to be who I am, 54% Able to use my spiritual gifts, 48% Feel loved and cared for, 38% Can voice my opinion, 39% Feel closeness and unity, 47% Able to help and serve people

■ Feel free to be who I am　■ Able to use my spiritual gifts　■ Feel loved and cared for
■ Can voice my opinion　■ Feel closeness and unity　■ Able to help and serve people

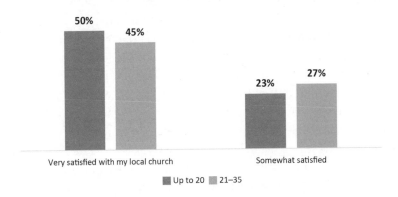

Figure 6. How Satisfied Are You With Your Local Church?

50% 45%

23% 27%

Very satisfied with my local church   Somewhat satisfied

■ Up to 20 ■ 21–35

INVOLVEMENT IN CHURCH MINISTRIES OR WITNESSING

Involvement is a crucial component in church member retention, especially when we talk about young people. Those who are involved in church life feel they are part of it. Sense of belonging is a very complex feeling, but without involvement—emotional and/or physical engagement—it is not possible to feel you are a part of anything.

Unfortunately, the data suggest that a majority of young people do not have any responsibilities in their local churches and are not involved in any church ministry during the week or on Sabbath. While some of them (37 percent of the adolescents and 41 percent of the young adults) hold an office in the local congregation, the results show that these responsibilities do not require their weekly involvement. Only 28 percent of the adolescents and 35 percent of the young adults were involved in a church ministry on the Sabbath during the last year. Even less of them (22 percent and 27 percent, respectively) helped with a church ministry during the week. However, the young adults were involved more in church ministries than the adolescents, although still not a majority.

The involvement of young people and their training for leadership are strategic objectives of the Adventist Church. A majority (66 percent average) of young people in each age group agreed or strongly agreed that they play an important role in decision-making in their local church, but less than a quarter strongly agreed. When asked if programs for preparing young people to become leaders exist in their local churches, conferences, or unions, a majority agreed. However, more people agreed that such programs exist on conference and union levels than on the level of their local churches. This is a point for local church leadership to think about.

The local church should be more intentional in involving young people in its ministry. It should create more opportunities for young people to serve with their talents, spiritual gifts, or professional knowledge. As other research shows, it is also important to teach them how to discover their calling and be a follower of Jesus in their workplaces using their gifts and skills to honor God.[6] As Figure 5 shows, only slightly more than half of the young people said they were able to use their spiritual gifts in their local church, and less than half in both groups said they were able to help and serve people in a meaningful way. Valuegenesis research in Europe found that there is a correlation between the longtime commitment of young people to the Adventist Church and supportive congregation where they can use their spiritual gifts.[7]

The survey also asked participants about their involvement in the church mission. A majority (about 70 percent) agreed or strongly agreed that they are involved in carrying out the mission of their local church. But in reality, more than 70 percent were not involved weekly in meeting the needs of non-Adventists in the community or witnessing to non-Adventists (*see Figure 7*). However, more of them, although again not a majority, were involved in forming new friendships with people outside of their church, possibly because of their contacts with peers in school or workplaces.

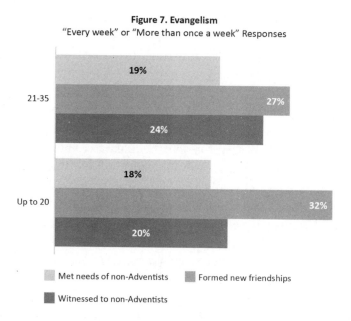

Figure 7. Evangelism
"Every week" or "More than once a week" Responses

- 21-35: 19%, 27%, 24%
- Up to 20: 18%, 32%, 20%

Met needs of non-Adventists   Formed new friendships
Witnessed to non-Adventists

Young people also answered the questions whether their involvement in evangelistic outreach to the community, efforts to meet the needs of the community, caring and nurturing church members, or reclaiming former members should increase. They agreed on all categories, but interestingly, reclaiming of former members scored higher than other categories in their response that it should increase greatly: 35 percent of the adolescents and 41 percent of the young adults said so.[8] Possibly, they have friends or know people who stopped attending their congregations and care about them. Pastors should use this potential.

DOCTRINES

The GCMS had some questions on the Seventh-day Adventist doctrines that helped understand how deeply rooted young people are in these fundamental beliefs. The results showed that:

- Overall, young people support Adventist doctrines. Total agreement ranged from 76 percent and up on most of the Adventist fundamental beliefs. These are very good results!
- Scores of the adolescents were lower compared with the responses of the young adults. In "strongly agree" responses the difference is 6-11 percent, a substantial difference.
- Although there has overall support for Adventist doctrines, scores in "strongly agree" responses varied (see Figures 8 and 9). The difference showed that young people were less confident in some fundamental beliefs than in others.
- There was confusion about the state of the dead.
- Overall, there was strong support for the Adventist lifestyle and biblical position on marriage.
- High acceptance of salvation through Jesus alone did not necessarily correspond with young people's relationship with Him and understanding of His total merits in the salvation of humankind.

Interestingly, the most popular doctrine for the young people was an Adventist doctrine about the Sabbath. "The true Sabbath is the seventh day (Saturday)" received the highest score in both age groups in overall agreement (93 percent for the adolescents and 97 percent for the young adults) and in "strongly agree" responses (76 percent and 83 percent respectively). Three other doctrines that broke a 70 percent ceiling of strongly agree responses for adolescents and an 80 percent ceiling for the young adults were: God created the universe, the head of the church is Christ, and salvation is through Jesus Christ alone.

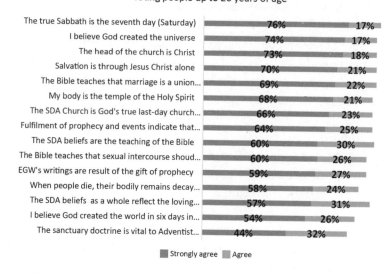

Figure 8. Adventist Doctrines
Young people up to 20 years of age

	Strongly agree	Agree
The true Sabbath is the seventh day (Saturday)	76%	17%
I believe God created the universe	74%	17%
The head of the church is Christ	73%	18%
Salvation is through Jesus Christ alone	70%	21%
The Bible teaches that marriage is a union...	69%	22%
My body is the temple of the Holy Spirit	68%	21%
The SDA Church is God's true last-day church...	66%	23%
Fulfilment of prophecy and events indicate that...	64%	25%
The SDA beliefs are the teaching of the Bible	60%	30%
The Bible teaches that sexual intercourse shoud...	60%	26%
EGW's writings are result of the gift of prophecy	59%	27%
When people die, their bodily remains decay...	58%	24%
The SDA beliefs as a whole reflect the loving...	57%	31%
I believe God created the world in six days in...	54%	26%
The sanctuary doctrine is vital to Adventist...	44%	32%

■ Strongly agree ■ Agree

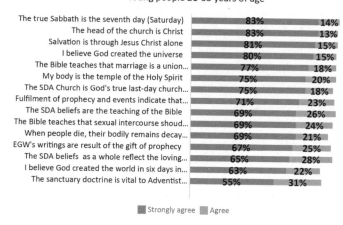

Figure 9. Adventist Doctrines
Young people 21-35 years of age

	Strongly agree	Agree
The true Sabbath is the seventh day (Saturday)	83%	14%
The head of the church is Christ	83%	13%
Salvation is through Jesus Christ alone	81%	15%
I believe God created the universe	80%	15%
The Bible teaches that marriage is a union...	77%	18%
My body is the temple of the Holy Spirit	75%	20%
The SDA Church is God's true last-day church...	75%	18%
Fulfilment of prophecy and events indicate that...	71%	23%
The SDA beliefs are the teaching of the Bible	69%	26%
The Bible teaches that sexual intercourse shoud...	69%	24%
When people die, their bodily remains decay...	69%	21%
EGW's writings are result of the gift of prophecy	67%	25%
The SDA beliefs as a whole reflect the loving...	65%	28%
I believe God created the world in six days in...	63%	22%
The sanctuary doctrine is vital to Adventist...	55%	31%

■ Strongly agree ■ Agree

LESS-SUPPORTED DOCTRINES

Adventist beliefs in the soon second coming of Jesus, the pre-Advent investigative judgment and heavenly sanctuary, Creation week, and the state of the dead received the least support in overall and strongly agree responses in both groups.

Jesus' Second Coming

Overall, 89 percent of the adolescents and 94 percent of the young adults believed that fulfillment of prophecy and events in the world indicate that Christ's coming is very near. Nevertheless, less than 40 percent strongly agreed that Jesus Christ would return in their lifetime. Interestingly, the adolescents were slightly more confident in that than were the young adults *(see Figure 10)*.

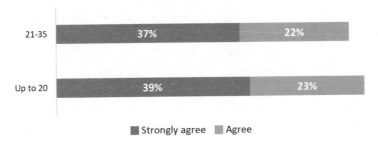

Figure 10. I Am Confident That Jesus Christ Will Return in My Lifetime

- 21-35: Strongly agree 37%, Agree 22%
- Up to 20: Strongly agree 39%, Agree 23%

■ Strongly agree ■ Agree

Pre-Advent Judgment

The least-supported statement and perhaps the least-understood doctrine by young people is an Adventist doctrine about the heavenly sanctuary. The statement "The sanctuary doctrine is vital to Adventist theology" received 44 percent of "strongly agree" responses by the adolescents and 55 percent by the young adults. As we see, the difference in the strong agreement between these groups comprises 11 percent. There were also other questions on the heavenly sanctuary in the survey (see Figures 11 and 12). Young people in both groups were quite confident about Jesus' role as our advocate, but not that many were sure regarding the beginning of the investigative judgment or its meaning.

Figure 11. The Heavenly Sanctuary
Young People Up to 20

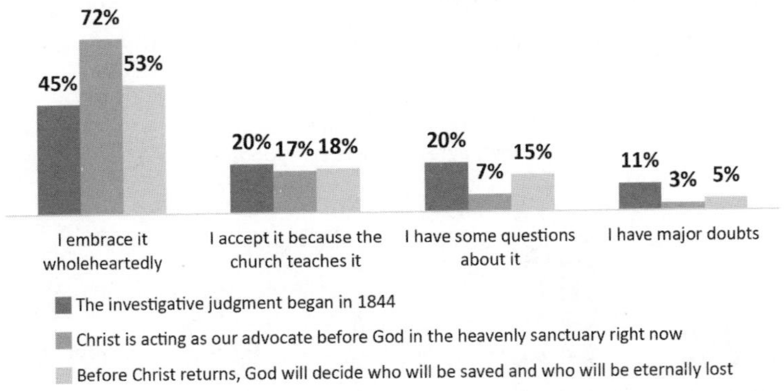

- I embrace it wholeheartedly: 45%, 72%, 53%
- I accept it because the church teaches it: 20%, 17%, 18%
- I have some questions about it: 20%, 7%, 15%
- I have major doubts: 11%, 3%, 5%

■ The investigative judgment began in 1844
■ Christ is acting as our advocate before God in the heavenly sanctuary right now
■ Before Christ returns, God will decide who will be saved and who will be eternally lost

Creation Week

Although young people were pretty confident that God created the universe, they were not that sure about the Adventist position on "I believe God created the world in six days of 24 hours each in the relatively recent past." The difference in "strongly agree" responses between these two statements is 17 percent in the young adults' group and 20 percent in the adolescents group *(see Figures 8 and 9)*.

The "Twenty-first Century Seventh-day Adventist Connection Study" on recent graduates also pointed out that our young people are more supportive of some doctrines than of others, such as "a six-day literal Creation, the inspiration of Ellen White, the sanctuary, the pre-Advent judgment, and the remnant identity doctrines."[9] It seems we need to share more information on these subjects, discuss them more with young people, and make sure they see them as sound, biblical, and relevant to their lives. Interestingly, in spite of this, the Sabbath doctrine, which is based on a six-day Creation week, was the leading doctrine for young Adventists.

State of the Dead

Research also revealed a lot of confusion on the state of the dead. Although a strong majority of both groups believe that when people die, their bodily remains decay and they have no consciousness or activity until they are resurrected *(see Figures 8, 9, and 13)*, more than a third in both groups agreed or strongly agreed that the soul is a separate, spiritual part of a person and lives on after death. Additionally, more than 20 percent of the young people believe that people who have died believing in Christ are in heaven right now. Some of the young people also believe that Christians may go to witch doctors and that the dead have powers to communicate with and influence the living. This shows that cultural traditions and previous beliefs sometimes coexist. Additional research has shown that in the territories with a long history of the Adventist Church and Adventist education more young people share biblical positions on these questions.

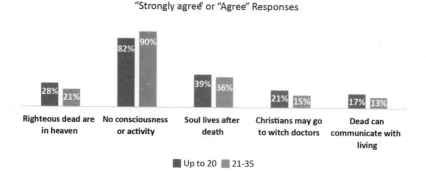

Figure 13. The State of the Dead
"Strongly agree" or "Agree" Responses

DISCIPLING, NURTURING, AND RECLAIMING

LIFESTYLE DOCTRINES

Healthy Lifestyle and Amusement

Young people understand well the value of basic doctrine for Christian lifestyle: "My body is the temple of the Holy Spirit" (see Figures 8 and 9). Responses to additional questions on Adventist lifestyle show that 79 percent of the young adults wholeheartedly accept the Adventist position on abstinence from alcohol, tobacco, the irresponsible use of drugs, consumption of unclean food, and a need to follow a healthful diet. Many of them (75 percent) also wholeheartedly agreed that Adventists should avoid amusement and entertainment that are not in harmony with the Spirit of Christ. These responses echoed with those of the adolescents: 69 percent accept wholeheartedly the Adventist position on alcohol, tobacco, and drugs; 73 percent on food; and 65 percent on amusement. We can note the 10 percent difference in responses of these two groups on the first and last statements. Nevertheless, in practice, an overwhelming majority supported the Adventist position on abstinence from alcohol and tobacco: 87 percent of the adolescents and 89 percent of the young adults said that they had not used alcohol in the past 12 months, and 96 percent of the adolescents and 97 percent of the young adults had not used tobacco.

Biblical View on Marriage

As Figures 8 and 9 show overall, 91 percent of the adolescents and 95 percent of the young adults believe that marriage is a union between a man and a woman. Less but still a strong majority in both groups believe that the Bible teaches that sexual intercourse should be exclusively reserved for marriage. This gives hope that the majority of Adventist young people hold biblical positions on marriage, although the adolescents again scored lower in "strongly agree" responses.

SALVATION THROUGH JESUS

In spite of the fact, that young people have a very strong opinion on salvation through Jesus Christ alone *(see Figures 8 and 9)*, almost half of the adolescents and two in five of the young adults do not believe that every person is born with tendencies toward evil or has a sinful nature *(see Figure 14)*. Additionally, about half in each group believe that following the health message ensures their salvation, and more than two thirds think that they will not get to heaven unless they obey God's law perfectly. A majority of young people in both age groups also believe that if they are to be saved, they need to be baptized into the Seventh-day Adventist Church.

Similar to other questions, the younger group again scores lower in "strongly agree" responses to the question about salvation through Jesus or the character of God. This shows that adolescents have less confidence in God or Jesus than young adults. An overwhelming majority of both groups (89 percent of the adolescents and 94 percent of the young adults) believe in a personal God who seeks a relationship with human beings. However, the difference in "strongly agree" responses between these two groups is 10 percent (63 percent and 73 percent, respectively). The same trend is seen in questions about salvation through Jesus Christ alone, or that people have a sinful nature, that they are saved the moment they believe and accept what Jesus has done for them, and that Adventist beliefs reflect as a whole the loving character of God. The difference in "strongly agree" responses between these groups ranges from 6 to 11 percent.

There is also less certainty in the younger group that prayer in the name of Jesus is the only way to defeat evil powers or demonic spirits: strongly agree responses score 9 percent less *(see Figure 15)*. Sadly, only 59 percent have such strong confidence in Jesus' power over evil powers.

The conclusion is that we need to help young people to raise their confidence in Jesus as their personal Savior, and encourage them to have personal experience and daily connection with Him. Although this subject is very important for people of all ages, the research shows that Adventist high school- and college-age young people extremely need it.

Figure 14. Salvation
"Strongly agree" or "Agree" Responses

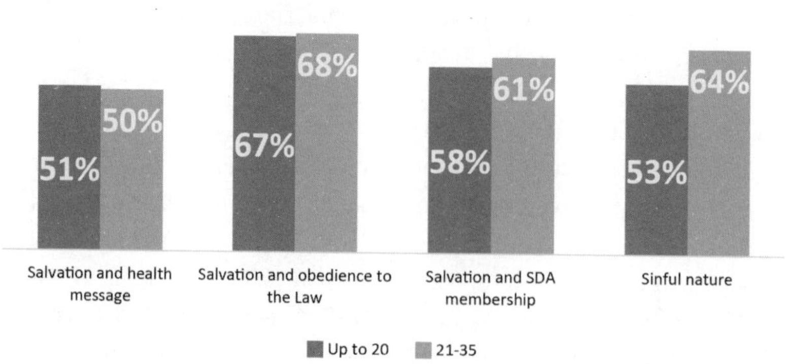

| Salvation and health message | Salvation and obedience to the Law | Salvation and SDA membership | Sinful nature |
| 51% / 50% | 67% / 68% | 58% / 61% | 53% / 64% |

■ Up to 20   ■ 21-35

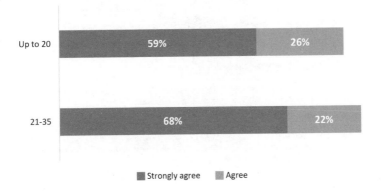

Figure 15. Prayer in the Name of Jesus Is the Only Way to Defeat Evil Powers and Demonic Spirits

Up to 20: 59% Strongly agree, 26% Agree
21-35: 68% Strongly agree, 22% Agree

Strongly agree   Agree

SPIRITUAL STRUGGLES, NEED OF SUPPORT, AND RECLAMATION

Many young people, looking back at the past 12 months, said that they have grown spiritually (Figure 16). But not all had this wonderful experience. Almost a third of the adolescents and more than a quarter of the young adults said that they had lost some important spiritual meaning that they had before or that they thought that they were in some way spiritually lost. Less of them but still about one in five said that their faith had been shaken and that now they were not sure what they believe. In times like these, young people need support from the church. However, a big percent (40 percent of the adolescents and 43 percent of the young adults) said that they had never received a visit from either of their pastor or an elder. This also shows a great need for having friends in the church. From another research on retention, we know that 62 percent of the young people said that they had drifted from the church gradually, half of them knew that they were drifting away, and the other half had not noticed.[10]

This means that most likely there was nobody close to them to note and rescue them from this gradual process until they drifted far away and became unchurched.

Thus, there is a group of young people in the church that needs support during their spiritual journey. And the church should help them make it! If they've stopped attending church, does it have a reclamation ministry? Are there members who are willing to visit them? As mentioned earlier, young people said that their involvement in reclaiming former members should increase. We need to use young people's enthusiasm to love those people back. And in saving others, they might save themselves.

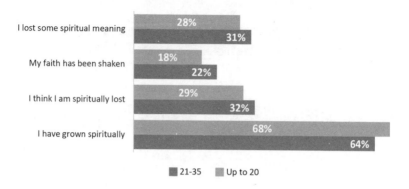

Figure 16. Spiritual Journey in the Past 12 Months
"Somewhat true" or "True for me a great deal" Responses

I lost some spiritual meaning — 28% / 31%

My faith has been shaken — 18% / 22%

I think I am spiritually lost — 29% / 32%

I have grown spiritually — 68% / 64%

■ 21-35   ■ Up to 20

CONCLUSIONS AND RECOMMENDATIONS

1. The statistics and research data show that high school and college students are groups at risk. We need to focus on the retention of all young people, but especially on the 16-20 age group in all aspects of their spiritual life and service. This group, Ambassadors, is the smallest club in church clubs for young people. And their responses in the GCMS were lower than responses of young adults practically in all questions.

2. Young people need mentoring and support during their spiritual journey. There should be intentional discipleship of young people in local churches. Pastors and youth leaders should model their spiritual lives, and help them create regular devotional habits and a vital connection with Jesus.

3. Local churches need to purposely create a safe environment for young people to feel loved and needed, to safely voice their opinion, ask questions, and be involved in the decision-making process in their local church. Then they can call such church their home.

4. Involvement in church ministry is crucial for young people's sense of meaning and belonging. Do we help them discover their spiritual gifts and give opportunities to apply them? Only if they feel they are making a valuable impact can they have this sense of belonging.

5. Belief in church doctrines should not be taken for granted if a young person has been baptized. The doctrines should be taught and discussed many times during young people's personal and

spiritual development. In the doctrines they should discover the loving and graceful character of God and Jesus, their personal Savior and Friend. Simply knowledge of doctrines cannot save; only Jesus can.

6. Young adults represent a unique group that is more mature than adolescents, more dedicated and more rooted in the church doctrines. However, their needs, especially those who have children, should not be neglected by the local church. Additionally, their professional skills and knowledge should be welcomed and applied in different areas of church life.

7. Reclamation is an important part of church ministry to young people. Its success depends on the intentional efforts of each local church to reconnect with those who are missing. Young people could be a vital force in this ministry to reach out to their inactive or missing peers and friends.

In conclusion, young people believe that the Seventh-day Adventist Church is God's true last-day Church with a message to prepare the world for the second coming of Christ *(see Figures 8 and 9)*. And fortunately, a majority see themselves attending a Seventh-day Adventist church for the rest of their life. Do you want to see them in your local churches, not just on pews but also on the podiums and at the pulpits being wholeheartedly involved? Do you want to see them leading the Adventist Church toward the second coming of Jesus? If yes, we need to help this happen. And we need to act now.

GALINA STELE, D.Min.

Galina Stele was born in Russia and worked many years for the Euro-Asia Division in different capacities: as a professor at Zaoksky Theological Seminary, Shepherdess coordinator, and director of the Institute of Missiology. She holds a D.Min. from Andrews University and currently works as research and program evaluation manager at the General Conference Office of Archives, Statistics, and Research. She is happily married to Artur Stele, they have a son and a 6-year-old grandson. Her special interest is in research, small groups, and youth retention.

ENDNOTES

1 General Conference of Seventh-day Adventists, Office of Archives, Statistics, and Research, *2019 Annual Statistical Report,* New Series (Silver Spring, Md.: Office of Archives, Statistics, and Research, General Conference of Seventh-day Adventists, 2019), vol. 1, p. 7.

2 You can find the meta-analysis report on the 2017-2018 GCMS total sample at http://documents.adventistarchives.org/Resources/Global%20Church%20Membership%20Survey%20Meta-Analysis%20Report/GCMSMetaAnalysis%20Report_2019-08-19.pdf.

3 Ellen G. White, *Testimonies for the Church* (Mountain View, Calif.: Pacific Press Publishing Association, 1948), vol. 8, p. 319.

4 Douglas Jacobs, Douglas Tilstra, Finbar Benjamin, Cheryl Des Jarlais, Mia Lindsey, Hollis James, Alan Parker, Sharon Pittman, and Octavio Ramirez, "Twenty-first Century Seventh-day Adventist Connection Study" Research Report (Robert H. Pierson Institute of Evangelism and World Missions, Southern Adventist University, 2013), p. 17, retrieved from http://southern .libguides.com/ld.php?content_id=26011451.

5 Stephen Sigg, "A Spiritual Home for Young People? The Adventist Youth and Their Church as Seen From the Valuegenesis Europe Data," *Spes Christiana: Valuegenesis Europe* 24 (2013): 148, 149.

6 David Kinnaman and Mark Matlock, *Faith for Exiles: 5 Faith for a New Generation to Follow Jesus in Digital Babylon* (Grand Rapids: Baker Books, 2019), pp. 36, 37.

7 Sigg, pp. 179, 180.

8 ASTR Blog "Global Research on Adventist Young People: Involvement in Church Life and Ministries," https://www.adventistresearch.org/blog/2019/11/global-research-adventist -young-people-involvement-church-life-and-ministries.

9 Jacobs et al.

10 "Leaving the Church: Why Some Seventh-day Adventist Members Leave the Church and Why Some Come Back" (Office of Archives, Statistics, and Research, General Conference of Seventh-day Adventists).

A Spiritually Vibrant Adventist Home

WILLIE & ELAINE OLIVER, Ph.Ds.

WHEN YOU THINK ABOUT SOMEONE who has influenced your faith, who do you think of?

I (Elaine) think about my grandmother, Gwendolyn Powell. She loved her church, her family, and most of all, Jesus. She knew no strangers, and never missed an opportunity to share her faith, with all of us in the household or anyone who came to our door: the mail carrier, the repair-person, the salesperson, or old and new neighbors. Now, to be sure, she would entice you with her wonderful baked goods: cookies, cakes, Jamaican sweet bread/buns, and coconut treats. I do remember her spiritual discipline of praying—three times a day. She would be on her knees first thing in the morning and last thing at night. Even at the ripe young age of 99 she was still visiting sick, shut-in, and elderly persons—praying with them and for them.

I (Willie) think about my dad—a pastor. He was a wonderful man, full of joy, patience, kindness, wisdom, a genuine love for people, and unconditional dedication to his family and his God. Everyone seemed comfortable with him because he had no pretense about anything. He was comfortable in his skin and made those who spoke with him feel comfortable as well. As a child I loved to hear him sing and pray at our family worships. His singing was joyful and filled with gratitude to God for His provision, presence, peace, and salvation. He loved to visit his members and neighbors; he was well known in the community as someone who would help if you had a need. Young and old alike would seek him out for counsel and encouragement. He was my spiritual hero and model, who made me long to be connected to the God he spoke about, prayed to, and preached about His imminent coming. There wasn't anything I could not talk to my dad about, and I experienced God through the care he demonstrated for my mom, my siblings, and me.

People that influence our faith are people we trust and look up to. It could be family members, close friends, or specific people that earned our trust, such as a church member or a pastor.

When we hear such words as **nurture**, **retention**, **discipling**, **reclaiming**, and even **evangelism**, we usually look at the organizational structure—the local church. However, our households of faith—our homes—can be centers of evangelism for nurturing faith in God and future commitment to the church.

Today's households are made up of multiple types of family formations. According to the U.S. Census Bureau, a household refers to "all the people who occupy a housing unit." So you could have family members who are related by birth, marriage, or adoption, in addition to friends, distant relatives, employees, coworkers, foster kids, boarders, or others living together in such a unit.

Households can also be classified by types, such as the nuclear family, the single-parent home, the extended family home, empty nesters, families with boomerang kids, single adults living alone, cohabiting couples, same-sex households, and urban families.

When we look at trends in such twenty-first century households, we can see that it is more common to have families with boomerang kids—married young adults who are moving in with their parents to save money. Single adults are living with roommates, and a number of young adults are creating an **urban** family by living together.

We also see millennials delaying marriage and family, and that post-Christian culture is shaping our children and adults. That becomes visible in declining church attendance.

People are using many available resources, such as Facebook/ YouTube/or Podcasts for faith formation. Such resources make it easy to invest in faith without going to a certain church. Access to Bible studies is available from various sources and is no longer dependent on someone's church or religion.

We do recognize there are multiple types of households that do not fit the traditional or stereotypical construct of family, which are now more the norm than the exception. Most people will progress through several types of household formations throughout their life span. Therefore, pastors and church leaders must have an interest in such diversity of households, since most of our churches do reflect them. Each of these household arrangements holds opportunities for discipling, nurturing, and reclaiming of members through the ability to form rituals and relationships within the household.

In 2018 the Barna Group conducted research on more than 2,000 Christian households to discover how faith is nurtured within households. The study unfolded powerful insights on how faith is handled in practicing Christian homes, and determined that all families can be categorized into four levels of spiritual vibrancy: dormant, hospitable, devotional, and vibrant.

Dormant households do not talk about God or faith together; they do not pray or read the Bible together regularly, and they do not welcome nonfamily visitors regularly. This level of spiritual vibrancy consisted of 28 percent of all families.

Hospitable households welcome nonfamily visitors regularly—several times a month—and they might participate in some spiritual activities, but not all of them participate regularly. This level of spiritual vibrancy included 14 percent of all families.

Devotional households talk about God or faith together; they pray and read the Bible together regularly, but they do not welcome nonfamily visitors several times a month. One third (33 percent) of all families belonged to this level of spiritual vibrancy.

Vibrant households talk about God or faith together; they pray together, read the Bible together regularly, and welcome nonfamily visitors several times a month. A quarter (25 percent) of all families consisted of this level of spiritual vibrancy.

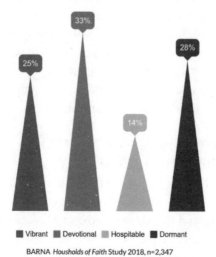

Levels of Spiritual Vibrancy

BARNA *Housholds of Faith* Study 2018, n=2,347

Barna's research findings also determined that while the size, shape, and trends of households are ever-shifting, the impact of the home remains the same in that it continues to play a pivotal role in instilling, nurturing, and shaping one's Christian faith. Ellen White states in *The Ministry of Healing*: "The well-being of society, the success of the church, the prosperity of the nation, depend upon home influences."[1]

The central theme of the Households of Faiths study[2] expressed how essential relationships are to practicing Christians who engage in thoughtful and transformative conversations about faith.

A previous study by the Barna Group,[3] conducted with 1,714 U.S. adults in 2017, revealed that most people are reluctant to talk about their faith. Some feel it is personal and private, some believe it's improper, some believe it may make them sound judgmental, and others simply are not interested in talking about faith. Consequently, many Christians have relegated conversations of a spiritual nature to the private sphere and usually only with people they already have an established relationship with, preferably with family members and close friends. This research underscores the power of intimacy in faith formation; in other words, people are more inclined to discuss their spirituality with those who they trust and know well.

Let's look at some other key findings of the 2018 Households of Faith study.

THE PRESENCE OF CHILDREN/MINORS CATALYZES SPIRITUAL VIBRANCY

As Jesus said: "Let the little children come to me" (Matthew 19:14).[4] When there are children present there is a sense of curiosity and wonder, which leads to greater opportunities to share faith and have meaningful and spiritual conversations. On the contrary, homes without minors have less give and take. Family members are more independent; therefore, interaction needs to be fostered with the intention to have real conversations and quality time for faith engagement.

FAITH FORMATION IS CONNECTED TO AND INCREASES WITH HOSPITALITY

Hospitality is the key indicator of a spiritually vibrant home. When people come together, conversations happen, ideas are exchanged, knowledge shared, and therefore it is the ideal place to share Jesus and His blessings with each other. That can sometimes be a challenge for couple households like empty nesters. They live more secluded lifestyles where meaningful exchanges happen between the spouses but rarely with anyone else. With intentional hospitable activities, these homes can become more vibrant. Another group that struggles with spiritual vibrancy are young unmarried adults that are living together, usually as housemates. They have more sporadic spiritual interactions, even if their homes are hospitable. Regardless of context and/or season in life, a spiritually vibrant home can be nurtured.

SPIRITUALLY VIBRANT HOMES ARE CHARACTERIZED BY FUN AND QUALITY TIME

People in these homes have meals together, share chores, play games, and sing together. They play sports and enjoy each other's company by doing common household activities. They carve out time for faith interactions, such as family worship, prayer, and Bible reading time. There is even vibrancy in their nonspiritual discussions.

FAITH HERITAGE IMPACTS CHRISTIAN BELIEFS AND PRACTICES FOR THE LONG TERM

Passed-down faith is good when there is a warm and emotional connection to the church. Spiritual struggle or wrestling with faith can also be a catalyst for faith development. Especially when it can be merged with positive memories of a church.

Let's take another look at what a spiritually vibrant home looks like.

Spiritually vibrant homes have meaningful quality time with their family members and housemates in addition to people from outside of the household. Family dinners, fun-filled activities, such as playing games, singing, sports activities, and reading books are a regular part of their lives. These families differ from devotional and hospitable households in that they combine both devotional and hospitable attributes. They are intentional about sharing such faith activities as family worship, prayer, and reading the Bible. They talk about feelings and have spiritual conversations; they engage in intentional spiritual coaching. Spiritual coaches look for opportunities to have reverent moments with individual household members; they share about God's forgiveness, discuss the Bible, maintain faith traditions of the family, and may also encourage church attendance.

WHAT DO OUR HOMES LOOK LIKE?

In 1990, 2000, and 2010 ValueGenesis Research studied the faith and values of young people attending Seventh-day Adventist high schools in North America. They looked at three aspects of teen life: family, school, and church. The ValueGenesis2 research revealed good news about the family in that approximately two thirds of the teen respondents reported their family life to be happy, loving, supportive, and warm, which is a slight increase from ValueGenesis1. These statistics are very important in that they continue to emerge as key predictors of spiritual maturity and long-term denominational loyalty.

WHY DO MEMBERS BECOME INACTIVE OR LEAVE THE CHURCH?

In 2014 the Office of Archives, Statistics, and Research (ASTR) at the General Conference conducted a research study on former and inactive church members. This research was called Leaving the Church study. In this study 48.9 percent of all participants were members for five years or fewer, 18.3 percent were members for six to 10 years, 12.3 percent were members for 11 to 15 years, and 20.4 percent were members for 16 or more years. When asked for their primary reason for leaving the church, 38 percent of the respondents reported marriage and family issues as primary conflict issues, 33.6 percent reported the death of parents, and 4.3 percent the death of other family members. Another 20 percent reported conflict in the church or conflict with other church members as a reason for leaving the church. More than half of those leaving the church reported relationship issues as primary triggers. A majority (82 percent) of all respondents reported attending church at least once or twice a week, with 36.2 percent attending more than once a week and 45.8 percent attending only on Sabbath. Less than half (41.9 percent) reported their level of engagement in church life as just an observer, and a quarter (25.7 percent) as a participant. More than half (63.6 percent) claimed to be involved in spiritual activities, such as family worship daily or one to three times a week. More than half (62.4 percent) prayed daily, and almost three quarters (72.1 percent) had personal Bible study daily or one to three times a week. When asked if they are open to reconnecting to the Seventh-day Adventist Church, 63.8 percent reported they are likely or somewhat likely to be contacted.

The study also revealed that 24 percent of inactive members had just drifted away without a specific reason. The young adults with 63.5 percent are the largest group of people who stopped attending church. The second-largest group with 35.1 percent is the middle-aged generation.

These specific ages indicate times of transitions in people's lives. The young adults are leaving home, graduating from college, living alone, getting married, and having children. The middle-aged members are becoming empty nesters and are looking for a new purpose in life after their children have gone to college.

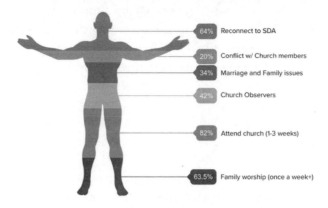

Profile of Members Who Left SDA Church

- 64% Reconnect to SDA
- 20% Conflict w/ Church members
- 34% Marriage and Family issues
- 42% Church Observers
- 82% Attend church (1-3 weeks)
- 63.5% Family worship (once a week+)

ASTR Study 2014 *Leaving the Church* , n=415

Roger Dudley stated the following in the book **Why Our Teenagers Leave the Church**: "The reasons for dropping out of the church seem to be highly interrelated. Those who choose to disconnect perceive the church as irrelevant because they sense they are unaccepted and their needs are neglected. They also feel unaccepted because they don't discern their church as attempting to provide them with relevant and targeted programming. The inconvenience of waking up early on Sabbath morning is another indicator that the church is oblivious to the reality of their lives. This combined with various personal issues and a very high distaste and disappointment with perceived intolerance, hypocrisy, and condemnation have estranged young adults from their church."[5]

The statement shows the church is very negatively perceived by the young people who are deciding to stop attending church. How can this negative perception be changed?

How can a spiritually vibrant Adventist home help with the nurture and retention of church members, especially with the retention of the young adults and the group of the middle-aged?

The creation of a warm and fun-filled environment has a great impact on building meaningful relationships with members inside and outside the family. It will bring family members and friends closer and give them opportunities to share conversations about real-life problems and faith experiences. Such will help grow faith and help provide a feeling of being valued and included. When families open their homes to others in the church, they create unique opportunities to show love and inclusiveness. These opportunities can help people at risk of leaving the church to feel valued. Newly converted friends that are included in family worship and faith conversations will experience spiritual practices that they may not have learned growing up and can help them to become active members in the church.

In the book *Valuegenesis:* Faith in the Balance, Roger Dudley underscores the importance of frequent family worship by stating: "Family worship seems to be a significant factor in helping youth develop a deep, rich, life-changing faith. It is interesting that something as simple to do as regular family devotions could be so helpful. Think what might happen if this family activity were reinstated in each household?"[6]

Age-appropriate family worship that is interesting, thoughtful, and applicable in combination with true examples of hospitality is the key to the retention of our children in the church. Creating warm and meaningful memories in connection to church life is a key component for nurture and retention.

Spiritual coaching can provide opportunities for real-life talk inside the family or with church friends in the privacy of the home. It can show the power of faith in an intentional caring, nonjudgmental environment. Honesty about feelings of hurt or guilt, disappointments, loneliness, and forgiveness can improve relationships and heal broken relationships.

Empty nesters could become family sponsors and provide spiritual coaching for teenagers in the church or families with young children.

Becoming a family sponsor or host for Spiritual Leadership in the Home studies will help other parents to become spiritual coaches. Giving parents practical tips for how to lead their family in Bible reading, faith-based conversations, and prayer; teaching them how to apply the Bible in their everyday interactions with their kids by practicing love, forgiveness, and caring for each other; and also how to create opportunities to discuss biblical principles will enhance their everyday life and spiritual development.

Spiritual coaching can help families deal with family problems and therefore help with nurturing and retention of church members.

In the following verses the Bible shares knowledge about how to connect with and treat others:

"These commandments that I give you today are to be on your hearts. Impress them on your children. Talk about them when you sit at home and when you walk along the road, when you lie down and when you get up" (Deuteronomy 6:6, 7).

"A new command I give you: Love one another. As I have loved you, so you must love one another. By this everyone will know that you are my disciples, if you love one another" (John 13:34, 35).

"Be kind and compassionate to one another, forgiving each other, just as in Christ God forgave you" (Ephesians 4:32).

"Therefore encourage one another and build each other up, just as in fact you are doing" (1 Thessalonians 5:11).

"And let us consider how we may spur one another on toward love and good deeds" (Hebrews 10:24).

"Offer hospitality to one another without grumbling" (1 Peter 4:9).

Let us take these words of wisdom to heart and focus on the people around us. When we teach our children about the Bible and how to develop a relationship with Jesus, our faith will also be strengthened. When we open our homes and are hospitable, we create opportunities to share with others what Jesus has done for us. When we support and encourage others, we build relationships and may even become friends. Then our homes will be vibrant homes that will impact the people around us, and we can see God working in each other's lives.

Proverbs 24:3, 4 says: "By wisdom a house is built, and through understanding it is established; through knowledge its rooms are filled with rare and beautiful treasures."

May the information presented impart wisdom and understanding to produce spiritually vibrant disciples of Jesus Christ, spiritually vibrant Adventist Homes, and spiritually vibrant churches. Let us lead by example so that faith that is sustainable will develop and can be passed down to the next generation.

WILLIE AND ELAINE OLIVER, Ph.Ds.

Elaine and Willie Oliver have been directors of the Department of Family Ministries at the General Conference of the Seventh-day Adventist Church since June 2010. Elaine Oliver is a licensed clinical mental health counselor (LCPC) and certified family life educator (CFLE) by the National Council on Family Relations. She holds master's degrees in clinical mental health counseling, counseling psychology, and higher and adult education, and has completed coursework for a Ph.D. in educational psychology. Willie Oliver is an ordained minister and a certified family life educator (CFLE) by the National Council of Family Relations. He holds a Ph.D. in family sociology with concentrations in gender and family and social stratification; an M.A. in pastoral counseling; an M.A. in sociology; and a B.A. in theology. He is an adjunct professor of family ministries at the Seventh-day Adventist Theological Seminary at Andrews University and at the Adventist University of Africa. The Olivers have been married for 35 years and have two adult children.

ENDNOTES

1 Ellen G. White, *The Ministry of Healing* (Mountain View, Calif.: Pacific Press Pub. Assn., 1905), p. 349.

2 Barna Resources, *Households of Faith* (2018), available at: https://shop.barna.com/products/households-of-faith, accessed Nov. 25, 2019.

3 Barna Group, *Spiritual Conversations in the Digital Age—Barna Group* (2017), available at https://www.barna.com/spiritualconversations, accessed Nov. 25, 2019.

4 Bible texts in this article are from the New International Version.

5 Roger L. Dudley, *Why Our Teenagers Are Leaving the Church* (Hagerstown, Md.: Review and Herald Pub. Assn., 2000), p. 66.

6 Roger L. Dudley and V. Bailey Gillespie, *Valuegenesis: Faith in the Balance* (Riverside, Calif.: La Sierra University Press, 1992).

Intentional Discipleship of Children & Teens

LINDA MEI LIN KOH, Ed.D.

IT IS THE DESIRE OF CHRISTIAN parents that their children will become faithful disciples of Jesus when they grow up. Hence, from their early years they bring them to church and involve them in many faith-building activities, such as Vacation Bible School, Sabbath School, Adventurers, children's camp, prayer conferences, and many others. We hope that the church and the teachers will disciple our children and help them grow their faith. However, when these children reach their teenage years, many of them left the church and some never to return. Where did we go wrong? Is it the parents' fault? Is it because the discipleship curriculum does not appeal to these youngsters anymore? These are questions that concern not only parents, but also church leaders and anyone who works with children and teens. Are we really losing many of our young disciples? What do statistics tell us?

STATISTICS ON YOUTH LEAVING THE CHURCH

A. Barna's Research of 2011[1]

This extensive study done by the Barna Group revealed some new insights into this huge issue facing the Church. In the book by Kinnaman, *You Lost Me*, *Why Young Christians Are Leaving Church and Rethinking Church,* the study revealed some of the following highlights:

- 1 out of 9 (11%) lose faith in Christianity
- 4 out of 10 (40%) leave the Church but still call themselves Christian
- 2 out of 10 (20%) disconnect from Church and express frustration about "church culture" and disconnects with society
- 3 out of 10 (30%) stay involved with church

Overall, the research uncovered six significant themes why nearly three out of every five young Christians (59%) disconnect either permanently or for an extended period of time from church life after age 15.

1. Churches seem overprotective
2. Teens' and twentysomethings' experience of Christianity is shallow.
3. Churches come across as antagonistic to science
4. Young Christians' church experiences related to sexuality are often simplistic and judgmental.
5. They wrestle with the exclusive nature of Christianity.
6. The church feels unfriendly to those who doubt

B. Lifeway Research study of 2017 [2]

A second study by Lifeway Research reported that the top 5 reasons for why youth leave the church were:

- Moving to college (34%)
- Church members seemed judgmental or hypocritical (32%)
- I didn't feel connected to people in the church (29%)
- I disagree with the church's stance on social and political issues (25%)
- My work responsibilities prevented me from attending (24%).

Indeed, these results look rather grim and discouraging for parents, Sabbath School teachers, and church leaders. So, what is the point of putting priority on nurturing the faith of children and teens when they leave the church after age 15?

Please don't give up yet! Ellen White reaffirms the value of nurturing children's faith when they are young:[3]

"It is still true that children are the most susceptible to the teachings of the gospel; their hearts are open to divine influences, and strong to retain the lessons received. The little children may be Christians, having an experience in accordance with their years. They need to be educated in spiritual things, and parents should give them every advantage, that they may form characters after the similitude of the character of Christ."

The Bible teaches that when Samuel was a child, he was growing in the knowledge of the Lord when he was living in the temple under the guidance of Priest Eli. Even Jesus, at age twelve, was growing in knowledge and favor with God and man. If it was vital for Jesus to do that when he was twelve, then it would be wise to look at the years of twelve, thirteen, and fourteen and be more intentional in discipling these youngsters.

PIVOTAL YEARS

Much research has shown that Christian discipleship is pivotal in the teen years. When the children were younger, it was not as difficult in discipleship, but when they hit the pivotal growth point of the early teen years, they start to develop their desire for freedom and independence. When they get to that point in maturity, we think maybe we should step back and let them take over. That would be a mistake!

If your twelve-year-old son recently learned to mow the lawn, you would not say to him, "Here is the lawn mower, so get to work." It's a serious tool and either one of the parents should show him how to use it, giving him all the safety tips. Thus, when we look at growing the faith of our teens, there must be someone who come alongside him to help him grow.

GOD'S DREAM FOR CHILDREN

Parents are chisels in the hand of God, shaping their children into the likeness of Jesus Christ. The Bible is filled with illustrations of individuals who trained and guided their children to follow God's way. Beginning with Genesis all the way to the New Testament, we find examples of God-fearing parents like Noah, Abraham, Hannah, Mary, Eunice, and others who intentionally shaped the faith of their children to keep the way of the Lord and to do what is right and just.

And Deuteronomy 6:4-7 tells parents to diligently teach their children the ways of God. "You shall talk of them when you sit in your house, when you walk by the way, when you lie down, and when you rise up," (NKJV).

In other words, intentional discipleship—deliberately filling our children's life with God's truth—is a vital part of parenting. God loves and cares for children and He has dreams for them that they be spiritually mentored by their parents; that they love Him with all their hearts; and that they obey His commands. Writer Allen S. Nelson in his article for Family Life Ministry identified three reasons why discipleship is important:[4]

1. **God Commands It.**

The Bible is filled with passages like Proverbs 22:6, 2 Timothy 3:15, and Ephesians 6:4 that show God's plan for children has always been that parents would be the *primary* disciple makers.

Sabbath schools, Bible camps, and other church programs can be helpful, but it can't take the place of parenting. Parents spend more hours with their children than anyone else and thus have greater impact on their lives.

Charles Spurgeon, one of the most influential preachers of the 19th century said, *"The first and most natural condition of things is for Christian parents to train up their own children in the nurture and admonition of the Lord."* [5]

2. If You Don't Disciple Your Children, The World Will.

Our children are exposed to messages from our culture, the internet, and mass media about how they should look, think, and act. We are influenced to look to our career, our possessions, sports, our children's popularity and accomplishments. We worship materialism instead of worshipping God. Public schools have removed God out of the classroom and society is talking about same-sex marriage. Parents, you need to seriously teach your children the Christian worldview and introduce them to the infallible truth of God's Word so that our children will be able to discern truth from error.

Ellen White cautions parents of today that: [6]

"It is a most grievous thing to let children grow up without the knowledge of God. Parents make a most terrible mistake when they neglect the work of giving their children religious training, thinking that they will come out all right in the future and, as they get older, will of themselves be anxious for a religious experience. Cannot you see, parents, that if you do not plant the precious seeds of truth, of love, of heavenly attributes, in the heart, Satan will sow the field of the heart with tares?"

We can't afford to let Satan sow tares in the hearts of our children. Can we? Parents, you must not let the culture dictate to you how you should raise your children. You need to intentionally train your children in God's way, to seek God's purpose for their lives, and to know Him as their Special Friend who can transform their lives.

3. True Christian Families Are Living Witnesses to the Community.

People living around you need to see that your family is different; that you worship God and honor Him in every aspect of your family life. Show your children real life examples of generosity, kindness, grace, prayer, and mission. Their friends will see that you all love Christ more than your computer. More than sports. More than popularity.

Ellen White also reminds us of the powerful effect of the family as a witness.[7]

> *"A well-ordered Christian household is a powerful argument in favor of the reality of the Christian religion, an argument that the infidel cannot gainsay. All can see that there is an influence at work in the family that affects the children, and that the God of Abraham is with them. If the homes of professed Christians had a right religious mold; they would exert a mighty influence for good. They would indeed be the 'light of the world..'"*

JESUS' METHOD OF DISCIPLESHIP

Many parents are asking, "Just how do we disciple our children and teens?" The answer to this question can be obtained from examining Jesus' method of making disciples. Jesus spent three years on earth discipling twelve men, shaping and growing their faith. Parents, grandparents and pastors who want similar results can glean from how Jesus trained his disciples.

1. Jesus Showed His Disciples How to Follow God

Jesus did not simply tell His disciples to follow Him; He showed them how to do it. He went out together with the disciples to show them how to teach, heal, and serve others. Jesus showed His disciples how to read God's Word, how to pray, and how to share their faith. He went out together each day to show them how to put those principles into practice.

Parents who are intentional in modeling after Jesus' method can try the following:

- Coming alongside our children to show them how to reach out to others and share the gospel. Teach your children some fun ways of sharing the gospel. Go with them on neighborhood prayer walks to show them how to pray for the neighbors, how to do door-to-door outreach to share a book or any other Christian literature.
- Modeling a lifestyle of prayer, personal devotions, and service. Provide them resources suitable to their age, such as a child or a teen devotional, prayer journal, etc. Encourage them to pray.
- Mentoring them to be leaders of the church.
- Giving them lots of opportunities to practice their gifts and talents at home and in the church. Encourage your teen to lead in family worship or leading song service.

2. Jesus Spent A Great Deal of Time with His Disciples

Jesus was not merely with His disciples in His spare time. Mark 3:14 says *"Then He appointed twelve, that they might <u>be with Him</u> and that He might send them out to preach..."* Jesus spent lots of time with his disciples.

In the late nineteen nineties, psychologists proposed the idea that busy parents can still be effective in parenting when they spend "Quality Time" with their children. Such time may be ten minutes a day or maybe longer. But many parents are starting to question whether time devoted to their children can be efficiently penciled into their calendars like their business appointments. According to Ronald Levant, a psychologist at Harvard Medical School in the same era, the idea of just having "Quality Time" is a great misconception.[8]

> *"I think quality time is just a way of deluding ourselves into short-changing our children. Children need vast amounts of parental time and attention. It's an illusion to think they're going to be on your timetable, and that you can say 'OK, we've got a half hour, let's get on with it'."*

Parents who really want to disciple like Jesus will need to spend "Quality Time" as well as "Quantity Time" with their children and teens. Teenagers especially need parents to guide them, communicate with them, and be present in their lives as they face many challenges related to their development and their striving for independence. Parents will need to sacrifice time, careers, hobbies, prestige, money, entertainment and possessions in order to be with their children. In reality, **"Quantity Time"** is what it takes to build deep relationships. Devoting time to our children will provide opportunities for teaching and molding their faith and beliefs. Parents can spend time doing some of the following activities:

- Having regular family worships. Spending time together in the evening for worships builds strong family bonds.
- Studying the Bible and Sabbath School lesson together. Having a family weekly Bible study is very beneficial for both parents and children in deepening their understanding of God's Word.
- Enjoying mealtimes and play times together enriches parent-child relationships.
- Talking and sharing concerns and issues as well as the joys and thankfulness (no gadgets, please!).

DISCIPLING, NURTURING, AND RECLAIMING

3. **Jesus Frequently Taught His Disciples Scripture and Showed Them How to Minister to Others.**

Jesus practiced Deuteronomy 6:7, but He took it to a new level: *"You shall teach them diligently to your children, and shall talk of them when you sit in your house, when you walk by the way, when you lie down, and when you rise up."* He frequently taught His disciples Scripture each day when they were walking down the sandy road to another town; He taught about the sower, the Good Samaritan and other things they saw along the way. He taught the multitude as they sat on the hillside; and He taught His disciples while they were fishing.

Parents who want to disciple like Jesus will constantly look for opportunities to pray, read scripture, sing songs, talk about the goodness of God, and show their children how to live through ministry to others. They can practice some of these ideas:

- Encouraging them to begin a personal relationship with Jesus through daily devotions, prayer and studying of God's Word. Get them a prayer journal.
- Helping kids discover their spiritual gifts and their passion for ministry.
- Equipping them to share their gifts in serving the church and the community.
- Training them to disciple their friends to become followers of Jesus.

The Barna Research Group Research fully affirms the values of these ideas as reported in their book, *Households of Faith,* a 2019 extensive study of practicing Christians and their living arrangements and routines.[9]

One of the goals of this study, conducted in partnership with Lutheran Hour Ministries, was to learn from households that appear to be exceptionally engaged in communal and consistent faith expression in the home. Barna developed a custom metric that sorts households by reports of collective, frequent engagement in key behaviors:

- Spiritual practices—defined here as praying every day or two and reading the Bible weekly all together.
- Spiritual conversations—defined here as talking about God and faith at least weekly all together.
- Hospitality—defined here as welcoming non-family guests regularly, or at least several times a month.

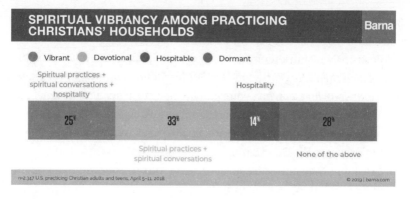

They found that households that participate in all of these activities at this frequency are what Barna refers to as **spiritually Vibrant**. A quarter of respondents in this study (25%) describes a household environment that is Vibrant. Others describe homes that are Devotional (only participate in spiritual practices and spiritual conversations), Hospitable (only practice hospitality) or Dormant (participate in none of the above), all of which are explored at length in the **full report**.

Vibrant households are those who engage in spiritual talks with their children, pray together as well as serve together as a family. It is true that intimacy and relationship in our family is a springboard to be able to talk about spiritual things. If we want to hold on to family, we need to hold on to God!

4. Jesus Sent Them Out on A Mission

The Gospel of Luke chapter 10 recorded that Jesus picked seventy other disciples from His followers and sent them out two by two to go ahead of Him into every city and town where He and His disciples planned to go. After Jesus had trained and prepared His disciples, he sent them out to preach and to share the gospel of salvation. The disciples were given opportunity to practice their skills learned from the Master.

In the same way, parents have the privilege and responsibility to teach and model to their children and teens the values of going on God's mission. They can be engaged in various ways of sharing the good news of salvation no matter where they are located. Have you tried some of the following?

- Providing opportunities for children to share Jesus with their friends and classmates.
- Showing them simple ways to witness, such as using the Wordless Book[10], Gospel Flipper-Flapper[11], animated tracts[12], etc.
- Leading them out to serve and get involved in compassion projects,

such as packing food and supplies for hurricane victims, distributing blankets to the homeless, etc.

- Providing opportunities for juniors and teens to go on mission trips overseas. It has been found that youngsters who went out to serve overseas return home with a new perspective of life, and increased gratitude for their families.
- Discussing & debriefing about what they have learned after going out on a mission trip.

Indeed, Jesus has shown us how we can be effective in disciple making. If we do not want the world to disciple our children, then we need to take our discipleship role more seriously by committing ourselves to intentionally discipling our children and teens. No matter how busy we are as parents, we need to make the spiritual discipleship of our children and teens a top priority. Research has shown that many children accept Jesus as their personal Savior before the age of 13. Hence, it is imperative that we nurture the faith of our children while they are young. Discipling our children and teens requires time, energy and intentionality; but it is worth it! Be an Intentional Disciple Maker!

LINDA MEI LIN KOH, Ed.D.

A native of Singapore, Dr. Linda Mei Lin Koh is currently serving as the Director of Children's Ministries at the General Conference of Seventh-day Adventists. She has twenty-four years of teaching experience both in Singapore and in the United States. Prior to her appointment to the General Conference, Linda has served for nine years as Director of Children's, Family, and Women's Ministries at the Southern Asia-Pacific Division based in the Philippines. Dr. Koh obtained her Ed.D degree in Educational Psychology and Counseling from Andrews University. She enjoys writing and has co-authored two books and has also contributed many articles for the *Adventist Review, Adventist World, Elder's Digest, Vibrant Life, Kids Ministry Ideas,* and other church publications. She loves children and is a strong advocate for children, often seeking to bring awareness of the need to put children first in our church so as to nurture and disciple them for Christ. She is married with two adult sons and six grandchildren.

ENDNOTES

1 Barna Group, 2011. https://www.barna.com/research/six-reasons-young-christians-leave-church/
2 Aaron Earls. https://lifewayresearch.com/2019/01/15/most-teenagers-drop-out-of-church-as-young-adults/
3 Ellen white, *Desire of Ages*, p. 515.

4 https://www.familylife.com/articles/topics/parenting/foundations/spiritual-development/4-reasons-you-should-intentionally-disciple-your-children/

5 Charles H. Spurgeon, *Come, My Children; A Book for Parents and Teachers on the Christian Training of Children*, Chapter 8; added to Bible Bulletin Board's "Spurgeon Collection" by Tony Capoccia at www.biblebb.com

6 Ellen White, *Adventist Home*, p. 320

7 Ellen White, *Patriarchs and Prophets*, p. 144

8 The Myth of Quality Time, *Newsweek*, May 11, 1997. https://www.newsweek.com/myth-quality-time-172948

9 Barna Research, *Household of Faith*, 2019.

10 Child Evangelism Fellowship. https://www.cefonline.com

11 Child Evangelism Fellowship. https://www.cefonline.com

12 Animated tracts, https://www.letthelittlechildrencome.com/child-evangelism-tools

Joining and Remaining:

A Look at the Data on the Role of Adventist Education

JOHN WESLEY TAYLOR V, Ed.D., Ph.D.

GIVEN THE EFFORT AND THE costs involved, Seventh-day Adventist parents sometimes wonder: "Does Adventist education truly make a difference? Do the benefits gained outweigh the expenditure? Is sending my child to an Adventist school an expense or an investment?"

Pastors and other church leaders also ponder: "Is Adventist education truly evangelism? Does it justify the resources that we invest? If so, how can we present a persuasive case for Adventist education to parents and other church members?"

Writing to church leaders and educators, Ellen White declared that the all-important issue in Adventist education is the conversion of the student.[1] While there have been studies, such as the CognitiveGenesis research,[2] which have examined the academic performance of students in Adventist schools, this article will focus on two key outcomes: accession and retention—joining the Adventist Church and remaining in the denomination.

So what do we know about access and retention, and the role of Seventh-day Adventist education? In short, there is a consistent and important relationship between attending an Adventist school and the likelihood that a child or youth will join the Adventist Church and then choose to remain a member. We'll take a look at the evidence.

JOINING THE CHURCH

In the biblical model, conversion is expressed through baptism.[3] Baptism, in turn, is a public statement of one's desire to formally join the church. Is there support for the role of Adventist education in accession to the church?

Adventist education is the longest and largest evangelistic event held by the Adventist Church. It is also one of the most effective.

Depending on the country and the educational system, the duration of a school day can range from five to nine hours, and a school year can range from 160 to 260 days.[4] An individual student could attend an Adventist school from a single year to perhaps 16 years or more. At minimum, if a student attends an Adventist school for just a single year, this represents an evangelistic opportunity of at least 800 hours. To use evangelistic terminology, this equates to a person attending an evangelistic series two hours per night for 400 nights. If a student, however, continues in Adventist education from first grade through university studies, the evangelistic potential could increase to more than 37,000 hours.

In Adventist education, 5,705 evangelistic sites specialize in children 5-12 years old, with 51,965 evangelists and 1,188,910 persons attending each day. Also, 2,336 evangelistic sites focus on adolescents 13-16 years old, with 36,711 evangelists and 583,946 in attendance. For youth and young adults, there are 167 evangelistic venues, with 14,103 evangelists and 142,530 attending. All told, Adventist education represents more than 8,000 evangelistic sites, with more than 100,000 evangelists involved and nearly 2 million in attendance each day.[5] Certainly it is the largest evangelistic endeavor of the church.

Is it effective? Each year for the past 10 years there have been at least 30,000 students, and in some years more than 50,000 students, in Adventist schools baptized during the school year, primarily in culminating events such as a Week of Prayer. The total for the 2006-2015 period was 427,313 baptisms.[6] To look at it another way, this is equivalent to a typical-size conference being established each year through the evangelistic ministry of Adventist education.

While only a few studies have compared attendance at Adventist schools with the baptismal rate of children from Adventist families, the ones that have examined this connection concluded that Adventist education does make a significant difference in terms of children and youth joining the church.

A 1990 study, for example, analyzed 844 children and youth from Adventist families in the Southern Union Conference of the North American Division.[7] Of those children and youth who had no Adventist education, 40.1 percent were never baptized. Of those with one or more years of Adventist education, 15.4 percent were never baptized; while in the group with 11 or more years of Adventist education, only 3.1 percent were never baptized (see Figure 1).

DISCIPLING, NURTURING, AND RECLAIMING

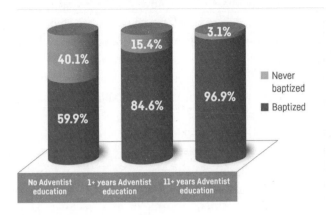

FIGURE 1. School Attendance and Baptism

Source: Kenneth James Epperson study

Another study conducted in 1985 of 807 children and youth from Adventist families in the Lake Union Conference of the North American Division found similar results.[8] Of those children and youth with no Adventist education, 38.3 percent never joined the church. In the group with some Adventist education, 4.6 percent never joined the church, while 100 percent of those in the sample who studied all 12 grades in Adventist education joined the church *(see Figure 2)*.

FIGURE 2. School Attendance and Church Membership

Source: Warren Minder study

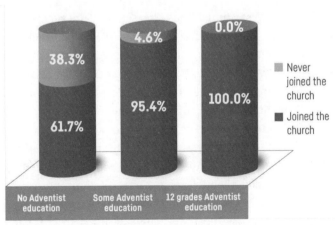

REMAINING IN THE CHURCH

While joining the church is foundational, retention is equally important. Sadly, many of those who join the Adventist Church subsequently leave the denomination. During the past 50 years (1965–2015), for example, there have been 34,385,004 accessions in the Adventist Church worldwide. During the same period, 13,737,205 people left the church.[9] This represents a net loss of 39.95 percent. In effect, for every 10 people who joined the church, four have slipped away.

The ratios are no better for young people. In the Youth Retention study that attempted to track more than 1,500 baptized 15- and 16-year-olds in the North American Division for 10 years (1988-1998), results indicated that in most of the demographic groups, at least 40 to 50 percent had left the church by their mid-20s.[10] Tragically, we are not just losing one of 10 coins, as described in Jesus' parable.[11] We are losing half of the coins! The question posed by the prophet Jeremiah becomes increasingly poignant: "Where is the flock entrusted to you, your beautiful flock?"[12]

We turn now to the matter of the retention of children and youth in the Seventh-day Adventist Church. Over the past three decades there have been at least seven studies that have examined the role of Adventist education in retention, with three of these studies conducted in the past seven years. Some of these studies have focused on specific regional populations, while others are more global in nature. Some present a snapshot in time, while others have taken a longitudinal approach. While each study has inherent limitations (as is the case with all studies), together they present a picture that is consistent over time and compelling.

One of the largest studies was the set of Valuegenesis surveys, conducted over a 20-year period, from 1990 to 2010.[13] Valuegenesis[1] data from 2,267 twelfth-grade Adventist students in Adventist schools in the North American Division, for example, showed that the more years of Adventist schooling, the greater the person's reported loyalty to the Seventh-day Adventist Church, his or her belief in the fundamental teachings of the church, and his or her intention to remain an Adventist at age 40. In the 2010 Valuegenesis[3] survey, 81 percent of all students indicated that attending an Adventist school was the most important factor that had helped them develop their religious faith, with the Adventist school ranking more highly than any other factor *(see Figure 3)*. Across all three Valuegenesis studies (1990–2010), a full 75 percent of Adventist students in Adventist schools believed that the chances of their remaining in the Adventist Church at age 40 were good to excellent.

FIGURE 3. Faith Development Factors

Source: V. Bailey Gillespie, Valuegenesis[3]

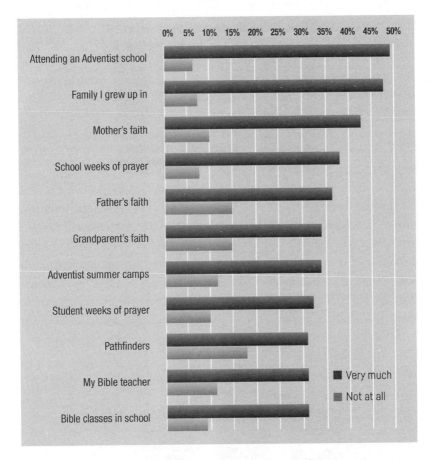

We have noted the Youth Retention study, which endeavored to follow high school students for 10 years, utilizing a sample about evenly divided between students in Adventist schools and in non-Adventist schools in the U.S. and Canada. One of the key findings of this research was that the number of years in an Adventist school was positively related to commitment to Jesus Christ and to commitment to personal Bible study, as well as to the statements "My relationship with Christ is stronger now" and "Religion is important in my life."[14] Furthermore, intention to marry an Adventist in students who attended an Adventist school was nearly twice the proportion of those who had not attended an Adventist school (83 percent versus 46 percent, respectively). At the 10-year mark the probability of leaving the Adventist Church was 3.9 times greater for those who had attended non-Adventist schools, compared with those who had attended Seventh-day Adventist schools (see Figure 4).

FIGURE 4. Youth Retention Study

FIGURE 4. Youth Retention Study
Source: Roger L. Dudley study

Remained in the Adventist Church 10 years later

Several doctoral dissertations have studied retention in the context of Adventist education. In Kenneth James Epperson's study, children of Adventist families in the Southern Union Conference who had no Adventist education were 4.5 times more likely to have infrequent or no church attendance, compared to those who had 11 or more years of Adventist education *(see Figure 5)*.[15] This is a significant finding, given that a lack of active involvement in the church is often a precursor to leaving the church.[16]

FIGURE 5. Church Attendance
Source: Kenneth James Epperson study

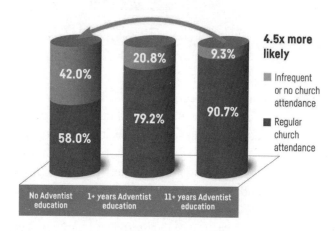

In 1990 Robert Rice carried out a longitudinal study in which he compared baptized Adventist youth in southern California who graduated from public high schools and those who graduated from Adventist academies.[17] Thirteen years after graduation, 37 percent of those who had graduated from public high schools remained in the church, compared with 77 percent of those who had graduated from Adventist academies *(see Figure 6)*. Rice also found that those who had graduated from Adventist academies were twice as likely to pay tithe (50 percent versus 26 percent), twice as likely to attend an Adventist church service regularly (59 percent versus 32 percent), twice as inclined to educate their own children in an Adventist school (59 percent versus 29 percent), and nearly three times more likely to have married an Adventist spouse (78 percent versus 27 percent), compared to those who graduated from a public high school.[18]

FIGURE 6. Retention and Baptism

Source: Robert Rice study

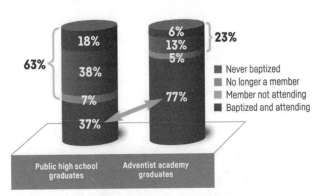

Warren Minder's study, conducted in the Lake Union Conference, also considered retention, identifying those who joined and remained, and those who joined but subsequently left the church.[19] In sum, only 50.8 percent of those youth from Adventist families who had not experienced Adventist education joined and remained in the church, compared to 98.2 percent of those who had studied all 12 grades in Adventist schools *(see Figure 7)*.

FIGURE 7. Retention and Membership

Source: Warren Minder study

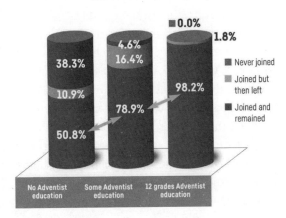

The Center for Creative Ministry recently conducted a global qualitative study in which 925 former or inactive church members were interviewed. Findings indicate that only 17 percent of lapsed and ex-members had received any form of Adventist education, compared to 56 percent of those who were current members.[20] This threefold difference provides evidence that those who have not experienced Adventist education are disproportionately more likely to become inactive or leave *(see Figure 8)*. The study concluded that one of the greatest retention issues for the Adventist Church relates to young adults rising into the middle class. These were individuals who joined the church when they were younger and had less education. As their education, predominantly in non-Adventist institutions, progressed, however, they quit attending regularly and eventually left the Adventist Church.

FIGURE 8. School Attendance of Former and Inactive Members
Source: Center for Creative Ministry study

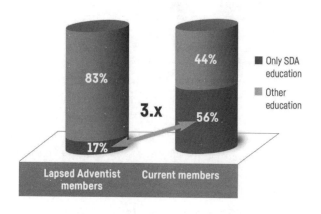

Global studies conducted by the General Conference Office of Archives, Statistics, and Research (ASTR) in 2013 and 2014 have also revealed key differences between ex-members and current members in terms of the proportion who have attended Adventist schools.[21] Current members were twice as likely to have Seventh-day Adventist tertiary education compared to ex-members who had studied at the tertiary level. Current members who had secondary education as their highest education were 2.5 times as likely to have studied in an Adventist school, compared to ex-members who had secondary education as their highest level of studies. Finally, current members who had elementary education as their highest education were three times as likely to have studied in an Adventist elementary school, compared to ex-members who had elementary education as their highest level of studies *(see Figure 9)*. This may suggest that early Adventist education is an especially powerful factor in retention.

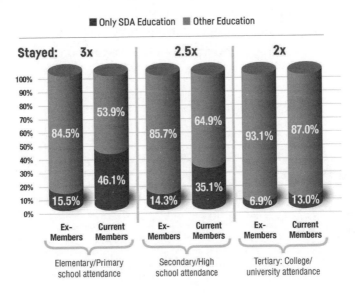

FIGURE 9. School Attendance of Current Members
Source: General Conference Office of Archives, Statistics, and Research

CONCLUSION

Although many factors undoubtedly relate to accession and retention, and further research, particularly in specific populations around the world, would be beneficial, the research that we have presents a persuasive conclusion: Adventist education is a consistent and important predictor of children and youth joining and remaining in the Seventh-day Adventist Church. As Ellen White observed: "In the highest sense the work of education and the work of redemption are one."[22]

In essence, Adventist education is mission. Through Adventist education, children and youth experience accession and retention, for the ultimate purpose of redemption *(see Figure 10)*. Consequently, the Seventh-day Adventist Church must reaffirm and uplift the central role of Adventist education in the evangelistic mission of the church.

Figure 10.

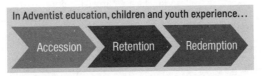

The prophet Isaiah wrote: "All your children shall be taught by the Lord, and great shall be the peace of your children."[23] The Hebrew word translated "peace" in this passage is *shâlôm*. While *shâlôm* does include the concept of peace, it incorporates much more—safety, well-being, health, prosperity, and happiness. *Shâlôm* is what we want for our children and youth. There is a condition, however. In order to experience *shâlôm*, our children and youth must be taught by God. Taught by God. Through Seventh-day Adventist education.

Adapted from a presentation at the 2017 Pan-African LEAD Conference in Kigali, Rwanda, February 15-19, 2017.

JOHN WESLEY TAYLOR V, Ed.D., Ph.D.

John Wesley Taylor V, Ed.D., Ph.D. serves as an associate director of education in the General Conference Department of Education in Silver Spring, Maryland, U.S.A. His grandfather, John Wesley Taylor III, joined the Seventh-day Adventist Church while attending an Adventist academy, and later, as a physician, served as a missionary in South America and Inter-America. Since that time, three generations have been educated in Adventist schools, have remained in the Adventist Church, and together have provided more than a century of service to the church.

ENDNOTES

1 Ellen G. White, *Fundamentals of Christian Education* (Nashville: Southern Pub. Assn., 1923), p. 436.

2 CognitiveGenesis was a longitudinal study conducted from 2006 to 2009 involving more than 800 Adventist schools in the United States, Canada, and Bermuda, with approximately 52,000 participating students in grades 3-9 and grade 11. Standardized achievement test results indicated that students in Adventist schools in the U.S. outperformed the national average in all subjects; for all grade levels, school sizes, and ethnic groups; and regardless of ability level. Furthermore, the more years a student attended an Adventist school, the greater the improvement in performance. This "Adventist advantage" in education became the subject of a PBS documentary *The Blueprint* by award-winning producer Martin Doblmeier. Further information on the CognitiveGenesis study may be found in J. Thayer and E. Kido, "CognitiveGenesis (CG): Assessing Academic Achievement and Cognitive Ability in Adventist Schools," *Journal of Research on Christian Education* 21, no. 2 (2012): 99-115. A summary is also available at http://adventisteducation.org/assessment/cognitive_genesis/overview.

3 Matthew 3:6, 11; 28:19; Mark 1:5; 16:16; Luke 3:3; Acts 2:38, 41; 8:12, 13, 36-38; 13:24; 16:31-33; 18:8. Unless otherwise indicated, Scripture quotations in this article are taken from the New International Version.

4 "School Days Around the World," https://norberthaupt.com/2012/04/20/school-days-around-the-world/; "School Days Around the World" (June 2015) infographic; http://elearninginfographics.com/school-days-around-world-infographic/. Total number of hours in school can range from 15,200 in Finland to 37,400 in China, which holds the record for both highest number of hours per day and highest number of days per year, at 9 and 260, respectively.

5 General Conference Office of Archives, Statistics, and Research, *2016 Annual Statistical Report: 152nd Report of the General Conference of Seventh-day Adventists* for 2015: http://documents.adventistarchives.org/Statistics/ASR/ASR2016.pdf.

6 Statistics provided by the Department of Education, General Conference of Seventh-day Adventists.

7 Kenneth James Epperson, "The Relationship of Seventh-day Adventist School Attendance to Seventh-day Adventist Church Membership in the Southern Union Conference" (Ed.D. dissertation, Loma Linda University, 1990). In this study 300 family units were randomly selected from the Southern Union Conference of the North American Division, and 210 families responded, representing a return rate of 70 percent. Of the individuals in the study, 40 percent had never attended an Adventist school. Children and youth from Adventist families who were baptized into the Adventist Church had attended an Adventist school for 8.06 years on average, while those children and youth who were never baptized into the Adventist Church had attended Adventist schools for an average of only 2.42 years, yielding a significant relationship (p<0.000) between the number of years in Adventist schools and baptism. The study also indicated that of those who were baptized, 2.6 percent were baptized prior to the age of 8, 63.7 percent were baptized between the ages of 8 and 15, while 14.2 percent were baptized between the ages of 16 and 23. The seventh grade was the most frequent grade level at which children were baptized, with 61.0 percent of those baptized having been baptized between grades 5 and 8.

8 Warren E. Minder, "A Study of the Relationship Between Church-sponsored K-12 Education and Church Membership in the Seventh-day Adventist Church" (Ed.D. dissertation, Western Michigan University, 1985). In this study 400 family units were randomly selected from the Lake Union Conference in the North American Division. The study reported a return rate of 71.8 percent and a sampling error of approximately 3.25 percent. The study found a significant relationship (p<.001) between the number of years in grades 1 to 12 that a person attended an Adventist school and whether or not the person was baptized into the Seventh-day Adventist Church. There was also a significant relationship (p<.001) between the church membership of each parent and baptism of the child, as well as between parental active involvement in the church and baptism of the child (p=.0011 for the mother; p=.0191 for the father). Minder also cited results from an earlier study, "A Study of Seventh-day Adventist Church Members," conducted in the Pacific Union Conference in 1962 (N=83,662; 68 percent return rate). That study reported that for young people who had attended all 12 grades at an Adventist school, 97 percent had joined the church, as opposed to 32 percent of the young people from Adventist families who did not attend any Adventist school during elementary and secondary schooling. Further, it was reported that in the group that had received some K-12 schooling in Adventist schools, 57 percent joined the church.

9 Figures provided by the Secretariat of the General Conference of Seventh-day Adventists.

10 Roger L. Dudley, *Why Our Teenagers Leave the Church: Personal Stories From a 10-year Study* (Hagerstown, Md.: Review and Herald Pub. Assn., 2000), p. 35. "At least 40 percent to 50 percent of Seventh-day Adventist teenagers in North America are essentially leaving the church by their middle 20s."

11 Luke 15:8-10.

12 Jeremiah 13:20, CEB.

13 Roger L. Dudley and V. Bailey Gillespie, *Valuegenesis1: Faith in the Balance* (Riverside, Calif.: La Sierra University Press, 1992); Roger L. Dudley and Janet Leigh Kangas, "Valuegenesis1: How Does Adventist Education Affect Youth Attitudes?" *Journal of Adventist Education* 52, no. 4 (April-May 1990): 24-29, 45, 46; Jerome Thayer, "The Impact of Adventist Schools on Students" (paper presented at the fourth Symposium on the Bible and Adventist Scholarship, Riviera Maya, Estado Quintana Roo, Mexico, March 16-22, 2008), http://fae.adventist.org/essays/iv_Thayer_Jerry.pdf. The Valuegenesis1 survey (1990) received responses from 10,641 Adventist students in Adventist schools and 457 Adventist students in non-Adventist schools in North America. Thayer subsequently

analyzed a subsample consisting of 2,267 twelfth grade Adventist students in Adventist schools. The report of a replication of the Valuegenesis1 survey in the South Pacific Division in 1993 is available at http://circle.adventist.org/files/download/VGCORERE.pdf. A further replication of the Valuegenesis1 survey was conducted in Puerto Rico in 1995, with reports available at http://digitalcommons.andrews.edu/cgi/viewcontent.... and http://digitalcommons.andrews.edu/cgi/viewcontent.cgi?article=1468& context=dissertations. See V. Bailey Gillespie, Michael J. Donahue, Ed Boyatt, and Barry Gane, *Ten Years Later: A Study of Two Generations* (Riverside, Calif.: La Sierra University Press, 2003); and V. Bailey Gillespie, "Valuegenesis2: Adventist Schools Do Make a Difference," *Journal of Adventist Education* 65, no. 1 (October/November 2002): 12-16. More than 16,000 Adventist students in grades 6 through 12 completed the second Valuegenesis questionnaire. The Valuegenesis3 survey (2010) received responses from more than 18,000 students in grades 6 through 12 in Adventist schools throughout North America (Bailey Gillespie, "Valuegenesis3 Update: Research Information Summary," Issues 1-5 [published by the John Hancock Center for Youth and Family Ministry, Riverside, California]).

14 Roger L. Dudley, "Understanding the Spiritual Development and the Faith Experience of College and University Students on Christian Campuses," *Journal of Research on Christian Education* 8, no. 1 (Spring 1999): 5-28; Roger L. Dudley, "Youth Religious Commitment Over Time: A Longitudinal Study of Retention," Review of Religious Research 41, no. 1 (1999): 110-121; Roger L. Dudley, "Christian Education and Youth Retention in the SDA Church," *Journal of Adventist Education* 62, no. 3 (February/March 2000): 8-13; Roger L. Dudley, *Why Our Teenagers Leave the Church;* Jerome Thayer, "The Impact of Adventist Schools on Students" (unpublished paper, 2008). This paper included a reanalysis of the Youth Retention study data. The Youth Retention study (Roger Dudley) began in 1988 with 1,523 baptized Adventist youth ages 15 and 16 in the United States and Canada. These individuals were surveyed each year in order to determine what factors were related to staying or leaving the church. When the study ended 10 years later, 783 (51.4 percent) of the original group, now young adults, completed the survey. Dudley speculated that many of the young people who dropped out of the study were no longer church members.

15 Epperson. Further analysis yielded a positive relationship (p<0.021) between Adventist school attendance and regular attendance at a Seventh-day Adventist church. Epperson also reported that children who had both parents as members of the Adventist Church averaged an attendance of 8.4 years in Adventist schools, compared to 1.19 years when only one parent was a member of the Adventist Church, representing a significant difference (p<0.000). For 53.6 percent of those who no longer regularly attended an Adventist church, neither parent was a member of the church.

16 Paul Richardson, "Survey of Former and Inactive Adventist Church Members," Office of Archives and Statistics (ASTR), publication produced by the Center for Creative Ministry, Milton-Freewater, Oregon, 2013: https://www.adventistarchives.org/2013-retention-study.pdf.

17 Robert W. Rice, "A Survey of the Relationship Between Attending Seventh-day Adventist Academies 9-12 and Subsequent Commitment to the Seventh-day Adventist Church" (Ph.D. dissertation, University of Denver, 1990). There were 264 participants in the North American Division study, representing a 70 percent return rate (65 percent for the public high school graduates and 75 percent for the Adventist academy graduates). In the study, 93 percent of those who graduated from an Adventist academy had spent the ninth grade in an Adventist school, whereas only 71 percent of those from Adventist families who graduated from a public school had spent the ninth grade in a public school. These statistics may indicate a tendency for certain Adventist families, whose children may begin high school in an Adventist academy, to shift enrollment to a public high school at some point during secondary education.

18 Data from the Youth Retention study yielded complementary findings in regard to tithe paying.

19 Minder. The sample (N=807), 215 individuals (26.6 percent) were not Seventh-day

Adventists. This group was comprised of 138 individuals (64.2 percent) from Illinois, Indiana, Michigan, and Wisconsin who had never joined the church and 77 individuals (35.8 percent) who left the church after joining. The study found a strong positive relationship (p<.001) between Adventist schooling and church retention, wherein increased years of Adventist schooling were associated with an increased probability of the person remaining in the church.

20 Richardson. Of the 17 percent of lapsed and ex-Adventists who had attended Adventist schools, 6 percent had attended an Adventist primary or elementary school at some point in their life, 7 percent had attended an Adventist secondary school, and 8 percent had attended an Adventist college or university. Participants were from Africa, South America, Europe, and North America.

21 Data for the school attendance of ex-members are based on the ASTR report "Leaving the Church: Why Some Seventh-day Adventist Members Leave the Church, and Why Some Come Back" (2014), a study that was conducted in all divisions of the church. Data for members are from the ASTR report "Global Church Member Survey" (2013), conducted in nine out of the 13 world divisions. The category "Other Education" for ex-members includes attendance at both Adventist and non-Adventist educational institutions, albeit these percentages were low: 7 percent primary, 7 percent secondary, and 5 percent tertiary (based on data presented by D.J.B. Trim at the LEAD Conference "Educating for Eternity" on October 6, 2016, in Silver Spring, Maryland, U.S.A.).

22 Ellen G. White, *Education* (Mountain View, Calif.: Pacific Press Pub. Assn., 1903), p. 30. This redemptive purpose perhaps led Ellen White to urge, "There should be schools established wherever there is a church or company of believers" ("Special Testimony to the Battle Creek Church" [1897], p. 40).

23 Isaiah 54:13, NKJV.

Published in *The Journal of Adventist Education,* 2017, Issue 3 (April-June).
Available at https://jae.adventist.org/en/2017.3.8

Living Up To Adventist Standards:

The Role Religiosity Plays in Wellness Behaviors of Adventist College Students

Alina M. Baltazar, Ph.D., M.S.W., L.M.S.W., A.C.S.W., C.F.L.E., is an Associate professor and M.S.W. program director in the School of Social Work and co-associate director of the Institute for the Prevention of Addictions at Andrews University.

Amanuel Dessie, B.S.W., M.S.W., is a student and graduate assistant in the School of Social Work at Andrews University.

Duane C. McBride, M.A., Ph.D., is a professor of sociology in the School of Social and Behavioral Sciences and executive director of the Institute for the Prevention of Addictions at Andrews University.

INTRODUCTION

Approximately a third of young adults (ages 18 to24 years) in the United States attend college.[1] College students make a variety of health decisions usually made without parental supervision.[2] Counseling centers on college campuses in the United States have reported increasing rates of depression and anxiety disorders.[3] A high percentage of college students experience depression (41 percent), and 63 percent reported overwhelming anxiety in national surveys.[4]

There is considerable concern today about how college students manage their own health. Obesity is at an all-time high, and the demands of a college schedule often significantly interfere with sleep, diet, and physical activity.[5] College students are generally healthy, so it can be difficult to be motivated to participate in these behaviors. Research has found negative health behaviors among college students are associated with having a mental illness.[6] Monitoring the Future conducts annual surveys among college students to monitor trends of alcohol and drug use.[7] They report that marijuana use is at its highest level in 35 years among college students with 43 percent reporting using during the past year. Alcohol consumption, especially getting drunk, has been going down for the same period of time.

A wide variety of research has also shown the protective effect of religion on substance use and other health behaviors.[8] Religiousness is multidimensional in nature and may play an important role in moderating the effects of major life events.[9] Research suggests that extrinsic religious-ness relates to depressive symptoms, and intrinsic religiousness relates to lower levels of depression. As students enter their college years, there can be a transition period in how they relate to religiosity, as they may move from the beliefs of adolescents to their beliefs as emerging adults.[10]

This paper presents results from a youth health risk survey conducted on a Seventh-day Adventist college campus in 2018 and examines the positive and negative influence of religiosity on wellness behaviors.

METHOD

A youth health risk survey has been distributed at Andrews University about every five years since 1990, using a purposive sample of representa-tive classes through the university. The goal is to examine health risk behaviors. Risk and protective factors are also identified. This paper presents results from the survey conducted in 2018 with an N of 650. Trained student workers entered into the chosen classrooms at the beginning of class and wrote a link on the board for students to enter their answers into their chosen device. The study was approved by institutional IRB.

The 21-item Depression, Anxiety, and Stress Scale (DASS) was used to examine mental health. The scale questions were rated on a four-point Likert scale of frequency or severity of the participants' experiences during the past week.[11] The scale has been found to be reliable and valid in a wide variety of international populations.[12] The scale identifies typical symptoms of these conditions.

Students answered questions about the frequency they engaged in a variety of health behaviors in a six-point scale from never to always. This study focused on four physical wellness behaviors known to affect mental health. Exercise was defined as moderate to vigorous cardiovascular exercise for 20 to 60 minutes a day. Water consumption was measured as eight cups of water per day and avoiding sugary drinks most of the time. Diet was defined as avoiding highly fatty, highly sugar, fried and processed foods majority of the time. For sleep, students were asked if they sleep, on average, seven to eight hours per night.

There were multiple questions regarding alcohol and substance use. This study will focus on annual reported use for the top two substances used by participants; alcohol and marijuana. For the purposes of this study, the answers were put into a binary of no and yes.

The religiosity internalization questions are from the Christian Religious Internalization Scale (CRIS).[13] This scale measures two types of internalization of religion. Introjection represents a partial internalization of religious beliefs and is characterized by self- and other-approval-based pressure. Identification represents adoption of religious beliefs as personal values. The question regarding commitment to Christ is just one question in which the participant identifies their level of commitment to Christ from none to fully developed on a four-point scale.

Multiple focus groups were conducted to help understand the results from the youth health risk survey. The questions examined in the focus groups included physical health, mental health, and substance use of college students and the role that religiosity plays. Students were recruited to participate in the study as part of a course requirement for some School of Social and Behavioral Sciences general education courses. There were multiple studies the students could choose from. Students were each given $20 as an honorarium for their time and were fed a meal. There were five focus groups, with four to 10 participants in each one. Participants could leave at any time, but none did. Each group was audio-recorded. The principal investigator asked the open-ended questions, and the graduate assistant took notes of nonverbal communication. A total of 39 participants took part in the qualitative portion of the study. The focus group participants were restricted to be self-identifying as Seventh-day Adventist, single, living on campus, and aged 18 to 25 in order to get a more homogeneous group of college students.

ANALYSIS

Data from the survey was downloaded into Statistical Package for the Social Sciences (version 24) for analysis. Only respondents who were Seventh-day Adventists (89 percent) were analyzed for this paper. The Seventh-day Adventist participants were very ethnically diverse, reflecting the ethnic diversity of the campus.

All religiosity questions were examined with mental health, and alcohol and marijuana use as the dependent variables. The religiosity questions were categorized as measuring level of commitment to Christ and internal or externally motivated religiosity. Only the statistically significant results are reported.

The focus groups were audio recorded to allow transcription. The principal investigator and graduate assistant then reviewed the transcripts independently and came up with a codebook. The initial analysis was accomplished by coding participants' themes throughout the data. The team used the classic constant comparison approach. This was facilitated with the qualitative software, QDA Miner. As the analysis progressed, researchers examined specific instances of the codes to clarify similarities and differences between the researchers' use of these codes. Then the top themes were identified.

SURVEY RESULTS

Wellness and Religiosity

Adding the moderate to very severe levels of depression shows that about a quarter of the Seventh Adventist students were depressed, with just under 20 percent anxious. *See Table 1.*

Physical wellness behavior results are reported as averages on a five-point scale. The measured physical wellness behaviors averaged somewhere between sometimes and often regarding frequency (exercise M=3.35, water M=3.89, diet M=3.59, sleep M=3.21). The only physical wellness activity that was statistically significant with mental health was sleep. Pearson correlations revealed the strength and direction of the relationship. There was a very small, negative correlation: when students reported getting less sleep, they were more likely to report anxiety (-.11, $p \leq .01$) and depression (-.15, $p \leq .01$). *See Table 2.*

For those who were not committed to Christ, 16 percent were moderately to very severely depressed; not sure if they were committed to Christ, 47 percent were depressed; committed life to Christ at a specific time but were no longer committed, 33 percent were depressed; commitment to Christ developed, 19 percent were depressed. These data suggest that uncertainty and the loss of commitment to Christ was more strongly related to depression than certainty of commitment or lack of commitment. *See Table 3.*

Pearson correlations revealed the strength and direction of the relationship between religiosity and mental health. Three variables that represented external (imposed by others) religiosity were positively related to higher stress, anxiety, and depression levels. Sharing faith for approval of others had a very small but statistically significant relationship, with increasing anxiety (.13, $p \leq .01$) and depression (.16, $p \leq .01$). Praying to avoid God's disapproval had a small statistically significant relationship with increasing anxiety (.20, p≤.01) and depression (.16, p≤.01). Attending church to avoid disapproval of others had a very small statistically significant relationship with increasing anxiety (.13, p≤.01) and depression (.10, p≤.05). The mental health variables were not statistically significant with any of the other religiosity variables, so focus groups were used to better explain the results. *See Table 4.*

Substance Use and Religiosity

Annual usage levels of alcohol in 2005 was 32 percent; marijuana, 8 percent. In 2012 alcohol use was 30 percent; marijuana, 16 percent. In 2018 alcohol use was 27 percent; marijuana, 19 percent. Annual use of alcohol has gone down slightly; marijuana use has more than doubled. These trends reflect general society trends of use among college students.[7] *See Table 5.*

Those who reported that they share their faith because God's important to them were less likely to consume alcohol in the past year (-.21, p≤.01), though while inversely related to marijuana use, it was not statistically significant. Those who reported they share their faith because they would feel bad if they did not were also less likely to consume alcohol (-.22, p≤.01) and marijuana (-.13, p≤.01). Frequency of church attendance decreased the likelihood of consuming alcohol (-.30, p≤.01) and marijuana (-.23, p≤.01), Bible reading and its relationship to alcohol (-.28, p≤.01) and marijuana (-.21, p≤.01), Sabbath School attendance and its relationship to alcohol (-.32, p≤.01) and marijuana (-.18, p≤.01), and attending religious programs and its relationship to alcohol (-.33, p≤.01) and marijuana (-.23, p≤.01). Believing God wants me to take care of my body (body is the temple) decreased likelihood of consuming alcohol (-.28, p≤.01) and marijuana (-.12, p≤.01), agreeing that the SDA church is the true church and its relationship to alcohol (-.31, p≤.01) and marijuana (-.19, p≤.01), and having a plan to remain an SDA and its relationship to alcohol (-.31, p≤.01) and marijuana (-.22, p≤.01). See Table 6. Overall, the results are consistent with previous research and show that consistent significant protective effect of religious practice, personal devotions, and religious commitment in regard to substance use.

FOCUS GROUP RESULTS

Perception of Substance Use

There were multiple themes identified in relation to substance use. The participants reported alcohol use is happening more than one would think, especially in the dorm. Because the SDA Church sets the standard of alcohol and drug abstinence and students know it is wrong, it happens undercover.

Students admit there is a cultural norm that while in college they are expected to experiment with alcohol in order to: cope with stress, escape from emotional distress, or to have fun in order to relieve boredom. It often depends on an individual's peer group. They didn't report peer pressure, but admitted that if their friends were doing it, they were more likely to do it so they wouldn't feel left out.

"I think one thing is although we are Adventists, we are also like 18 or 20 something, and generally people associate college with fun and a lot of the idea of college is like drinking and getting drunk, all these recreational activities, and some people maybe they wanna experiment, some people they are not necessarily set in their faith, so this isn't something they can't do." FG3 participant quote summarizing perception of substance use.

Perception of Physical Health

Physical health can be a challenge for many stressed-out and overwhelmed college students. They associate physical health with going to the gym and know that is it important, but they are young and feel invincible. They know it is a good thing, but find it is challenging with everything else they have to do in college. Their peers can have a positive and a negative influence on whether or not they are physically active.

"I think the majority of us kinda almost like think it's impossible, cause we are like drowned with work or school stuff, and we have to do this and that. We also wanna be socially active. So it's kind of like at least the working-out part or like taking care of ourselves properly kinda gets pushed to the bottom." FG2 participant summarizing the perception of physical health by the participants.

Perception of Mental Health

There were three major themes that were identified by the participants in relation to mental health. The most commonly identified theme was the knowledge that resources to address mental health challenges are available on campus. Another point raised was the promotion of the counseling and testing center on campus grounds. This was identified as beneficial for students by helping to create awareness of mental health. The third major theme that participants reported was the issue of stigma on campus. Even though resources are available on campus, participants reported that the stigma decreases the chances of them getting help.

"It's something that I guess students kinda take for granted—they just expect you to go to class and be OK with everything that happens, and there is a lot of drama that happens in college, a lot more than what I would have liked to happen in college, but you have to be able, to nonetheless, and from personal experience I should have gone and talked to a counselor, not just for my own mental health but because of the student persona of, oh, you don't need to do that, you'll be OK, you'll work through it. I didn't, and I should have." FG1 participant quote summarizing participants' understanding of mental health.

Role of Religion

One of the major themes identified from the focus group discussions under the role of religion on wellness behaviors was that religion sets standards and helps to resist the temptation and to cope with stress. The participants further reported that if a student has internalized religion, it helps in setting a standard, which can help them make smart decisions living a healthy life.

The focus group participants identified the religion can cause guilt and/or lead to rebellion if a person has not internalized this value. Participants stated that if religion is not well understood and internalized by college students, it can often lead to a feeling of guilt and shame.

In addition to this, participants stated that the feeling of religion being pushed down on them can often have an oppressive feeling on college students. Thus, these types of feelings can further lead a student to rebel against or find coping in other activities that go against the standards set by religion.

"I think the church tends to shame people into doing things a lot of the time. It is not do this because it is good for you. It is more do this because if you don't you aren't doing good. . . . Instead of shaming someone into doing it, just encourage them to live a godly life." FG4 participant.

DISCUSSION

In the United States, alcohol use is decreasing and marijuana use is increasing among college students.[7] Participants in this study show the same trends in alcohol and marijuana use, with annual use of alcohol decreasing and marijuana use more than doubling over a 13-year period. Students at this SDA university have significantly lower rates of alcohol (74 percent of the average college students versus 27 percent of SDA college students) and marijuana use (43 percent of the average college students versus 19 percent of SDA college students), but the focus group participants report it still happens, though under cover, which makes it harder to keep students who do use safe from the dangers.

Physical health is not a high priority for college students. In the survey, participants reported on average that they "sometimes" exercised regularly, drank enough water, ate a healthy diet, and got enough sleep. Youth development and stress interferes with improving the physical health of college students. Since they are young and much less likely to suffer from chronic health conditions, their health is a low priority. Especially with the multiple stressors they are dealing with from school and having to maintain a social life.

Depression and anxiety rates are increasing among college students. A sizable amount of participants in this study report moderate to very severe levels of depression (24 percent) and 18 percent had anxiety (nearly one out of five), though these are almost half of national rates for college students.[14] There is stigma against getting help for mental health challenges.

Though religiosity is typically seen to have a positive influence on mental health, there have been studies that have found some negative influence.[15] This study supports both types of findings. External pressure is related to higher depression rates in this study. Religiosity does set standards as found in the focus group, but if those standards are not internalized, it can lead to an individual struggling to meet those standards, and when that does not happen, it could affect mental health. The higher the individual's commitment was to Christ, the lower the depression rates, except for those who have no commitment at all. That group had the lowest depression rates (16 percent). According to research, nonbelievers typically have higher rates of suicide and depression, but a recent research study found that those who are nonbelievers for intellectual reasons, as opposed to emotional reasons, had lower rates of depression.[16] In this study those who had doubts about their commitment to Christ had the highest levels of depression (47 percent). It is hard to know if the depression caused an individual to doubt their commitment to Christ or the doubts led to a lack of certainty about their world that could worsen depression. Among those who reported their commitment to Christ was developed, only 19 percent were depressed. Being committed to Christ could give a sense of purpose and certainty about their world, though still one out of five of them suffered from depression.

CONCLUSIONS AND RECOMMENDATIONS

Religious faith and belief can be helpful to wellness, but if it feels forced or the individual has doubts, this study found that there were higher rates of depression and anxiety, and that could lead to rebellion. The focus groups helped to shed light on the importance of internalizing religiosity. Though a lot of religiosity at a Seventh-day Adventist university is external with its expectations, those standards do help a person live a healthier lifestyle, according to the focus groups. That external pressure becomes a problem when the individual hasn't completely internalized the beliefs that led to those standards and expectations.

Seventh-day Adventist health standards are clear, but college students have a hard time implementing them. Expectations are high from all sides: parents, peers, religion, and society. There is a normalization for even SDA college students to relieve that pressure and have fun through alcohol use, though at much lower rates than other colleges. They don't see the need to spend the time and effort to take care of themselves physically. In working with this population to address these issues, it is important to keep these developmental and cultural issues in mind. Church leaders need to listen and hear what they are trying to tell us about the pressure they are under. We need to help them find a healthier balance with all of their responsibilities and look for better ways to cope with stress besides alcohol use, gaming, or Netflix.

Spiritual growth is a process that needs support and guidance. Young adults are trying to figure this out. Their generation is coming of age in a world with ever-increasing rates of those who do not have any religious affiliation (23 percent).[17] They are trying to figure out where they fit in. Standards are important, but they need to understand where these standards come from and how they fit into today's society.

As a church we need to be more supportive and understanding of those who struggle with depression and anxiety, and encourage them to get help from trained mental health professionals. The focus group participants felt Andrews University's counseling center did a good job of that by talking about mental health issues openly. All church educational institutions and churches should do the same, because the stigma is still an issue that can be addressed by talking about it more openly in order to normalize the struggle, even for Christians.

ALINA BALTAZAR, Ph.D.

Alina M. Baltazar (Ph.D., M.S.W., L.M.S.W., A.C.S.W., and C.F.L.E.) is the Master of Social Work program director and associate professor in the Social Work Department, and the director of prevention education at the Institute for the Prevention of Addiction, at Andrews University. In addition she provides psychotherapy services in the community part-time at Life Coach Psychology in Berrien Springs, Michigan. She received her Ph.D. from Michigan State University in the area of human development and families studies, her Master of Social Work from the University of Michigan with a focus on aging, and her B.A. in psychology from Andrews University. She is also a certified family life educator. Baltazar currently teaches clinical social work classes and a personal relationships course at Andrews University. In the past she has taught in the areas of behavioral sciences and family studies. She has published and presented research in the areas of parental and religiosity's influence on youth health risk behavior, parenting, pastoral family stress, domestic violence, and mental health. She has worked as a licensed clinical social worker for more than 23 years in the areas of medical and psychiatric social work, and psychotherapy. She has been happily married to her high school sweetheart for more than 25 years, and is the proud parent to three young men ages 21, 18, and 15.

ENDNOTES

1   N. A. VanKim and T.F. Nelson, "Vigorous Physical Activity, Mental Health, Perceived Stress, and Socializing Among College Students," *American Journal of Health Promotion* 28, no. 1 (2013): 7-15.

2   E. M. Glowacki, S. Kirtz, J. H. Wagner, J. D. Cance, D. Barrera, J. M. Bernhardt, "HealthyhornsTXT: A Text-Messaging Program to Promote College Student Health and Wellness," *Health Promotion Practice* 19, no. 6 (2018): 844-855.

3   American College Health Association, "National Survey of Counseling Center Directors" (2014), International Association of Counseling Services, Inc., Monograph Series No. 9V, retrieved from http://0201.nccdn.net/1_2/000/000/088/0b2/NCCCS2014_v2.pdf.

4   M. E. Duffy, J. M. Twenge, and T. E. Joiner, "Trends in Mood and Anxiety Symptoms and Suicide-related Outcomes Among U.S. Undergraduates, 2007-2018: Evidence From Two National Surveys," *Journal of Adolescent Health* 65, no. 10 (2019): 590-598.

5   J. Calestine, M. Bopp, C. M. Bopp, "College Student Work Habits Are Related to Physical Activity and Fitness," *International Journal of Exercise Science* 10, no. 7 (2017): 1009-1017.

6   J. S. Young, C. S. Cashwell, and J. Shcherbakova, "The Moderating Relationship of Spirituality on Negative Life Events and Psychological Adjustment," *Counseling and Values* 45, no. 1 (2011), doi.org/10.1002/j.2161-007X.2000.tb00182.x.

7   J. E. Schulenberg, L. D. Johnston, P. M. O'Malley, J. G. Bachman, R. A. Miech, and M. E. Patrick, "Monitoring the Future: National Survey Results on Drug Use, 1975–2018: Volume II, College Students and Adults Ages 19–60" (Ann Arbor, Mich.: Institute for Social Research, The University of Michigan, 2019), retrieved from http://monitoringthefuture.org/pubs.html#monographs.

8   M. Townsend, V. Kadder, H. Ayele, T. Mulligan, "Systematic Review of Clinical Trials Examining the Effects of Religion on Health (Review Article)," *Southern Medical Journal*, December 2002, pp. 1429+, Gale Academic Onefile, accessed 24 Nov. 2019.

9   G. W. Allport, "The Religious Context of Prejudice," Journal for the Scientific Study of *Religion* 5 (1966): 447-457.

10 Center for College Mental Health Annual Report, "Annual Report" (2015), https://ccmh.psu.edu/files/2017/10/2015_CCMH_Report_1-18-2015-yq3vik.pdf.

11 Barney G. Glaser and Anselm L. Strauss, The Discovery of Grounded Theory: Strategies *for Qualitative Research* (Aldine Publishing Company, 1967).

12 S. B. Oswalt, A. M. Lederer, K. Chestnut-Steich, C. Day, D. Ortiz, "Trends in College Students' Mental Health Diagnoses and Utilization of Services 2009-2015," *Journal of American College Health* (2018), doi: 10.1080/07448481.2018.1515748.

13 R. M. Ryan, S. Rigby, and K. King, "Two Types of Religious Internalization and Their Relations to Religious Orientations and Mental Health," *Journal of Personality and Social Psychology* 65, no. 1 (1993): 586-596.

14 Duffy, Twenge, and Joiner.

15 J. Levin, "Religion and Mental Health: Theory and Research," International Journal of *Applied Psychoanalytic Studies*, doi: 10.1002/aps, 2010, retrieved from http://baylorisr. org/wp-content/uploads/levin_religion_mental_health.pdf.

16 J. O. Baker, S. Stroppe, and M. H. Walker, "Secularity, Religiosity, and Health: Physical and Mental Health Differences Between Atheists, Agnostics, and Nonaffiliated Theists Compared to Religiously Affiliated Individuals." *Social Science Research* 75 (2018): 44-57.

17 Pew Research, "America's Changing Landscape" (2016), **https://www.pewforum.org/ 2015/05/12/chapter-1-the-changing-religious-composition-of-the-u-s/#atheists -and-agnostics-make-up-a-growing-share-of-the-unaffiliated**.

TABLES

TABLE 1

DASS Scale Results

	Stress	Anxiety	Depression
None	75%	67%	63%
Mild	10%	14%	12%
Moderate	6%	8%	12%
Severe	7%	4%	5%
Very severe	2%	7%	7%

TABLE 2

Wellness Behavior Frequencies

	Exercise	Water	Diet	Sleep	Vitality
1. Never	5%	3%	3%	8%	8%
2. Rarely	21%	13%	14%	25%	18%
3. Sometimes	31%	24%	33%	26%	35%
4. Often	22%	24%	33%	26%	35%
5. Very Often	10%	17%	16%	12%	10%
6. Always	8%	16%	7%	6%	5%
MEAN	**3.35**	**3.89**	**3.59**	**3.21**	**3.22**

TABLE 3

Depression and Committment to Christ

	Not committed	Not sure	Committed at one time	Fully committed
Depressed*	16%	47%	33%	19%

*p≤.01

TABLE 4

External Religious Pressure and Mental Health

	Stress	Anxiety	Depression
Share faith for approval of others	.12**	.13*	.16*
Pray to avoid God's disapproval	.12*	.20*	.16*
Attend church to avoid disapproval of others	.14*	.13*	.10**

*p≤.01, ***p≤.05

TABLE 5

Trends in Annual Substance Use

	2005	2012	2018
Alcohol	32%	30%	27%
Tobacco	12%	7%	6%
Marijuana	8%	16%	19%

The Need for Loving and Supporting Local Churches

Church Statistics and Research Findings

D. J. B. TRIM, Ph.D.

SOME OF THE DATA PRESENTED HERE were included in presentations to the 2013 Nurture and Retention Summit; to the Annual Councils of 2014, 2015, and 2017; and to division nurture and retention meetings in the Northern Asia-Pacific and the Trans-European Divisions (2014 and 2017). There will thus be familiarity with some points made in this chapter, but some statistics are new or updated, while in addition it does not hurt to be reminded of things that one has heard before. This is especially the case when the data are so sobering.

From 1965 through 2018, a 54-year period, the total number of church members has been 39,100,507. For the purposes of tracking losses we start in 1965, because up until 1964, our statistical reports recorded only the total membership and accessions. Starting in 1965, however, we have recorded the number who were disfellowshipped and gradually we started adding more clarity too. We started to break down accessions into baptisms, professions of faith, and, since 2018, re-baptisms of former members as a signal of the importance of reclamation; but we also gradually added reports of numbers of deaths, of missing (as well as those dropped from membership), and what are rather blandly called adjustments, which generally result when audits are done and the figures do not work out as they should. So, that means from 1965 through the end of 2018, we have 54 years of data. This is a very large and robust data set. The trends and the trajectories are clear. In those 54 years, a total of more than 39 million people have been Seventh-day Adventists. *(Figure 1)*

These are not people who were raised Adventist but not baptized. They are not people who thought about joining the church. These are people who were full members of the Seventh-day Adventist Church. Of those, just under 24 million stayed. As of the end of 2018, the number who left is more than fifteen million: to be precise, 15,132,505 *(Figure 2)*. And that is the best-case scenario, since in some parts of the world (including territories with very large book memberships), membership audits have not been completed, indeed are very far from complete. When they are completed, and the people who in their own mind left years ago are registered in our statistics, our losses will be still higher. So our own statistics are telling us that our net loss rate is, at minimum, 39%.

FIGURE 1

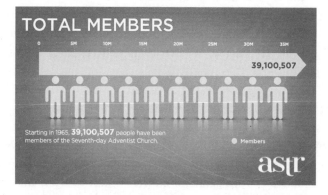

FIGURE 2

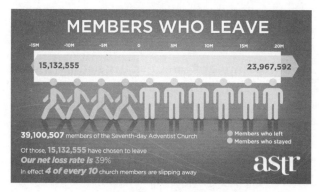

I am truly at a loss as to what to say about this. I've thought about it a lot. Indeed, I am now concerned that perhaps, by sharing this appalling statistic regularly—that 4 of every 10 church members leave, that 2 of every 5 leave—that maybe it has become too familiar. Maybe now church leaders take it for granted.

I say that, because there are still parts of the world that prefer not to carry out membership audits, which is really burying ones head in the sand about the reality of what is happening. There are parts of the world that still hold massive evangelistic campaigns without having put in place networks of support for the new members won by evangelism. And so I don't know what to say anymore. Back in 2013, when I recognized that we had this detailed data going back to 1965 and ran the numbers, I did not expect the losses to be this bad. But having checked my figures twice, I thought, "Well, this will surely be greeted with sackcloth and ashes. It will surely have an effect—it will result in changes." Having presented these statistics regularly in my yearly report to Annual Council, I know that there is a wave of shock that goes around the room—but I conclude now that it does not leave the room. Awareness of the terrible statistics of loss has not produced a widespread change—or at least not yet. Hence my concern that, as a result of my reporting, church leaders take the appalling loss rates for granted—that familiarity has bred complacency.

So, truly, I am at a loss as to what to say, what do, to arouse a sense of alarm and of urgent need for action. The only thing I can think of to say about this is that these are not numbers, they're people. And they're our family members. I would guess that 99% of church members have close family members who are not in the church. And we are not talking about the in-laws of in-laws, we are talking about brothers and sisters, sons and daughters, sometimes even parents. I don't know else to say, because this fact should motivate us to do something.

* * *

At any rate, those are the figures: the latest statistics we have, coming not from those who are negative about the church and want to share bad news; they are the results of the church's official statistical reporting systems. We should not—I hope we cannot—close our eyes to what our own careful and time-honored systems are telling us.

Furthermore, these statistics show us that global accessions and net losses have developed in step with each other *(Figure 3)*. There are certain key dates: 1997 was when net losses in a year first exceeded 200,000; 1999 was the first year that net accessions were more than 1 million. It dropped back but then has been solidly above one million *per annum* since 2005. But 2005 was also the first time that net losses reached 800,000 in a year. In 2010 there was a major drop in losses, probably because it was a GC Session year. There were more than 950,000 members deducted in 2014, the peak year for losses. There was a major drop in losses in 2016, probably reflecting GC Session (this time a delayed effect), before losses rise again.

FIGURE 3

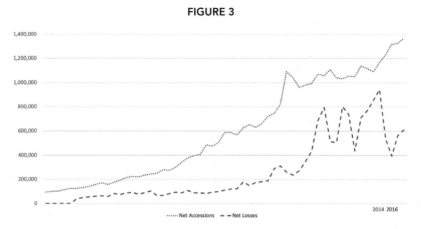

What I just want to suggest is that the two track each other: not exactly to be sure. That is partly because, for a long time, losses and audits were not a priority, though in the mid 2000s they began to be. Once losses began to be recorded in significant numbers, one can see *(Figure 3)* that when there is a spike in accessions, a couple of years later, there is a spike in the losses.

This becomes plainer when we look not at the last 54 years, but at the last 25 years. It is really in the last 25 years that the church has had explosive growth and also that it has given an increasing priority to audits. Figure 4 shows accessions and losses for the period 1994-2018 but calculated as five-year moving averages; this smooths out the peaks and troughs that are inevitable since annualized growth can be volatile for a number of reasons. Accessions and losses track each other more clearly once we use five-year moving averages, since losses come later than the accessions. The two diverge recently but that is because of the effect of reduced audits after the 2015 General Conference Session (with new officers coming in, who did not immediately prioritize audits); I have therefore also shown the actual losses, which in 2017 and 2018 have risen again.

If the lines in Figures 3 and 4 showed less of a relationship we might conclude simply that losses come mostly from long-term church members, whose departures cannot be predicted. But the fact that losses track accessions indicates that there is a missing link in the cycle of discipleship, for though we do not know when those who are registered in reports as losses actually left, the statistical data suggests that we are bringing people in *and then losing them*. Looking at this, some people might say,

"Well, since losses track growth, we should not put any focus on growth in evangelism." That would be an incorrect conclusion to draw from these data. But what they *are* telling us is that if we organize major evangelistic campaigns, we *also* need to have major discipleship programs that go hand in hand, step in step with them. That's what I think these data are telling us. We have to grow but we have to grow holistically. We have to close the circle of the discipling cycle.

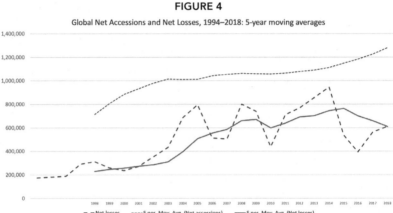

FIGURE 4

Global Net Accessions and Net Losses, 1994–2018: 5-year moving averages

I am often asked, "What might our membership be if we retain better?" It is a very hard question to answer, but in the Office of Archives, Statistics, and Research, we have undertaken a very rough projection. It assumes that we *retained 80% of members instead of 60%*. But then it also takes as its assumption that think all those additional people who stayed would *also* bring in new members, at the same rate as our accessions per member rate; and those new members would stay and they would bring in new members, and so on ad infinitum. Having used these assumptions for growth and retention, we then used standard mortality rates to calculate an estimated number of deaths—these are not, in fact, going to be that great, simply because, again, most of the growth has come in the last 25 years and so most new members would not have died. The end result is a rough projection that world church membership now would be 42.5 million, which is double the current reported membership of 21.4 million. This gives us a sense of what would happen if we had a significant improvement in our retention rate: it would have a significant and positive impact on our church growth.

* * *

DISCIPLING, NURTURING, AND RECLAIMING

Having considered statistics of members who left, the obvious question is: why did they leave? We have conducted two major global studies and the results have been very widely shared, I will just address a couple of points, to make the crucial point that the people who left, on the whole, didn't do it because they had abandoned belief in the seventh-day Sabbath. They didn't depart because they had abandoned belief in God. They didn't leave because they'd become predestinarian Calvinists or believed that God tormented people in hell for eternity. They slipped away because they weren't supported in times of trial or crisis; they left because they weren't loved.

In the studies of lapsed or ex-members, when asked "What was your view of Adventist Church at the time you left?" *(Figure 5)*, the most frequent response, almost one in four, was "I thought highly of it but I couldn't measure up." The second highest, of just over one in five, was "I thought highly of it but I had lost touch." For just over one in six, the church had simply become irrelevant, while one in seven felt the church was cold and inflexible. Only a fraction thought the church lacked integrity. Rather than a conscious rejection of an organization whose values they reject, members just slip away when they feel they can't fit in, aren't wanted, or aren't valued.

FIGURE 5

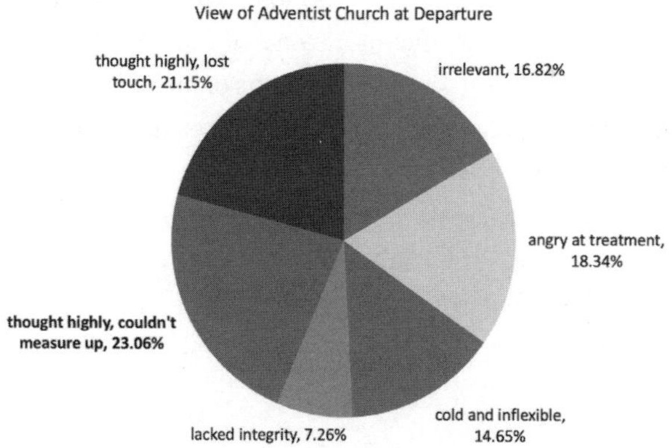

View of Adventist Church at Departure

thought highly, lost touch, 21.15%

irrelevant, 16.82%

angry at treatment, 18.34%

thought highly, couldn't measure up, 23.06%

cold and inflexible, 14.65%

lacked integrity, 7.26%

In the research, a question was asked about life events in the year leading up to the decision to stop attending church. This question is not "*Why* did you stop attending?", though that question is also asked (see below), but people may not always know themselves and so we wanted to probe factors that may have influenced people as they moved from church attendance to non-attendance. As Figure 6 shows, a very large percentage experienced some very stressful life event in the 12 months before they stopped attending church.

FIGURE 6

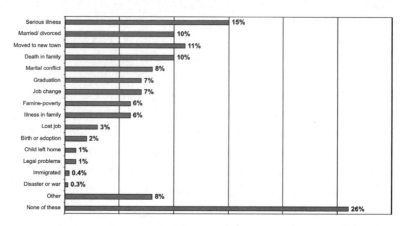

When those who took part in the research *were* asked why they decided to stop attending church, many different answers, were given, which is not surprising. However, the largest single answer, given by 28% of respondents, is that there was no big issue, "I just drifted away".[1] Table 1 shows only the responses that were in double digits of percentages (there were a number of other reasons cited by respondents that were only minor, including, for example, worship styles, arguments about which are not as significant a cause of member loss as some have supposed). Also significant were perceptions of lack of compassion for the hurting, and acknowledgment of "moral failures on my part."

TABLE 1. *Most Important Reasons for Deciding to Stop Attending Church*

28% No big issue; I just drifted away

25% Lack of compassion for the hurting

19% Moral failure on my part

18% I did not fit in

14% Too much focus on minor issues

13% Conflict in the congregation

12% Moral failures of members

11% Moral failures of leaders

11% Pressure from family or friends

10% Race, ethnic or tribal issues

DISCIPLING, NURTURING, AND RECLAIMING

What is perhaps most noteworthy is that almost all the different factors shown in Figure 6 (all but the last) can be understood as articulating, in different ways, essentially the same underlying cause. As a colleague observed in the GC research oversight committee, when we first reviewed this research, all the cited reasons reflect different manifestations of the same problem. Simply put, many local churches are not as loving and supportive as they ought to be when their members suffer stressful life events, or when, as they walk with Christ, they fall off the narrow path[2]—yet after all, "there is no one who does not sin" (1 Kings 8:46).

In the research, former members were also asked why they left. The previous question was about why they **stopped attending church services**. This question asks people who are no longer members why they came to **depart the denomination**. They were asked to name primary, secondary, and minor factors. Figure 7 shows the weighted results. Perceived hypocrisy in other church members ranks the highest; but because this reflects people not living up to the standards they avow, it is consistent with the view that church members leave because they do not receive the support they feel they need in time of crisis. So too, even more so, is the factor ranked third, a lack of friends in the local church. But especially striking is the word that occurs in these results, again and again: conflict. Five of the top ten weighted factors, and seven of the top thirteen, are different forms of conflict. This underscores the recommendation of the 2013 Nurture and Retention Summit that training in conflict resolution and reconciliation be provided widely and at all levels of church structure. Unfortunately that has been implemented very sporadically.

FIGURE 7

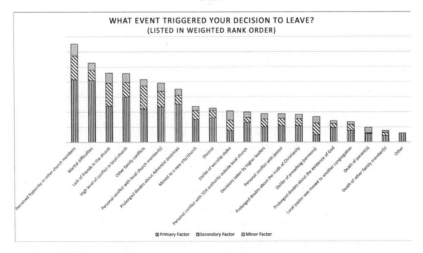

The picture that emerges from former Adventists is clear. Church members go through stressful life events, they experience conflict. As a result, they stop attending church—often intending that to be a temporary measure until personal or family illness passes, or conflict diminishes. But what happens when they stopped attending? The distressing results are tabulated below.

TABLE 2. *"What happened when you stopped attending church?"*

40% No one contacted me
19% A church member came to visit me
17% A local elder came to visit me
15% A local church member contacted me by phone
10% An Adventist relative made contact
9% The pastor came to visit me
6% The pastor contacted me by phone or Email
3% An Adventist, not a local member contacted me
2% I received a letter in the mail

For four of ten respondents (by a curious chance the same percentage who leave), no one contacted them. Only 6% contacted by the pastor. Now, this is data from around the world, not primarily from North America. My local church has its own pastor for discipleship and six pastors, as many large churches in the United States have. In contrast, in some parts of the world, there are six churches to a pastor, or more. Nevertheless, 6% seems very low—too low. Pastors do not have to do all the work, of course; indeed, they should be training elders and church members to help nurture other church members. As Table 2 also reveals, however, that is hardly happening either. Not quite one in five former Adventists was visited by another church member, or by an elder.

This finding should not surprise us. For pastors to know to train elders and use small groups for discipleship they would need to have been trained themselves. They also need to know nurture and retention are a priority. Yet in our 2012–2013 global study of pastors, in which pastors all around the world were surveyed, 53% said they never received training in nurturing and retaining in their bachelor's degree. Of those who've gone to a postgraduate course, again, 53% said there was no training in those areas in their graduate study. We can't be surprised if members aren't being trained because the pastors themselves don't know what they should be doing—and when nurture, retention, and discipleship are not being dealt with in their training, they will conclude that it is not a priority. And we have other evidence too that, indeed, they do not see it as a priority.

In last year's worldwide church members survey (a survey of more than 60,000 church members worldwide, in every division),[3] the question was posed: "Is training on nurturing and discipling of church members offered through my local church?" Very pleasingly, 64% responded, "Yes, it is." But that means that in 36% of churches, more than one third, training is not being offered. And really, we would want that figure who say "yes, it is" to be much higher, if the loss rate is to be lowered from 39%. Another question in last year's church member survey as posed as a thesis statement: "In my local church, I feel loved and cared about" (Figure 8). In response, almost half answered that this was very true, with another 13% choosing between somewhat true and very true; but 29% say it is only somewhat true; only 9% answered no, but the fact that only 62% agreed with this strongly suggests 38% feel it is problematic. We praise God that 62% feel that their local church quite considerably loves and cares about them, but, again, we would like it to be much higher. If more people feel more loved and cared about, if there are fewer incidents of hurt, then fewer members would leave.

FIGURE 8

In my local church, I feel loved and cared about...

■ Not true at all   ■ Not true at all-somew...   ■ Somewhat true   ■ Somewhat true-very true   ■ very true

* * *

Might they come back?

Our study of lapsed members and former members suggests that most have not found new religious homes (Figure 9). Instead, 40% say they're nominally Adventists but never attend church. Just under one in ten state they are active in another Christian church (with another 2.3% being inactive in another Christian denomination). Less than 1% have joined a religion other than Christianity. The remaining 23% report no definite religious affiliation, adrift on a sea of faith.

Thus, most former Seventh-day Adventists have not invested in another faith community. And we can guess why that is so when we remember how unimportant doctrinal disagreement was as a factor precipitating departure.

How aware are they of developments in Adventism? Nearly half of those who took part in our studies report very little or no knowledge of what is happening in the Seventh-day Adventist Church. But just over half claim to be knowledgeable and 18% say they have detailed knowledge. This means they are still interested. There is an adage that the opposite of love isn't hate, it's apathy. These people still feel the pull of the faith community they once were part of. Indeed, more than three quarters of former Adventists report themselves as being open to reconnecting, *if* the approach were made in the right way.

FIGURE 9

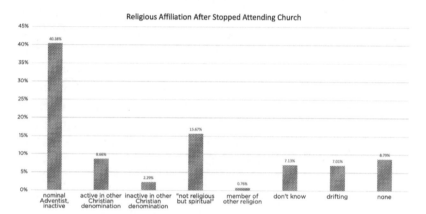

Given the statistics with which we started and these research results, we can say with confidence that there are millions of people who have left the Adventist Church. These are people who largely share our doctrines and our presumptions. We need to reach out to them with the love of the heavenly Father—the Father of the prodigal son in Luke 15, who was welcomed back with warmth and love, and without question or quibbling.

* * *

What has been shared so far are from significant, even huge, data sets. But to close, I will share, as I did during my presentation at the Nurture and Retention Summit, some of the reaction to the summit on social media. There were many tweets, including by somebody who must have taken to Twitter, especially for the purpose of commenting on the summit, because they had not tweeted before it began and at that point they had no followers. The tweets vigorously complained that, at the

DISCIPLING, NURTURING, AND RECLAIMING

summit, we were simply indulging church leaders by all getting together in a comfortable location, and that all we were doing was talking.

One such tweet:

More effort went into NR summit than in reclaiming members. Did you know one phone call, email, or postcard would have brought me back? If received when I stopped going. It has been years and I have not heard a word yet tons of effort for a platform to blow hot air.

Another:

How many of the church resources go into the Nurture And Retention Summit when the simple answer is to make a personal connection? Is the summit teaching people how to use a phone? Over five years and no one from the church has tried to make a connection after we stopped going.

And so on and so on. Yet what was clear was that whomever was tweeting was watching the live stream of the summit. They were a church member who had been hurt and for whom perhaps nobody cared, for certainly nobody had sought them, in sharp contrast to the good shepherd, who left the 99 sheep he had in order fo find the one that had strayed.

In the summit we did not train people to pick up the phone; most of those attending were from divisions and we wanted to inspire them to start declaring nurture a top priority in their fields, and to inspire their union and conference or mission counterparts to do the same. It was essential to share with church leaders because if they don't declare wholistic disciple-ship to be a top priority we will continue to hemorrhage members.

But we certainly wanted church members who watched the lives-tream, and we want everyone who is reading this book, to pick up a phone. Every pastor needs to make discipleship a priority in their local church(es). If they lack the skills themselves they need to be trained. Then they need to train their elders and church members that, if other members aren't at church, show concern: call them up. And if pastors can't or won't prioritize this, church members can take the initiative themselves. There is one final research finding that is striking: we know from other research that the 60% of members who *were* visited after they stopped attending church are more likely to express openness to reconnecting. The lapsed or former member who is visited might not come back to church the next Sabbath—but they are more likely to return at some point in the future.

* * *

Many important strategies were shared at the 2019 Nurture and Retention Summit and are elaborated in this book. They were and are important and valuable. But the bottom line is that we have to care about our brothers and sisters in Christ and we have to let them know that we care.

Moreover, the millions of lapsed and former Seventh-day Adventists worldwide, who already believe much of what we believe, who in many cases are all around us, are waiting for us to reach out. They are waiting for us to love them with the love of the shepherd and the father of Luke 15.

DAVID TRIM, Ph.D., F.R.Hist.S.

Dr. D. J. B. Trim is Director of the Office of Archives, Statistics, and Research at the General Conference of Seventh-day Adventists, a position to which he was elected by Annual Council in 2010. Born in Bombay, India, to missionary parents, he grew up in his father's homeland of Australia, before moving to his mother's homeland of Great Britain. He is a graduate of Newbold College (BA cum laude) and later served on the faculty there for ten years (1997-2007), teaching BA courses in history, literature and religion, and MA courses in mission and hermeneutics. He then held the Walter C. Utt Chair of History at Pacific Union College; since 2014, he has been an adjunct professor of church history and mission at the Seventh-day Adventist Theological Seminary, at Andrews University. His Ph.D. is from the University of London (2003). His publications include ten books along with many book chapters and articles, in both scholarly and church publications, while he presents "This Week in Adventist History" on the Hope Channel. Dr. Trim was the first Seventh-day Adventist to be elected a Fellow of the Royal Historical Society and has held visiting fellowships at the University of Reading, in Britain, and the University of California at Berkeley, in the United States. He is married to Wendy, a native of California; they have an adult daughter, Genevieve, who lives in Berlin, in Germany.

ENDNOTES

1   Figure 6, "Most important reasons for deciding to stop attending Church", is based on a qualitative study: the reasons given were not answers that those surveyed were asked to choose, but the researchers' summaries of different answers, based on their analysis of the interviews.

2   Cf. Ellen G. White, *Acts of the Apostles*, p. 565.

3   See http://documents.adventistarchives.org/Resources/Global%20Church%20Membership%20Survey%20Meta-Analysis%20Report/GCMSMetaAnalysis%20Report_2019-08-19.pdf

Barnabas: Epitomizing Discipling and Nurturing

ANTHONY R. KENT

BARNABAS IS LUKE'S LEVITE HERO of Acts! While one Levite, in the good Samaritan parable, wouldn't cross a road to help a victim of a violent robbery, Barnabas crisscrossed cities and countries discipling and nurturing individuals, communities, and churches. Barnabas' courage, character, and commitment enabled him to be the ultimate human change agent of the book of Acts. The inspiring story of Barnabas is a not-so-subtle invitation to disciples of every era to emulate the amazing ministry of the "Son of Encouragement."

The book of Acts is the Hollywood of the New Testament. But it's a wholesome Hollywood! After a few words of introduction, it's a case of "Lights, camera, action!"

It has stars. It's action-packed from start to finish. Many of its scenes, although written 2,000 years ago, could easily be major Hollywood blockbusters of the twenty-first century.

When Luke graphically describes the ascension of Jesus from the Mount of Olives (Acts 1:6-12), the outpouring of the Holy Spirit in the upper room (Acts 2), or the shipwreck of Paul and his companions in the Mediterranean (Acts 27:13–28:2), it's as though there are film clips embedded into the text. But these events are more compelling than modern movie scenes! Paul's epic shipwreck takes two weeks, and Paul the hero oversees the safety of all passengers and crew, and although he's bitten by a viper he barely flinches, and it's the snake, not the hero, who dies!

The key words that we remember from Acts are from the scripts of action sequences:

- "Men of Galilee, why do you stand gazing up into heaven? This same Jesus, who was taken up from you into heaven, will so come in like manner as you saw Him go into heaven" (Acts 1:11, NKJV).

- "Silver and gold I do not have, but what I do have I give you: In the name of Jesus Christ of Nazareth, rise up and walk" (Acts 3:6, NKJV).
- "Nor is there salvation in any other, for there is no other name under heaven given among men by which we must be saved" (Acts 4:12, NKJV).
- "Lord, lay not this sin to their charge" (Acts 7:60, KJV)

Of all the stars that Luke introduces to us in Acts, there is none more significant than the star of discipling! And he has a nickname to prove it! And he's better than any Hollywood star! He's someone we can trust, emulate, and use as a positive role model. Best of all, he's not the creation of some scriptwriter's imagination—he's real! His principles, morality, and motives are always good, wholesome, encouraging, and inspirational! He's not just *acting*, verbalizing memorized words from a script—he's living the Christian life, the authentic real life, of a disciple maker.

We are introduced to this character for the first time in Acts 4. It's helpful to read the wider context of his introduction—how Luke brings him onto his stage. For Luke, introductions are important.[1] Besides, Luke shares important information about nurturing and discipling people in this introduction to a great discipler:

"Now the full number of those who believed were of one heart and soul, and no one said that any of the things that belonged to him was his own, but they had everything in common. And with great power the apostles were giving their testimony to the resurrection of the Lord Jesus, and great grace was upon them all. There was not a needy person among them, for as many as were owners of lands or houses sold them and brought the proceeds of what was sold and laid it at the apostles' feet, and it was distributed to each as any had need. Thus Joseph, who was also called by the apostles Barnabas (which means son of encouragement), a Levite, a native of Cyprus, sold a field that belonged to him and brought the money and laid it at the apostles' feet" (Acts 4:32-37, ESV).

It's a beautiful picture! And in this inspiring picture of the apostles and believers—there is only person, one individual, whose identity surfaces to the top for specific mention. Most likely he represents best the characteristics of the group.

This is the first glimpse we have of Joseph, who was given the nickname of Barnabas.

Nicknames often tell the story of a person very succinctly. The most obvious feature of a person can be captured in a simple nickname—like

Sons of Thunder! Positive nicknames are generally a good sign that the individual is well appreciated and regarded by their peers. (Among teenagers, it's not unusual that the most popular receive nicknames.) And as readers of Acts will discover, there is every reason to regard and appreciate Barnabas highly, and he was aptly called Son of Encouragement. Barnabas is referred to 23 times in Acts, and he emerges as one of Luke's heroes, one of the great heroes of the early followers of Jesus.[2]

Why? Because he was a discipler and a nurturer!

Barnabas was a Levite. Some tend to look down on Levites, but there is no reason to have a negative opinion of Barnabas. Who were the Levites?

According to Darrell L. Bock, "Levites were often wealthy and very well educated, but not all were priests. . . . Levites served in the temple, keeping watch over the gates, policing the area, instructing, and copying the Torah."[3] The roles and functions entrusted to Levites, protecting the assets of the Temple, teaching the Torah, and copying it—well before the days of printing presses—indicate that Levites were generally respected and trusted in the community.

We are not told where Barnabas' land was located. It could have been in Judea or on his home island of Cyprus. It appears that the injunction against Levites owning land was widely relaxed by the first century. Even in the time of Jeremiah, we have the example of Jeremiah being a priest and purchasing a property (Jeremiah 32:7-12).

So Barnabas sold his land, without any fuss or fanfare, and laid **all** the proceeds at the feet of the apostles. This honest, generous, and unassuming approach of Barnabas stands in stark contrast to what follows immediately in Acts—the story of the deceitful **Ananias and Sapphira**. It is a little disappointing that many of us may know the story of the unfaithful Ananias and Sapphira better than the remarkably faithful Barnabas.

But there is another important contrast in Luke's account. Readers of Acts are soon to read of garments being placed at the feet of a young man named Saul (Acts 7:58). These items of clothing are not intended for the poor or needy, like the proceeds of Barnabas' assets. Instead, these are the robes of those stoning Stephen, the dedicated deacon and disciple. The disparity in the introduction of Saul (who later became known as Paul) and Barnabas is truly jolting! Luke appears to be highlighting the extreme background differences of these two people. Saul was doing all he could to control, thwart, and destroy the disciples of Jesus. Barnabas was completely the opposite, doing all he could to resource, grow, and develop Jesus' disciples. These two earnest, zealous, Jewish, religious men, having completely opposite opinions about Jesus, are soon to meet each other. Careful readers of Acts anticipate this meeting and are intrigued by the clash. They wonder, Who will win out—Saul or Barnabas?

So Barnabas gave all the money from the sale of the land to the leaders of Jesus' followers—no strings attached! Barnabas had no expectations of controlling the expenditure of the money nor controlling the leadership. And it wasn't a case of paying money to the clergy leaders so that Barnabas could have the excuse to do no ministry. These points are very apparent in Acts 11:22. It's the church in Jerusalem that *sends* Barnabas to Antioch—the church body maintained control, and Barnabas was a willing servant, following the directives of the Holy Spirit and the body of Christ.

What else is revealed about Barnabas?

Acts 11:22-24 describes him as "a good man, full of the Holy Spirit and of faith" (verse 24, NKJV), as well as being a very fruitful evangelist. Colossians 4:10 informs us that Barnabas was a cousin of John Mark—this is the Mark who wrote the Gospel of Mark, the youthful disciple of Jesus. The *Seventh-day Adventist Bible Dictionary* introduces to us a tradition that identifies Barnabas as one of the 70 (or 72 in some translations) sent out by Jesus, as recorded in Luke 10:1.[4]

In Acts 9 Luke records the much-anticipated first meeting of Saul and Barnabas. They meet in Jerusalem. Although they once had vastly different opinions about Jesus and His followers, Saul had encountered the resurrected and ascended Jesus on his journey of persecution to Damascus. Instead of implementing persecution in Damascus, Saul as a recipient of the gift of the Holy Spirit (verse 17) and newly baptized (verse 18) became a proclaimer of Jesus (verse 20). The persecutor suddenly became the persecuted. In the dead of night Luke describes Saul dramatically fleeing from Damascus (verse 25). Saul makes his way to Jerusalem and encounters the "Son of Encouragement." This first meeting of Saul and Barnabas provides us with a great insight into Barnabas' methods of operation as a disciple of Jesus and essentially as a disciple maker:

"And when he [Saul] had come to Jerusalem, he attempted to join the disciples. And they were all afraid of him, for they did not believe that he was a disciple. But Barnabas took him and brought him to the apostles and declared to them how on the road he had seen the Lord, who spoke to him, and how at Damascus he had preached boldly in the name of Jesus. So he went in and out among them at Jerusalem, preaching boldly in the name of the Lord. And he spoke and disputed against the Hellenists. But they were seeking to kill him. And when the brothers learned this, they brought him down to Caesarea and sent him off to Tarsus" (verses 26-30, ESV).

All the disciples, except Barnabas, were afraid of Saul! Although Jesus' followers in Jerusalem had all those beautiful attributes of dedication (Acts 2:42-47; 4:32-35)—initially **they shunned Saul!**

Risking potential damage to his reputation, Barnabas was fearless! His treatment of Saul was exemplary! For good reason the text of Acts singles him out and highlights his virtues as a discipler and nurturer! Acts 9:27 describes how Barnabas took Saul and brought him to the apostles. This carries the idea that Barnabas "took him under his wing."[5] Barnabas' ministry to Saul, instead of ruining his reputation, enhanced his reputation as a "son of encouragement"! Not that his support of Saul was motivated by the desire to enhance his reputation.

It appears that Barnabas was not afraid to risk or lose his life in his ministry of discipling potential followers of Jesus. Clearly this speaks to an assurance that Barnabas had—a profound awareness that his life and destiny were in the hands of his Savior, Jesus, and that nothing would fall upon him that was outside of heaven's plan for him.

If we reflect on Galatians 1:18, Saul visited Jerusalem on this occasion for 15 days, so it is reasonable to assume that Barnabas didn't just support him for one initial meeting (which may have lasted for minutes or hours), but most likely the best part of two weeks! In this context, particularly in the Jerusalem of this era, two weeks could be a long time. For example, Jesus, in less than a week, was welcomed into the city triumphantly and yet within that same week was crucified by an angry mob. Jerusalem was a dangerous and volatile city, and Barnabas was prepared to associate closely with Saul, who could well have been regarded as a traitor by one group or a wolf in sheep's clothing by the opposing group. Either way, Barnabas was willing to support a marginalized individual and risk being personally isolated.

Barnabas also verified Saul's story of transformation.[6] Sometimes it can be very difficult to tell our story—it can be difficult to "blow our own trumpet" or "ring our own bell," because it can appear that we are bragging. But Barnabas helped Saul confirm his astonishing—no, let's call it what it was: miraculous—Damascus road experience.

It can be even more difficult to tell our story, particularly if it is an amazing miraculous story, to a sceptical audience. And the apostles were sceptical!

So Barnabas showed Saul/Paul how to share his extraordinary testimony to this rather untrusting audience. And Paul was to learn from

DISCIPLING, NURTURING, AND RECLAIMING

this mentoring, because years later, as recorded in Acts 22, Paul shares his testimony confidently before persecutors in Jerusalem; and as recorded in Acts 26, once again Paul boldly proclaims his conversion testimony before the unbelieving Agrippa.

Clearly Barnabas was an important mentor and discipler for Saul. And Saul, at the time of this visit to Jerusalem in Acts 9, was viewed very suspiciously by most of the followers of Jesus. During this time in Jerusalem, Saul continued to be somewhat of a nuisance; he was problematic, and his life was in danger. This passage concludes with Saul, to avoid being murdered in Jerusalem, being sent back home to Tarsus. Saul being shipped back to Tarsus is reminiscent of the colloquial cliché, "Go back to wherever you came from!"

In Tarsus, Saul remained in obscurity. We are not told what he did during that time— in Luke's account he does nothing to distinguish himself; he remains inconspicuous, unseen, and unheard.

The next occasion that we read of Barnabas is Acts 11:22. Barnabas is sent by the church in Jerusalem to the fledgling work being done in Antioch. Barnabas does his ministry well in Antioch and is warmly received and appreciated by the community.

In Luke's record of Barnabas' ministry in Antioch, it is very easy to miss the importance of the next brief reference to Barnabas: "So Barnabas went to Tarsus to look for Saul" (Acts 11:25, ESV).

We are not told how Barnabas traveled from Antioch to Tarsus. If he went by land, it was 148 miles (238 kilometers)! If he traveled approximately 20 miles (30 kilometers) per day, which was the typical travel length of a day's journey, it would have taken Barnabas eight traveling days! Walking 20 miles (or 30 kilometers) was not regarded as a suitable Sabbath activity on a day of rest, so the likely time length of the journey was longer than eight days. By any measure of the era, traveling from Antioch to Tarsus was a substantial journey!

It is also probable that Barnabas traveled at his own expense. Paul was to later write in 1 Corinthians 9:3-7 that he and Barnabas did not receive wages when they were ministering—even their expenses don't appear to be covered! Barnabas was a remarkable man, donating all the proceeds of the sale of his property and then ministering as a self-funded volunteer. So, not only did Barnabas undertake this considerable journey to look for Saul, it is likely he provided his own travel expenses.

Luke adds these details: "And when he had found him, he brought him to Antioch. For a whole year they met with the church and taught a great many people. And in Antioch the disciples were first called Christians" (Acts 11:26, ESV).

The words "and when he had found him" reminds us of Luke's earlier wording in his record of Jesus' parable of the lost sheep. In fact, the phrasing of the Greek in Acts 11:26 is identical to Luke 15:5.[7] The text may also imply that Barnabas needed to do some careful, thorough searching to find Saul. And then Barnabas brought Saul back to Antioch. Barnabas' return trip was most likely more than 300 miles (nearly 500 kilometers)! Why did Barnabas make this extensive, arduous journey? For one reason: to reach out to Saul so he could disciple and nurture him!

Barnabas returned to Antioch with Saul, and there he taught, trained, nurtured, discipled, and ministered with Saul for a year.

It would also appear that Luke wants to ensure that his readers don't miss the significance of this ministry at Antioch. He writes: "The disciples were called Christians first in Antioch" (Acts 11:26). This ministry of Barnabas—teaching, training, nurturing, and discipling—appears to trigger that all-important, timeless, identifying badge: *Christian!* Clearly Barnabas' Christlike ministry is an all-important association with the word "Christian."

God blessed both of these mighty workers, Barnabas and Saul/Paul, in their ministries. The Christians at Antioch received this very important instruction from the Holy Spirit: "Set apart for me Barnabas and Saul for the work to which I have called them" (Acts 13:2, ESV).

Barnabas and Paul had very effective ministries. As well as being nurturers and disciplers, Barnabas and Paul were evangelists—sharing the gospel and the knowledge of salvation with those who were unfamiliar with Jesus. The only recorded speech we have of Barnabas is an evangelistic message he copreached with Paul at Lystra (Acts 14:15-17)—to a pagan audience. This is important because it illustrates that Barnabas was not just focused inwardly, toward those within the church. All people were of interest and significance to Barnabas; he was a "son of encouragement" to all.

How important was the nurturing, discipling, and training offered by Barnabas? The following comments offered by Ellen G. White illustrate the importance of this type of ministry: "Experienced workers today do a noble work when, instead of trying to carry all the burdens themselves, they train younger workers and place burdens on their shoulders."[8]

And so Saul grew, under the blessing of God, empowered by the Holy Spirit, and under the training, nurturing, and discipling of Barnabas. Ellen White also writes of the Paul tutored, nurtured and discipled by

Barnabas: "Paul's heart burned with a love for sinners, and he put all his energies into the work of soul winning. There never lived a more self-denying, persevering worker."[9]

We know well the extraordinary ministry of Saul/Paul: apostle, missionary, evangelist, pastor, teacher, trainer, biblical author, humanitarian aid worker—the list goes on! Paul was certainly an amazing servant of God. It's perfectly reasonable to wonder: What would have happened to Paul had not Barnabas made that long journey to Tarsus to find him, disciple him, and nurture him?

Luke also describes Barnabas as a key person in the discipling, nurture, and reclamation of another very important New Testament character, John Mark (Acts 15:36-39). John Mark, better known as Mark, had deserted Paul and Barnabas during an earlier missionary journey (Acts 13:13). Mark could so easily have been lost to the Christian cause. Mark could have been seen as lacking moral fiber, perhaps a backslider. But Barnabas saw the potential of Mark, this youthful disciple of Jesus, and was eager to offer him some encouragement, further training, and another opportunity.

Ellen G. White provides this valuable insight: "This desertion caused Paul to judge Mark unfavorably, and even severely, for a time. Barnabas, on the other hand, was inclined to excuse him because of his inexperience. He felt anxious that Mark should not abandon the ministry, for he saw in him qualifications that would fit him to be a useful worker for Christ. In after years his solicitude in Mark's behalf was richly rewarded, for the young man gave himself unreservedly to the Lord and to the work of proclaiming the gospel message in difficult fields. Under the blessing of God, and the wise training of Barnabas, he developed into a valuable worker."[10]

Paul was afterward reconciled to Mark and received him as a fellow laborer. He also recommended him to the Colossians as one who was a fellow worker "unto the kingdom of God," and "a comfort unto me" (Colossians 4:11).

Again, not long before his own death, Paul spoke of Mark as "profitable" to him "for the ministry" (2 Timothy 4:11). History tells us that Mark, inspired by the Holy Spirit, was to author one of the most significant pieces of Christian literature: "The Gospel According to Mark"— the "Mark" of the New Testament. This was a new genre of literature. It was an innovative way of telling the story of Jesus and also instructing and nurturing people into being disciples of Jesus. The majority of biblical scholars agree that Mark's Gospel account was source material for the Gospels that were later written by Matthew and Luke.[11] Imagine if Barnabas had not taken Mark "under his wing" and Mark had not written his Gospel? Imagine a Bible without the Gospel of Mark, and without Mark's Gospel, I wonder what the Gospels of Matthew and Luke would have been like.

There is an obvious and natural question we need to ask: Where would the Christian faith be without the discipleship, nurture, and reclamation ministry of Barnabas?

The Barnabas who nurtured, discipled, trained, and mentored Mark. The Barnabas who nurtured, trained, discipled, and mentored Saul/Paul to be an apostle, missionary, evangelist, pastor, teacher, trainer, biblical author, and humanitarian aid worker!

When we consider the ministry of Barnabas, we can't help pondering what the Christian Bible would look like if Barnabas had not been the "son of encouragement" to Paul and Mark, who ultimately were both very significant authors of the New Testament.

Having reflected on the life, ministry, and priorities of Barnabas in the early church, we should consider our own personal ministries and the church of today. Some very appropriate questions to ask ourselves are:

How much stronger and healthier would the church be today if we retained the evangelistic emphasis but also were more effective with our discipling, nurture, and retention?

How can we emulate Barnabas' ministry in the church today?
What could happen in the church today with an effective ministry of discipleship, nurture, and reclamation?

ANTHONY KENT

Anthony Kent has specialized in discipleship-based evangelism in Western secular settings, as well as being an effective church planter in irreligious cities. He has ministered and pastored in varying contexts: inner-city, suburban, regional, and rural isolated churches. Prior to being elected to the General Conference Ministerial Association in 2005, Anthony was the ministerial secretary for the South Pacific Division. His ministry is always enhanced by his devoted wife, Debora, and their two young adult daughters, who continue to keep him very humble.

ENDNOTES

1 For example: Luke's introductions to his Gospel (Luke 1:1-4) and to the book of Acts (Acts 1:1, 2) are very important. Similarly important are Luke's introductions of John the Baptist (Luke 1:5-25, 39-45, 57-80), Jesus (Luke 1:26-56; 2:1–4:15), and Saul/Paul (Acts 7:58; 8:1-3; 9:1-25).

2 Darrell L. Bock, *Acts* (Grand Rapids: Baker, 2007), p. 216.

3 *Ibid.*

4 "Barnabas," *Seventh-day Adventist Bible Dictionary* (Washington, D.C.: Review and Herald Pub. Assn., 1960, 1979), p. 121.

5 Bock, p. 369.

6 Craig S. Keener, *Acts: An Exegetical Commentary 3:1–14:28* (Grand Rapids: Baker, 2013), vol. 2, p. 1689.

7 Both Luke 15:5 and Acts 11:26 have καὶ εὑρών.

8 Ellen G. White, *The Acts of the Apostles* (Mountain View, Calif.: Pacific Press Pub. Assn., 1911), p. 368.

9 *Ibid.,* p. 367.

10 *Ibid.,* p. 170.

11 Robert H. Stein, *Mark* (Grand Rapids: Baker, 2008), p. 16.

Connecting With the Disconnected

BRIAN LITZENBERGER

WHY ARE TWENTY-FIRST CENTURY young people leaving the church? Another just-as-important question is why the unchurched are seemingly unreachable. The traditional church mind-set of expecting young people and unchurched alike to believe as we believe, act as we act, and to become like us is failing miserably. This presentation will discuss the best way to connect with the disconnected and show how important it is to no longer operate under the "this is how we have always done it" ideology.

As I was preparing to present, my wife was challenging me saying, "You need to provide a solution." To which I replied, "There is no blanket, 'silver bullet' solution that will quickly and easily resolve this particular challenge. The solution is connecting with Christ personally and intimately. In other words, the problem today is not programmatic—it is the absence of a personal and intimate relationship with God and others, in that specific order."

Somehow we have come to confuse knowledge about someone as a relationship. Interestingly enough, this seems to be accepted only in religious circles; when it comes to our relationships on earth, it is a completely different story. I have yet to find an individual that would be willing to let someone else date their beau for them, yet this is what we have come to do with God every week.

The question of why and where our young people are going has become a main topic of discussion. Recently as I was working with a Sabbath School class, I sat down with them and asked them three questions:

Question 1: How do you feel when you come to church?
Answer: "We feel like people here have written us off." Upon further explanation, it was discovered that one of the Sabbath School leaders had

told the young women attending the Sabbath School that they should plan on being pregnant shortly after they graduate from high school. One of which was my daughter, who asked me, "Dad, is that really what they think of us in church?" To which I replied, "Not in this house!"

Another replied that the church was hypocritical: "We are constantly being told what we need to do and how we are supposed to love and respect others, but we are not treated with love and respect."

Question 2: How do you feel about God and religion?
Answer: "It doesn't really make sense to me." When I asked them if they shared their doubts and struggles, they quickly replied, "I don't feel as though I can do that without being judged." Let me stress that these answers are coming from young people.

"I don't know; I am always being told what I should believe about God, and how important it is to have a relationship with God, but I don't see other people able to talk about how their relationship with God has helped them."

"I don't know how to relate to the Bible."

Question 3: If you were in charge of your Sabbath School, what would you do differently?
Answer: "Food!" Yes, we are definitely dealing with teens! The next answer may surprise you. "We want to be involved in more than just collecting offering. We want to be of service; we want to get into the community and do something. We want to make a difference."

These are the young people that are leaving the church. The bottom line: their needs aren't being met. Teenagers have a desire to question. If they do not feel safe enough in church to ask those questions, or if they ask and we can't answer those questions, where do they go? Google.

The knee-jerk response has typically been to seek out the newest and latest program that will resolve the problem. For example, where I come from there is a new program the conference is promoting and conducting training. It's called "A New Kind of Leader." In truth, it is a great concept and program, but it is nothing more than new wine in an old wineskin. Right on the cover of the book it states, "What you believe can make a difference in somebody else." With young people, it is not about what you believe—it is what they believe and whether or not they have ownership of what they believe. It seems that lay leaders somehow have this idea that we need to give them everything and just tell them what they need to know, molding them into what we believe is the best for them, disregarding whatever does not fit into our vision. Great program, but it is completely missing the mark. It is not a program that listens, understands, empathizes and comforts. It is not meeting the needs of these young people.

Six reasons young people are leaving the church:

1. isolationism
2. shallowness
3. anti-science
4. sex
5. exclusivity
6. doubters

Of these six, the most common ones that I have personally dealt with in my ministry work are:

1. **Shallowness:** Many young people think church is boring, finding it irrelevant. Biblical concepts are unclear, and God is absent from their church experience.
2. **Exclusivity:** Church is exclusive, it does not agree to disagree, and I am forced to choose between my faith and my friends. One person my wife and I have worked with stated, "I feel like church is a private club. If I do not believe exactly as they do in every way, I will never be accepted."
3. **Doubters:** Young people think church is not a safe place to express doubts. This was just discussed. Many young people both in and out of the church have serious doubts they want to discuss, but they have no one they feel they can trust to talk to.

I would like to point out that these are answers that have come from both young people inside the church as well as the secular community. In fact, many in the secular community have come from a Christian or church background, whether it be Saturday or Sunday. They were raised in a home that attended a weekly service. However, when their stories are told, one finds out they were raised in a home in which their concept of God came from a father who was abusive, beating on them or their mother, maybe even sexually abusing them. Then, come Saturday or Sunday morning, the whole family gets dressed up, drives to church, and presents themselves as the perfect Christian family. While there they are told of a

God who is loving, peaceful, compassionate, and kind. The emerging question should be obvious. "If God is loving and caring, why is He allowing this to happen to me?" The end result is an unspeakable animosity, distrust and even hatred toward Christianity and the church in general.

There is another statistic produced by the Barna Group conducted in 2012. Six out of every 10 young people will leave the church permanently, starting at the age of 15. Now, you might say to yourself, "That is in those other churches; we as Adventists don't have that problem. We have a thriving children's ministry and teenage program; our teenage classes are packed every week." In many cases their parents are forcing them to come, and the young people feel as though it is just not worth the argument. But, hey, they are in church, right? Great, they are here. The problem is that they have mentally checked out.

The truth is that they are living my own story. I mentally checked out of church at the age of 15. I went through the motions of being a good Adventist child. I was able to fake it, and as a teen who was successful at faking my faith, I started to wonder how many others were doing the same thing. I guarantee you this is still the case. I have stood up in front of young people after sharing my story and asked, "How many of you feel differently?" Not one young person raised their hand. The fact that these phenomena are occurring makes it more dangerous than if they were to physically be gone. We are lulled into a sense of false security, thinking that everything is OK, and then we are blindsided when our young people disappear.

John 4:35 states, "Look around you and see how the fields are ripe for harvesting" (NRSV). Jesus had to teach this concept to His disciples. Today we have come together because we recognize this fact both in the youth that is leaving our church and our inability to reach out and connect with the unchurched. So it's not just our young people we can't connect with— it's the people outside the church and in the community we are having trouble reaching. "The harvest is plentiful, but the laborers are few" (Luke 10:2, NRSV). This statement is just as true and applicable today as it was when Christ first came. The following three reasons show these statements to be applicable:

1. **In society today, people need and seek out a satisfying worldview and spiritual fulfillment.**

    If you have a hard time understanding this one, go spend some time with people in a secular community. My secular ministry was with bikers, and let me tell you, they are searching . . . and so is everyone else. The social media idea and all the knowledge highway that we have that did not exist when I was growing up has disconnected us from human relationships. People are out there searching for understanding and connection.

This world is getting scary, and people are wondering what in the world is going to happen. Doomsday theories, conspiracy theories, the list goes on and on. The same thing was happening when Jesus arrived on this earth. The Israelites under Roman rule did not feel much different than many today. The people were looking then (as they are today) at what was being offered, and found it to be empty. There had to be something more, they just didn't know what that something was until Christ appeared.

2. **Many churches fail to gather a harvest because they cannot perceive the harvest.**

Most churches continue "doing church" as usual, assuming that most people in the community are Christians, further assuming that their ministry is merely the nurturing and caring of said Christians. Often church leaders and their members are in denial (or simply choose to ignore) the number of pre-Christians, unchurched Christians, and hurting young people both in the church and in the community. More often than not, many of these do not even know many unchurched people. Another point and problem that remains quietly in the background that should be considered: just because someone is in our church does not mean they are a Christian who has experienced a true conversion.

3. **Christianity has too few laborers to gather the harvest.**

In most traditional churches, including my own, we ask our people to share the good news and invite people to church, or various outreach programs our church is conducting. They either don't do it, or they go out (that) that day, hand out flyers about the event, return to the church, and are done.

As leaders, we gently push and prod our members to share their faith and invite, but they don't do it.

We may even provide good evangelism training. Our members take the training, like it, and believe that sharing their faith is important, but they still don't do it.

There are two main reasons this happens. The first is that many, including I myself at one time, have attempted to labor and have come out of the harvest empty-handed. When my wife and I first started doing the biker ministry, we went out with copies of *Steps to Christ*, the way I had been taught. I was raised with Ingathering. As a Pathfinder, every year we would go out Ingathering and hand out books. After leaving the church and returning, I went back to my root concept and understanding of evangelism. So we bought a bunch of *Steps to Christ* books, put our name and contact information inside, and begin handing them out. Ninety-nine percent of the responses were "That's religion; I don't want anything to do with it." This went on for two years, and we finally began to ask ourselves, "What are we doing wrong?" Two years we went through this, and we're thinking, *Wow, what are we doing wrong?* At this point many give up in discouragement.

My wife and I were that discouraged; however, rather than give up, we decided to look at Christ's ministry and emulate whatever we were led to discover. After an inductive look at Christ's ministry, we decided it was time to get out of God's way with our own ideas of how to reach people. We decided we were just going to mingle and fellowship without an agenda. Our spiritual agenda became like Christ's. We met people, built relationships with them, meeting whatever needs they had as best we could. We comforted when the need arose; we laughed and mourned with them. Our new ministry philosophy was affirmed that weekend when God placed a ready soul in our path to be harvested. We prayed through the sinner's prayer with him as he accepted Christ. God's Spirit showed up, and let me tell you, that is the most amazing experience my wife and I have ever had.

The second reason for traditional evangelism failure is largely a result of the first: many traditional churches are no longer able to reach, receive, retain, and grow receptive people in their own individual ministry areas.

The root causes are essentially that harvesting and nurturing has changed, and we have no idea how to harvest or nurture the change. So we continue to go with what we know, we attempt to do the same thing, sometimes wrapping it up in a shiny new package. It may work for a moment, but in the very near future, we find it ending in failure. We fail to gather a harvest; sometimes, at a costly expense, we often brutally damage or destroy whatever "sprouts" may be or have been developing. Again, I make this statement based upon personal experience working with people, both young and older, in the secular community as well as our own church youth.

There are several reasons for this occurrence. Christians tend to assume the following:

1. What motivated us will motivate them.
2. The approach that reached me (us) is the approach that will reach them.
3. They already know what we are talking about.
4. Those we are witnessing to will like the church well enough to be able to respond affirmatively to our effort.

Did you notice something interesting? That list of reasons is all about us, isn't it? Our approach is all what we think should be happening. It isn't what we think will work—it is allowing God to lead and use us in the way He knows we need to be used. Our evangelism efforts continue to utilize and rely on these traditional approaches, both within our own programs, ministering to our young people, and reaching out to the community. The results of these approaches are yielding declining and/ or completely zero results. Other churches have just given up on these approaches, not bothering to replace them.

At this point the results should come as no surprise. Our own youth, who have grown up in the church, are leaving the church, and a vast majority of churches have not reached or discipled any really unchurched or secular person.

"But our church has grown in membership." That may very well be; however, is that growth from our witnessing effort, or is it from transfer of memberships from other churches? The final question: How many members are on the books but not seen in church?

Let's keep it simple and ask, "Is it the goal of a 'traditional church' for people to be religious and 'become like us'?" This includes believing, behaving, having the same experience as we have. With this goal in mind, do we focus mainly on theology and doctrine, handing people the glasses with which to decipher God's Word the way we think they should decipher it? This does not promote or encourage a personal and intimate relationship with Jesus.

In our ministry efforts and preparations to receive others into our church family, have we stopped to consider just what people, youth, and unchurched may be perceiving when they experience "traditional church"?

The gravitational pull of our human nature is self-serving. It does not look to serve others. Church congregations are made up of humans. Unless a personal and intimate relationship with Jesus is developed, the church as a body will seek to focus on its own needs and wants. Unchurched as well as our youth are seeing the hypocrisy. They are hearing the words, but not seeing the actions. Unless we are willing to be honest about ourselves and our shortcomings, giving up the idea that we need to be the perfect example of Christianity, and begin our walk with Christ at the center of our personal lives, we will never be anything more than Seventh-day Pharisees.

Consider their approach for a moment: "I know the law, and that law is going to make me good enough to get me into a relationship with Christ." We all know how well that worked out for the Pharisees. Keeping the law was all well and good, but they were not keeping it because of their love for God—they were keeping the law because of their love for themselves.

Our "knee-jerk" solutions to the youth problem in our church have typically been one of the following two. The first is not unfamiliar to me, as it is the same that I experienced growing up: we ignore it. We ignore the situation, hoping that youth and young adults will somehow right themselves when they are older and have their own children. All this advertises to the young people is that leaders, parents, and church members have missed the significance of the times and the needs of the young people, choosing instead to call it a phase they will hopefully grow out of. The truth is that this has been going on a lot longer than many want to admit; the proof of this lies in the fact that we are here having this discussion.

The second "knee-jerk" solution is that we exhaust all efforts to appeal to the teens and young adults. Great, we recognized the need and are addressing the problem. However, this approach excludes the older members and "builds the church on the preferences of the young people, and not on the pursuit of personal and intimate relationship with God. . . . One response I received from parents and a pastor was "Hey, at least they are at church." The facts of that particular program and philosophy: Two of the girls in this particular Sabbath School became pregnant by two of the boys, and a half dozen others are into drugs and have disappeared.

Let's continue to be honest: maybe it goes beyond the needs and wants of members; maybe it boils down to preferences. Have any of you ever tried to lead beyond the preferences of the church members? In fact, maybe it is not even the church members, but a specific patriarchal member or the patriarchal member and their following. Here is a result of personal experience.

We were working with a church in California where a singular pastor and I were trying to combat the things we have identified thus far.

The church had already completed a health survey and was found to be deficient in all eight areas. I was working with the youth and assisting the pastor. As we began to implement new strategies, our voicemails from a patriarchal member and his following blew up, our e-mails blew up, and we started having meeting after meeting. The church was called into a general session by the head elder; the pastor was seated by himself in front of the church, facing the congregation area, while the rest of the congregation, led by the elders, began to fire accusation after accusation at the pastor. That is how terrible it was. The bottom line is that many feel as if it is their right to have the church fit into their tastes and whims, and the church body as a whole suffers because of it.

Attempting to keep a congregation happy will not work for three primary reasons:

1. This method of Christianity is killing the church.
2. Attendance is stagnating or on the rapid decline as people drift further and further from Christ. In fact, if we are to be completely honest, this is less of practicing Christ's likeness and more of making the same mistakes the Pharisees did; we are replicating them exactly.
3. It is WRONG! We cannot please everybody in our church, and if we are trying, we are wrong. The bottom line: when our preferences begin causing people to leave the church (the church is the body of Christ, not a building, denomination, or religion) and keeps the unchurched people from the promise of Christ's free gift of salvation, it is time to change our preferences and make Christ our preference of priority.

My wife and I are both very passionate. She hates the way I drive—she thinks I should be going one direction, which, in her opinion is the better and shorter route between point A and point B. I personally feel it is about the journey, not the destination, and if a wrong turn occurs, not a big deal. She feels it is necessary to criticize and hound me. This at times turns into quite the "discussion." One particular day this began to occur when something suddenly dawned on me. I simply stated, "Honey, I am not going to argue with an opinion." I must admit I felt a bit smug because this statement ended the discussion. More important, however, I had discovered a powerful tool in communication and leadership. There is no point in arguing opinions. Arguing in this manner is simply trying to prove that our opinion is more right than the other and that we will do whatever it takes to make sure we convince the other person that we are right.

This correlates directly into our Christian experience, doesn't it? Some of the most volatile meetings I have ever attended on a regular basis are church board meetings. What a mess. I wonder at times: "Where is Christ in all of this mess?" The apostles warn and encourage us to not be divisive, to be kindhearted, to love and encourage each other . . . and then you sit in a church board meeting and wonder, *Are we as Christian brothers and sisters living this concept right now?* It's not like you can stand up and say, "Is Christ in this meeting with us right now, because it certainly doesn't feel like it."

So the million-dollar question is What do we do about this? We focus on the fundamentals. At the beginning of a training camp in July of 1961, Vince Lombardi, recognized as one of the greatest football coaches of all time, stood up in front of 38 professional football players. Mr. Lombardi held a football out in front of him and said, "Gentleman, this is a football."

The Green Bay Packers, having lost a substantial lead and the championship to the Philadelphia Eagles the preceding season, would, six months later, defeat the New York Giants 37-0 to win the NFL championship. They would never again lose another playoff game, and would go on to win five championships in a seven-year period, including three in a row. Vince Lombardi never coached a team with a losing record.

As Christians, what is our fundamental? It is developing our personal and intimate relationship with Christ. It always has been. Christ depended solely on His relationship with God; in turn, He taught His disciples to depend on the same through Him, and then the Holy Spirit. I have to ask (and I am not trying to be antagonistic), When did we lose sight of this fundamental? This is what our primary focus is supposed to be, and it works. Do math Christ's way: He started with four disciples, then multiplied by three. Then those 12 turned to 120, who were gathered in a room praying. God poured His Spirit out upon them, and 3,000 were added to their number . . . in one day. At the very core of this success was absolute dependence and trust in Christ, letting Him take care of the details. God's math, God's work, not ours; I believe that can still happen today if we would simply plug back into what we should be plugged into to begin with.

What is to be gained from focusing on that single fundamental? We will be an open conduit that will allow Christ to use us when and where he knows we need to be used. We will begin to emulate his love and compassion to others. We will begin connecting with them in a way that will attract and not push away.

There are six ways that Jesus connected with people:

1. **Affirmation**—Whenever Jesus approached somebody one-on-one, He affirmed them as a human being.

2. **Acceptance**—He accepted them for where they were at. They did not need to meet a bunch of standards to be accepted by Him. "Come as you are right now; I will make the change." He appreciated them for who He created them to be, not what they were at that moment.

3. **Appreciation**—He appreciated them for who He created them to be, not where they were at. We see God showing appreciation at Jesus' baptism: "This is My beloved Son, in whom I am well pleased" (Matthew 3:17, NKJV). A paraphrase of Paul's letter to the Romans is "I love you; here's what I appreciate about you . . ." Paul goes on to list that the whole world is talking about you. As a sports coach, we would call this a positive coaching method. When we affirm the positive, we spend a whole lot less time having to correct the negative.

4. **Affection**—Appropriate affection. Every single time Christ was one on one with somebody, there was a physical touch involved. He knelt down with a leper. He helped him up, He put sod on the eyes, He put a child on His lap, there was always affection and always physical touch. In a world today that is starving for affection, people are finding it in very unhealthy and negative ways, seeking out physical forms of affection that provide a fleeting moment of euphoria and pleasure, as opposed to a long-term love relationship with Christ and His body (the church). This is where our young people are going, they are looking to fill a God-shaped hole that they don't know how to fill. So they are seeking anything and everything they can to fill it. Only to find more emptiness.

5. **Availability**—Christ *always* made Himself available. Nicodemus, the rich young ruler, the children, the Samaritan woman at the well—the list goes on and on. In working with alcoholics and addicts who are recovering, one never knows when they will need support. Our phone has rung at 2:00 in the morning. My wife would roll over and say, "I will go put a pot of coffee on." I would then spend the next two plus hours talking to someone because they were in crisis and wanted to go drink.

6. **Accountability**—So then each of us shall give an account of himself to God. This is so important. What exactly are we going to

be held accountable to? Whether or not we have a personal and intimate relationship with Christ. Remember what Christ said, "I am not going to know you if you don't know Me. If you haven't spent the time to get to know Me I don't know you." It is not through anybody else. Abraham had a covenant with God, then God had to make a covenant with Isaac, and then Jacob. Why? Because it is not transferable() . . . it is individual.

This is the core fundamental that we need to return to. Back to basics for Christians is not a football, but Christ. The previous presentation was on stewardship. As the presenter was speaking, I was thinking, *We could have done this together*. Most people hear the word "stewardship" and immediately think of money. We are stewards of time, we are stewards of people and how we relate to them, and we are accountable. If God were to audit our stewardship of His creation and desire for all to know Him, what would those results be?

Are we truly caring for people? The only way to unselfishly and truly care for people is to connect with Christ personally and intimately. Only then will we be able to start looking at others and seeing them the way God sees them. We have to connect with Him.

We can have all the programs in the world, and they will do no good. Nothing is going to happen, because it is something we are attempting to do, not something that we are living . . . and that is the difference.

BRIAN LITZENBERGER

A military veteran of 10 years, Brian Litzenberger served in the United States Army and the United States Coast Guard. While serving in the Army, he was trained as a recruiting and retention NCO. Honorably discharged in 2001, Litzenberger spent the next few years working in public safety. He is a certified EMT and worked in that field for four years. Over the years, Litzenberger has volunteered his time to Pathfinders, Cub Scouts, and coaching youth sports: volleyball and lacrosse. Brian Litzenberger and his wife have been ministering in the secular community of alcoholics and addicts for 20 years. They founded a motorcycle club that was focused on introducing Christ into the 12 steps of Alcoholics Anonymous. Currently he works with the pastor of his local church in developing a small-group ministry and teaching the youth Sabbath School. Litzenberger has been asked, on several occasions, to speak at conference Pathfinder events and local churches. He holds a bachelor's degree in interdisciplinary studies, with an emphasis in religion, criminal justice, and psychology, and is currently working on his master's degree in pastoral ministry.

People Behind the Numbers

A Positive Perspective on Membership Auditing

EDWARD HEIDINGER and CHARLES RAMPANELLI

FUNDAMENTAL CONSIDERATIONS

As a church, our greatest treasure are people (Malachi 3:17). They were entrusted to us by God as His flock (John 10:16), His family (1 John 3:1, 2).[1] It is our duty to work for their salvation.[2]

"The Secretariat has information about these members. However, the information is relevant when it is updated and used. The more this information about our members, the more effective pastoral care becomes. Thus, up-to-date member data provide key information for more effective pastoral work."

"What man of you, having an hundred sheep, if he loses one of them, doth not leave the ninety and nine in the wilderness, and go after that which is lost, until he finds it?" (Luke 15:4).

What is the situation of the sheep?
She is lost.

What is the pastoral attention?
The pastor goes and finds her.

How does the pastor know that the sheep is lost?
He has to count them!

Misunderstanding of the needs and challenges faced by members can cause problems. We need to know the members and their individual characteristics. An option that helps us keep up-to-date member data for pastoral work is the Permanent Review Program. This is a simple means of working through which members can be taken care of permanently,

DISCIPLING, NURTURING, AND RECLAIMING

analyzing their condition, establishing and executing plans to reach and develop them.

HOW TO CONDUCT THE PERMANENT REVIEW PROGRAM?[3]

As a solution for this, the Special Revision Group (SRG) can be a great tool. The Special Revision Group is a permanent subcommittee that works with the local church directive committee.[4]

Special Revision Group—Composition:
1. Four to six members chosen by the church board.
2. Suggestion: pastor, elder, clerk, treasurer, and two or three more members who are familiar with the congregation.
3. It should operate permanently. The board may replace the members as needed.

Responsibilities of the SRG
1. Screen all names in the membership records, classifying them in one of these auxiliary lists:
   - Regular Frequent Members
   - Regular Nonfrequent Members
   - Attends Another SDA Church
   - Absent Members List
   - Members to Rescue
2. Update the five lists every 12 months.
3. Meet to follow up on the progress of the Permanent Review Program.
4. Present a report of the work done to the church board—once every three months. This should be one of the first items of the agenda.

Responsibilities of the Church Board[5]
1. Appreciate the reports presented by the SRG.
2. Appoint a person responsible to lead the work in favor of each group list.[6]
3. Define what types of service/care should be provided to the members of each list.
4. The committee may follow the evolution of each list by checking the increase or decrease of members in each list. Quarterly you can devote time to this task. In addition, for example, you can conduct deeper studies and plans for specific groups or special

age groups. In a quarter, rescued youth can be targeted for special actions. At the next meeting, seniors who are classified as infrequent regulars may be involved. And so on.

5. Provide a list to the pastor/elder with the names of the members who left the church, to be considered for the Reunion Project (rescue of former members). In a church with many members, a subcommittee to work with a large number of members to be rescued may be formed.

Responsibilities of the Church Clerk

1. Provide an updated membership list from ACMS (Secretariat System) and the forms for the five auxiliary lists used for the activities of the SRG.
2. Participate in the elaboration of the five auxiliary lists as member of the SRG.
3. Based on the auxiliary lists, update each member's record on ACMS after the SRG has submitted its report in the church board.
4. Update membership ranking during the period between the SRG meetings. This classification will be validated by the executive committee, whenever analyzed on its agenda.
5. To include on the executive committee's agenda quarterly the membership rating analysis. The secretariat may even suggest specific studies to assist the committee in planning the care of its members. Newly baptized members, absent from Sabbath School, new generation, not frequent because of work (those who travel, for example), age or health, among others.
6. Monitor the progress of the work done with the members of the five lists. The secretariat, by constantly updating member rankings, can view and assist in monitoring, supervising, and caring for members with the knowledge of the context surrounding the members. Therefore, in a large church, a larger team is likely to be needed to assist the local church secretary.

The Five Auxiliary Lists

These lists are confidential. Only members' names, without additional data, should be submitted to members of the SRG and of the local church executive committee. This is a very important issue, because while the classification does not define a specific action for the church, information confidentiality will protect members and will provide church leaders with the time and privacy to engage in the rescue and development of their brethren.[7] Members must be classified on ACMS based on them.

In this working view, members can be classified into five groups: Regular Frequent Members; Regular Nonfrequent Members; Attends Another SDA Church; Absent Members List; Members to Rescue. Next, you can see a brief description of who would form each group and some suggestive actions for them.

Regular Frequent Members

Members who attend frequently
Newly baptized members (past 12 months)
Other members

Procedures:
- Update the information on their membership records.
- Have a permanent visitation plan.
- Involve them in church ministries.
- Although these members are attending church, be careful that they do not change their ranks by helping them to stay connected to Jesus in a life of real discipleship.[8]

Regular Nonfrequent Members

Members with irregular attendance
Members with difficulty of locomotion
- Elderly members
- Members who are ill
- People with special needs

Procedures:
- Update the information on their membership records.
- Develop a visitation plan that meets the needs perceived for each case.
- Involve them in church ministries, especially Sabbath School.

NOTE: Try to create condition so that they may become regular, frequent members.

This may be one of the groups that should pay more attention to their potential risk. If something is not done for them, they will probably change their ranking, and it will not be to the frequent ranking.

Attends Another SDA Church
Members to be received
Members to send

Procedures:
- Members to be received: Follow the process as outlined in Chapter 4 and move their name to the regular members' list.
- Members to send: Inform the church where they currently are members, through ACMS, that they desire a transfer and wait for this church to send the letter of yransfer.
- Members who are attending a church other than the church where they are registered at may be at risk of not receiving the pastoral care and attention needed to develop their lives with God and the community of believers.

Absent Members List
Members who have not attended church services for more than six months and whose whereabouts are unknown

Procedures:
- Post the list on the church's bulletin board and publish on ACMS.
- Distribute this list to church officials and other members who can help.
- After you have spent at least two years with no success in locating the member, and exhausted all resources in this search, follow the process of the *Seventh-day Adventist Church Manual* and remove the name from the auxiliary list.
- Perhaps because they are not permanently monitored by the church, either in a Sabbath School class or by the local church executive committee, these members have entered a challenging situation, where removal will probably be the end result.

Members to Rescue
Members who are not living in harmony with church doctrines

Procedures:
- Organize the Reunion Project, which includes a visitation plan.
- In case the member returns, move their name to the auxiliary list of regular members.
- The rescued member must be involved in an active discipleship

plan, in saving others, to be developed and not to return to his or her state.[9]

- After having made every effort to rescue,[10] but have had no success, apply the corresponding disciplinary measure according to the procedures specified in the *Church Manual* and remove their name from the auxiliary list.

Currently, all members of the South Brazil Union Conference are classified under ACMS in one of five groups. Reviews, meetings, plans, and actions at all levels within this framework are a result of this desire to better shepherd its members.

But how can you rank all members of a region with more than 2,000 churches? In addition, how to continue the process started so that the data is updated and used for the best results?[11] To reach this destination requires a road and a vehicle.

PLAN FOR EXCELLENCE—THE ROAD[12]

In order for the secretariat to continue with the plan it had begun, to execute it with excellence, something more was needed. We did not expect only punctual actions, but a process. In addition, new clerks in local churches needed full instruction and in a short time for the movement to continue.

For this, we needed a way, a guide that would tell us what was expected of a secretary/clerk. This route should be simple and understandable, but complete and involve the day-to-day work of the secretariat.

Then the idea came from a secretary! Why don't we have a program of excellence, with requirements to be met, with points for each activity?

The name of the excellence program in Portuguese is *Secretaria Nota 1000* (in English, it could be translated as "Class A Clerk"). The goal is to motivate and encourage the local church secretariat to do its job with excellence.

One of the great secrets to the effectiveness of this plan is a year-round monitoring and follow-up process.[13] Only launching of the excellence plan is not enough. Quarterly reports, controls, and incentives are fundamental.

At first, all the secretaries of the local churches communicated directly with the conference. The work was getting clearer and clearer, but it was still necessary to speed up the information, instruction, and execution of the secretariat's activities.

Within the excellence plan, each activity has a specific score totaling 1,000 points (hence the name in Portuguese). The higher the challenge and importance of the item, the higher the score. Some items, because they are only partially fulfilled and a partial score is still achieved. Others require full compliance for the score. A gift recognition is given to each secretary who reaches 1,000 points. However, the greatest prize is to know that work is done with excellence, for our God is worthy of it.[14] The more the secretary gets involved in doing the work effectively, the more joy and energy are involved, bringing positive results to the local church and the care of members.[15]

The requirements in the plan of excellence broadly involve the work of the local church secretary. When the plan began, he had simpler items. Over the years (this program began to be implemented in 2014 in the North Santa Catarina Conference, and in 2016 throughout the South Brazil Union Conference) the level of difficulty of the items was increasing, as well as the development of the local church secretaries. In addition, the percentage of secretaries who reach the highest score increases year by year. In addition, 7 standard requirements for all conferences, and they are free to add additional items as indicated by the local need.

To assist the secretaries of the local churches, 6 of the 9 Conferences of the South Brazil Union Conference have a Secretariat Auditor, being one of the main activities to assist in the process of classifying and analyzing the list of members. In addition, a simple manual has been prepared with guidelines on how to accomplish each of the excellence plan requirements. These guidelines include images of the secretariat's system for carrying out actions in the office, as well as advice for conducting activities, such as preparing for the local church board. One of the most commonly used items in this material are the suggestive models of agenda and vows for the minutes of the local church (one of the requirements of the plan of excellence).

Below is a comparison of the requirements of the years 2014, 2017, 2018, 2019, 2020. In 2015 there was only one change, indicated below. The requirements of 2016 were the same as 2015 requirements.

Class A Clerk—2014
1. Use the ACMS frequently (at least once a month—in 2015 this item has been expanded to at least twice a month).
2. Attend the trainings.
3. Register the church officials in the ACMS.
4. Update the membership registry.
5. Register the baptismal cards in the ACMS.
6. Register the church in the ACMS.

7. Complete the integrated report on a quarterly basis.
8. Conduct the reunion project.
9. Have a discipleship plan for the newly baptized.
10. Participate in the committees and write the minutes.

Class A Clerk—2017
1. Participate in the trainings (regional, integrated, district, etc.).
2. Register the officers in the ACMS.
3. Update the list of members.
4. Update the member registry (address, contact, pictures, etc.).
5. Register the ACMS baptism cards.
6. Keep the church record updated on the ACMS (updated church and mailing address, church contacts, service times, church picture, etc.).
7. Complete the integrated report of the departments on the requested dates.
8. Conduct the reunion project (actions to rescue people away from the church).
9. Enroll 100 percent of Sabbath School members.
10. Standardized committees and registries.
11. Participate in committees.Keep the book of minutes updated. Keep the book of acts updated.Keep the wedding book updated.

Class A Clerk—2018
1. Register the baptismal vow forms on ACMS.
2. Update the membership lists on ACMS.
3. Update membership records on ACMS.
4. Register officers on ACMS.
5. Complete the ACMS integrated report for departments by the requested date.
6. Organize the reunion project.
7. Enroll 100 percent of members in Sabbath School.
8. Prepare church board agendas.
9. Prepare book of minutes according to standards.
10. Keep the book of minutes updated.

Class A Clerk—2019
1. Biannual classification of members on ACMS.
2. Analysis of CRM/discipleship in the monthly agenda of the church board.

3. Register the baptismal vow forms on ACMS.
4. Update membership lists on ACMS.
5. Integrated reports.
6. Reunion project.
7. Prepare minutes according to standard.

Class A Clerk—2020

1. Review the updated rank in the committee (quarterly).
2. Analysis of the CRM in the executive committee (monthly).
3. Register baptism cards in the ACMS (soon after they are forwarded).
4. Update the list of members in ACMS (throughout the year).Complete the integrated report in ACMS (January, April, July, and October).
5. Carry out the reunion project/rescue of the Estranged (throughout the year).
6. Prepare the standardized book of minutes (throughout the year).

DISTRICTS SECRETARIAT—THE VEHICLE[16]

At this point we felt the need for a means through which the clerks, who by now knew the way, to know how to move in it. We felt they needed someone who could accompany and aid in their difficulties.[17] That is how the idea for district secretaries came about!

The process of implementing the district secretaries program is relatively simple and quite natural. We can divide it into four parts:

I. Appointment
II. Training
III. Mission
IV. Motivation

I. Appointment[18]

The profile and the character of the district secretary are important to the choice and performance of this task.[19] Experience and technical knowledge are important in this function, but accessibility, availability, agility, and ability to relate and motivate are much more. The position of the clerk is technical. The position of district secretary is one of leadership. Demand and profile are different.

The process by which a district secretary is elected may vary. It may happen through a voting process among church clerks, but we have seen good results when we ask for the suggestion of the district pastor. This brings authority and support to the district secretary.

II. Training

The district secretary will need to be trained, instructed, and closely monitored, especially after their appointment. Because the profile and demands of this function are different from those of a church clerk, district secretaries need to know exactly what is expected of them, what tools they will have and how to use them.

Training can occur in a few ways:
- Annual meeting of district secretaries
- In person, by the executive secretary, auditor or conference secretariat, especially for those newly appointed
- Videoconference meetings (Zoom, Skype, etc.)
- Online tests/quizzes about the *Secretariat's Guide and Church Manual*

Among the tools available to the district secretary are:
- Teamwork
- Quarterly and annual incentives
- Quarterly and annual evaluations (Class A Clerk)
- Follow-up through telephone and WhatsApp
- Quarterly meetings
- Occasional visits
- Assistance from District pastor
- Support from the Conference
- Much prayer, friendship, relationship, and love

III. Mission

The district secretariat is the vehicle, but the road is the plan for excellence. To maximize results, the district secretariat must have a very clear and measurable mission.

The district secretaries measure their efficiency as local clerks develop in the plan for excellence, the Class A Clerk.

This is where the vehicle finds a road to excellence. District secretaries knows that a large part of their job is to help local church clerks reach their goals during the year in each church of their district.

IV. Motivation

Keeping the group happy, integrated, and motivated is just as important as the previous items. Suggestions to be practiced:
- Annual awards for those who reach a percentage of the proposed goals

- Annual meeting in a pleasant place[20]
- Quarterly meetings with the purpose of interaction of clerks in their districts/regions
- Sporadic visits from Conference employees in their homes
- Phone calls
- Contact via WhatsApp messages and groups
- Make funds available for their work
- Total availability, fast and priority service to this group

The system of district secretaries will not lessen the work of the conference executive secretary, but will exponentially increase the results achieved in the pursuit of excellence and the salvation of people.

CONCLUSION

Seeing people as the church's greatest treasure is necessary, but dealing with numbers in this context is a challenge. Seeing only inputs and outputs is not enough. We need to know the current context of the members we have. Excellent and sustained commitment by the church secretariat and leadership is also needed to do better than what has been done so far.

Some actions have shown good results, but steady progress is vital in this process. These things (plan for excellence and district secretaries) help us to see people behind numbers.

EDWARD HEIDINGER

Edward Heidinger was born in Peru on October 2, 1978. He is married to Susana Heidinger and has two daughters: Priscilla, 14, and Rebekah, 7. He has two bachelor's degrees: business administration (1999) and theology (2003). He holds a master's degree in theology (2016) and is beginning his doctoral studies in ministry at Andrews University. He was a district pastor; field department director and executive secretary; union department director, executive secretary, and president; assistant to the president and (currently) executive secretary of the South American Division.

CHARLES EDSON RAMPANELLI

Charles Edson Rampanelli, Brazilian, was born on October 21, 1978. He is married to Márcia L.B.G. Rampanelli and has two children: Júlia M. G. Rampanelli, 13, and Guilherme G. Rampanelli, 10. He has a bachelor's and a master's degree in theology from the Brazil Adventist University, and has been a pastor since 2000. He has worked in several areas of ministry: as an auxiliary pastor, a pastor in the educational area, a district pastor, and departmental director in several areas, as well as executive secretary in local conferences. He is currently the executive secretary of the South Brazil Union Conference.

DISCIPLING, NURTURING, AND RECLAIMING

ENDNOTES

1 Ellen G. White, *Principles for Christian Leaders,* pp. 16-18.
2 In the last days, there will be only one remnant. John says of these that they "keep the commandments of God, and have the testimony of Jesus" (Revelation 12:17, KJV).
3 *Church Secretarial Guide,* chapter 10, South American Division.
4 *Seventh-day Adventist Church Manual,* p. 132.
5 *Ibid.,* p. 131: "Study membership lists and initiate plans for reconnecting (reclaiming) members who have separated from the church."
6 About the care in dealing with people who have departed from the church, see Thom S. Rainer, *The Book of Church Growth,* p. 284.
7 E. G. White, p. 134.
8 See Jim Howard, *Discipleship Handbook,* p. 3.
9 "Christians who are constantly growing in earnestness, in zeal, in fervor, in love—such Christians never backslide" (Ellen G. White, in *Review and Herald,* June 7, 1887).
10 About the job to save the saints, see John Piper, *Brothers, We Are Not Professionals,* pp. 121-127.
11 To analyze the role of leadership to start and continue the process with the purpose of developing people, see Colin Marshall and Tony Payne, *The Trellis and the Vine,* pp. 102-110.
12 *Secretary's Agenda 2019*—South Brazilian Union Conference.
13 "Those who are placed in responsible positions should feel it their duty to recognize talent. They should learn how to use men, and how to advise them" (Ellen G. White, *Christian Leadership,* p. 57.
14 "We must strive for excellence because it is the excellence that honors God. It is the excellence that inspires people" (Bill Hybels, Axioms, p. 251).
15 About the trust placed in the team and its results, see Stephen M. R. Covey, *The Speed of Trust,* p. 230.
16 Participation of Harry James Streithorst, executive secretary of the North Santa Catarina Conference.
17 About the importance and the foundation of today's leading leaders, see Emilson dos Reis, *How to Lead,* p. 30.
18 Choosing people to form a team is a challenge. Some pitfalls and advice to assist with this process can be found in Mike Bonem and Roger Patterson, *Leading From the Second Chair,* pp. 94-97.
19 "The Lord will use humble [people] to do a great and good work. Through them He will represent to the world the ineffaceable characteristics of the divine nature" (Ellen G. White letter 270, 1907).
20 About work and recreation, see Greg McKeown, *Esssentialism,* p. 96.

The Care and Rescue of Members Who Have Left the Church

Reencounter Project

EMANUEL GUIMARÃES

THE CHURCH, THROUGHOUT ITS HISTORY, has developed various methods of evangelism to reach people and has achieved great growth, yet many members have stopped attending church, departing from God's ways. Apostasy is a real problem in practically every denomination.

When we analyze a local church, we find basically three ways or methods of growth.

The first way is growth by evangelism. We reach out to new members through public and personal evangelism. Public evangelism is like fishing with a net—the fisher seeks large numbers of fish; personal evangelism is like a fisher catching one fish at a time. In public evangelism the retention rate may be higher or lower depending on the location and ability of the local church to receive these new converts. In personal evangelism, however, retention rates are higher.

The second way is biological growth: we grow up with children of church members born of believing parents in Adventist faith and doctrine. In countries in which the birth rate per family is currently low, this factor has been reflected in the aging of the church because there are not many children and young people, and so the biological growth is very low.

The third way of growing a local church is to increase the number of members by transfer. Members move for many reasons and circumstances; they ask for their transfer letter and are received into the new community, increasing the regular number of members of that community.

A NEW METHOD

The local church grows by evangelism, biological growth, and transfers. But there is a new and extraordinary way or method that seeks to evangelize and bring back to the good shepherd's fold those who have stopped attending church and turned away from God's ways. It is the evangelism that we call the Reencounter Project, with excellent results and wonderful experiences.

There is currently a lot of research on the loss of church members. But a survey, which caught my attention, was conducted in São Paulo, Brazil, with two groups of people: those who left the church and turned away from God and have not returned yet; and those members who departed from the church, returned, were rebaptized, and are today firm in the faith.

REASONS MEMBERS LEFT THE CHURCH

With the first group of members, who left the church and have not yet returned, various reasons were given similar to the various surveys already conducted on loss of church members— problems such as relationships, personal problems, and many other issues with very small rates. Some of these answers are understandable, but most of the reasons were not relevant, considering that many still had a hurt heart and feelings.

The second group of members is composed of former members who have returned to the church, were rebaptized, and are now firm in the faith. They cited several factors similar to research already conducted. But one important and crucial question was asked: What was the main reason or motive that caused you to actually leave the church?
The answer presented two very relevant points: (1) a spiritual crisis in their life; (2) a personal decision to abandon the faith.

REASONS THE MEMBERS RETURNED

The reasons former members return to church are interesting and important for the local church to understand its missionary and spiritual role in the rescue. The following points were cited in general terms:

1. 1. They missed the fellowship with church members. The sense of community and fellowship greatly marks the lives of church members.
2. 2. They felt a stronger desire to return when they encountered a very warm, cordial, and Christian church reception.
3. 3. Music plays an important role in life, and many felt strongly influenced by music to return.
4. 4. Other variable factors were cited, in very small percentages and similar to the surveys already conducted.

But a crucial and important question was asked directly to those who left the church, returned, and are firm in their faith today: What was the strongest, most relevant feeling or factor that made you really decide to go back to God's ways?

The impact of the answer is very impressive and enlightening. They answered that the main factor was discovering that someone was constantly praying for them, not giving up interceding before Christ so that they would be impressed to return. And a second main reason was finding out that someone in the church really cared about them personally, showing Christianity and patience, and seeking to fulfill their necessities.

Basically, we can conclude that most leave the church for spiritual reasons and return for spiritual reasons. Certainly, it is the action of the Holy Spirit through people who have interceded in prayer that touches the hearts of former members.

Redeeming members who have left the church has to do with spiritual matters and is a way to develop missionary discipleship.

If we begin a great movement of faith, prayer, and work ,"*many who have strayed from the fold will come back to follow the great Shepherd.*"[1]

The cause of spiritual decline and lack of involvement in mission that have led many to apostasy is the loss of evangelistic passion. A vision of discipleship in the local church toward this rescue ministry is decisive. Christ's parables illustrate God's desire to save those who are lost.

Herbert Lockyer, quoting F. W. Boreham, makes an interesting observation: "*Mathematics are cold and unconvincing and cannot explain everything. The lost sheep represented 1 percent loss— one out of a hundred; the lost silver meant a 10 percent loss—one out of ten; the lost son was a 50 percent loss—one in two.*"[2]

It doesn't matter if it's just 1 percent, 10 percent or 50 percent losses. The most important is who goes to get the lost ones who have left the church. Our greatest mission is to go out and seek the sheep that has strayed from God's ways. In fact, the sheep knows it is lost, but it does not know the way back, and it desperately needs help. Ellen White wrote: "*The sheep that has strayed from the fold is the most helpless of all creatures. It must be sought for by the shepherd, for it cannot find its way back. So with the soul that has wandered away from God; he is as helpless as the lost sheep, and unless divine love had come to his rescue he could never find his way to God.*"[3]

FAITH, PRAYER, AND WORK

Caring for and rescuing members who have left the church is a discipleship and retention process that involves faith, prayer, and work. The process of growth in faith applies to these three points as well. According to Ellen White: *"For the disheartened there is a sure remedy—faith, prayer, work. Faith and activity will impart assurance and satisfaction that will increase day by day."*[4]

Rescuing of members who have strayed from the ways of the Lord is a biblical calling. James wrote: *"My brothers and sisters, if one of you should wander from the truth and someone should bring that person back, remember this: Whoever turns a sinner from the error of their way will save them from death and cover over a multitude of sins"* (James 5:19, 20, NIV).

The church must challenge its leaders to apply this principle of discipleship and spiritual growth for their members to grow in faith, seeking to save those in the family of faith as well. And the church will be strengthened with mission-oriented actions in which pastors play a key role. *"The best help that ministers can give the members of our churches is not sermonizing but planning work for them . . . . If set to work, the despondent| will soon forget their despondency; the weak will become strong; the ignorant, intelligent, and all will be prepared to present the truth as it is in Jesus."*[5]

MEMBERS' PARTICIPATION IN THE REENCOUNTER PROJECT

The involvement of members of the church in the care and rescue of former members develops a very contagious evangelistic and missionary passion for the following reasons: 1. The community of faith and the sense of a large family is a very strong feeling in the church, so losing a member is very painful for those who really love one another. John wrote, "By this everyone will know that you are my disciples, if you love one another" (John 13:35, NIV). This Christian love is not inert when it knows that there are sheep of the Lord Jesus needing to be rescued. 2. The low operating cost of reunion evangelism facilitates the local church's involvement in this rescue ministry. 3. The friendship factor has a strong influence on the members. Many of them have developed fraternal relationships for a long time; some have even grown up together in that local community and this is a facilitating factor for Reencounter Project evangelism. 4. Knowledge of the doctrine speeds up the process of preparation for rebaptism, as they need only a few reinforcement studies at some issues in their Christian journey.

Tangible Results

In the experience developed over the past five years in the Central Brazil Union and in the South American Division, results show great gospel victories in the lives of members who returned to the church and were rebaptized through the Reencounter Project. In the Central Brazil Union 18.2 percent of all baptisms achieved were the result of redemption of members by rebaptism. In South America it was 12.9 percent; this represents 154,202 rebaptisms. This is a very important factor in church growth rates.

REENCOUNTER PROJECT STRATEGIES

With the awakening to search for members who left the church, some strategies were developed:

1. **Reencounter Project Held in Partnership With the World Ten Days of Prayer Project**

    The local church is prepared three to six months before rebaptism. A church preparation sermon is preached for the work of visitation and intercessory prayer by distributing the names to the visiting team. A lecture on visiting members who have left the church is very important at this stage of preparation. During these months leading up to the Ten Days of Prayer, church members intercede and regularly visit former members. On the first Saturday of the Ten Days of Prayer, members participate in the local Ten Hours of Fasting by interceding specifically for the people they are praying for and visiting in recent months, so they decide to rebaptism. These special days DVDs with testimonies of returning church members are delivered to the former members, along with other QRCode materials and brochures, which will facilitate contact with other important materials to inspire and nurture these brethren in their faith-building. At the end of the Ten Days of Prayer, we have a great Reencounter baptism ceremony.

    This project is very effective because the focus on prayer and caring for the former members is the biggest return factor in reconnecting with members who have left the church.

2. **Reencounter Through Sabbath School Class**

    At the beginning of the year, the church secretary and the elder in charge of evangelism of members who left the church make a list of irregular members and those who have left God's ways. Sabbath School teachers receive names that are distributed per class. Names are passed on to visitation pairs formed within the class. Members receive the prayer card, visit, and plan for intercession for members who have left the church. Each month of the year a rebaptism is performed through the

Sabbath School class responsible for that month. Thus, throughout the year the rescue is carried out. The Reencounter Project follow-up is done through the Sabbath School card, which mentions each Saturday the members for whom the class is praying and working for to be back on church.

3. **Reencounter Project in the Evangelistic Weekend in the Local Church**

The local church schedules in its annual calendar a special weekend to hold the Reencounter Project. In this weekend's schedule a baptism is held to appeal to former members to return to the church. Prior to the program, invitations with QRCode with beautiful testimonies and DVDs are distributed. It is very important to have a careful preparation in the program and sermon, as they must focus on those who have left the church. This evangelistic weekend is very practical and easy to be carried out in the local church.

4. **Reencounter Project Through Youth Prayer Week**

Youth Prayer Week is done with an emphasis on evangelism for those who have left the church.

Young people and church members are looking in advance to visit and invite formers members to attend this special week. They receive QRCode invitations that feature beautiful testimonies videos and DVDs are distributed.

Powerful altar calls are made for former members to return to the church. After this week, the church continues helping and supporting those who answered to the appeals.

5. **Public Evangelism Caravan**

Church members visit former members and invite them for a one-day evangelism program. They deliver invitations and DVDs. An evangelist pastor preaches each night in a different church within the Caravan project.

The preparation of the members for the baptisms that are performed on this special night is done months in advance for the Caravan day. The evangelist makes special altar calls to those who left God's ways to return to the church.

After the Evangelistic Caravan, the church continues to assist those who accepted the appeal.

6. **Robe of Faith Project**

This project is very interesting and very effective. Because former members are visited and receive a Robe of Faith kit that includes a baptismal robe, a DVD with beautiful experiences of people who have returned to God's ways, and an invitation to the Reencounter meeting.

All former members are included in the local church members' intercession project. After being assisted and followed up, they are rebaptized. The robe they received as a gift is donated by the rebaptized member to someone who needs to return to God's ways.

There are several actions that result in the redemption of members who have left the church. And how can we apply this? Choosing and experimenting with the local church the method that is best for each reality. The tried methods encourage us to make the Reencounter:

- Accomplished in partnership with the World Ten Days of Prayer Project
- Through Sabbath School classes
- Conducting the Reencounter Project on a special weekend at the local church
- With Youth Prayer Week
- Through the Caravans of Public Evangelism
- Personal Evangelism with the Robe of Faith

MATERIALS PRODUCED FOR THE REENCOUNTER PROJECT

Materials were prepared for two groups of people: church members and former members.

Church member materials:

- **Intercessory Prayer Card:** Church members are challenged to pray for two or three former members and to visit them. The card is placed on in their Bible for constant remembrance.
- **Sermons:** 1. Motivation and appeal to church members—is for training on how to carry out the Reencounter project. Usually it is preached three to six months prior to Reencounter Project Day. 2. Reencounter Sermon—It is designed for Reencounter Day for the purpose of reaching former members.
- **Sabbath School Membership Card:** There is a special space to write the names of those who are away from the church. Each Saturday the teacher and class intercede in prayer. Class members are assigned to visit and pray with them. So the work is done all year round.

The materials for former members are: Invitation card with QRCode, website with exclusive materials and a specific Facebook link for contacts, and testimonies from those returning to the church.

All these actions are aimed solely at seeking and rescuing those who were once in the church. To strengthen new members and prevent dropouts after baptisms or rebaptisms, members are enrolled in the Discipleship School in the "New Creature" Project, where they learn about worship; Sabbath sanctification; tithes and offerings; personal health care and how to preach the gospel.

The Reencounter Project has reached thousands of members who once left the church. But our challenge is to seek every sheep that is far from God's ways and bring it back to the good shepherd's fold. This is the challenge of love for the mission that Christ has given us all.

EMMANUEL GUIMARÃES

Emmanuel Guimarães has served the church in several areas, as a pastor, evangelist, ministerial secretary, publishing ministries, Global Mission, Sabbath School and personal ministries, health, ADRA, and during the past nine years he has been executive secretary of conference and union (Central Brazil Union Conference). He holds a master's degree in leadership from Andrews University and in theology from UNASP in Brazil. He is the author of several books and articles on church growth. His joy is to train people to preach the gospel and also to rescue members who have left the church. He appreciates reading and swimming. He is married to Lourdes and has three married daughters, Jacqueline (physiotherapist), Gracielle (lawyer), Viviane (physician), and a granddaughter, Julinha.

ENDNOTES

1   Ellen G. White, *Testimonies for the Church* (Mountain View, Calif.: Pacific Press Pub. Assn., 1948), vol. 6, p. 401.

2   F. W. Boreham, in Herbert Lockyer, *All the Parables of the Bible* (Grand Rapids: Zondervan, 1963), p. 282.

3   Ellen G. White, *Christ's Object Lessons* (Washington, D.C.: Review and Herald Pub. Assn., 1900, 1941), p. 187.

4   Ellen G. White, *Prophets and Kings* (Mountain View, Calif.: Pacific Press Pub. Assn., 1917), p. 164.

5   Ellen G. White, *Testimony Treasures* (Mountain View, Calif.: Pacific Press Pub. Assn., 1949), vol. 3, p. 323.

Discipling, Nurturing, and Reclaiming

DISCIPLESHIP

During the past few decades Seventh-day Adventist membership records have reported a loss of about 40 percent. Even worse, more than half of those who left were considered missing or unknown. One can rationalize that in some cases it was an accumulative loss that was reported during membership or statistical auditing, but that doesn't acknowledge whether it was a two- or three-year loss or an ongoing loss of 10 or 20 years.

Membership loss is not unique to this denomination. In recent years North American mainline denominations have lost one third of their membership. Christian leaders attribute the current situation to faulty discipleship. The foundation problem of the church is that it embodies superficial discipleship. The Apostolic church had a simple but very effective organization, and discipleship had high standards. They did not have a clear separation between clergy and laity, because all believers constituted the people of God. In contrast with the early church, today we have an exhaustive institution, but the discipleship criteria are so low that we don't even call it discipleship, but membership. As such, it is understood as a lifetime involvement or a paid subscriptions kind of participation despite constant renewal of allegiance.

We believe that every Christian must be a disciple following the Master. Subsequently, one should obey His command to make other disciples. A disciple should become a leader, influencing another in the disciple-making process. Jesus called us not only to be His disciples but also to make disciples. This should be obvious, because it is not possible to be a true disciple of Jesus without making disciples. This is not optional, and at the same time it should be understood, not as a duty, but as a privilege.

The Great Commission is our mission (Matthew 28:18-20). Our call is to make disciples. The disciple's goal is to form new disciples. This is the process of discipleship, in which the spirituality is developed by a personal relationship. This course of action is more effective in groups. They can promote diversity, recognizing people's differences. This can strengthen the group, providing "an environment in which people can learn and grow as they work and share together."[1]

The disciple is an equipper whose heart has been wonderfully and meticulously shaped by God as a magnificent piece of work, a real masterpiece. "As water reflects the face, so one's life reflects the heart" (Proverbs 27:19, NIV).

The mission of the church is to announce salvation through Jesus Christ, because "there is no other name under heaven given to mankind by which we must be saved" (Acts 4:12, NIV). The testimony of the disciples was so powerful that the people "realized that they had been with Jesus" (verse 13, NKJV). Likewise, In order to fulfill the goal of witness for Jesus, the primary function of the church is to train their members how to spend time with Jesus and share this good news of salvation with others in order to reach out to the world and call in new disciples for Jesus. "Every church should be a training school for Christian workers."[2]

The lifelong task of ministry or service is the real objective of life. "Christ's followers have been redeemed for service. Our Lord teaches that the true objective of life is ministry."[3] The multifaceted process of making disciples has to be developed in a close relationship between the Master and the disciple. As with disciples of Jesus, the starting point of this process is spending time with the Master and being transformed by Him. Only after this personal experience, can we be equipped to witness for Him. In the equipping course of action the equipper becomes able to equip, the disciple becomes a disciple maker. Jesus operates in His follower, equipping him or her to become a disciple. Jesus operates through His disciples, as they become equipped disciples making more disciples. "The church is God's appointed agency for the salvation of men. It was organized for service, and its mission is to carry the gospel to the world."[4]

The task at hand is intrinsic and yet, at the same time, very intricate. The question would be "Do you have in your local church a disciple-making process to reach out, assimilate, equip, and send disciples?" If you do, the follow-up questions would be "Is it working? And how do you know it is working?"

NURTURING

The 2015-2020 Seventh-day Adventist Church Strategic Plan—Reach the World—reflects several strategic issues related to the need of strengthening pastoral care, spiritual growth, and discipleship. Many local churches lack robust mechanisms for member care, especially for those who are at risk of leaving the church. Local churches need pastors to equip elders and members collectively to provide pastoral care for each other. Discipleship programs should be greatly strengthened, with baptism being the beginning of a life as a fruitful disciple of Jesus Christ. A baptismal certificate must be understood as a birth certificate, not as a graduation diploma. In recent years research has shown that among those who left, 40 percent said nobody contacted them; only 9 percent reported they were visited by the pastor, and 17 percent by a local elder. Some of them may have forgotten any attempt to be reached, or they were trying to blame others for their decision. However, it is crucial to reconsider the importance of pastoral care.

The pastoral role in the context of Ephesians 4 is to equip the saints for their ministry. Paul presents the pastor, not as a performer of ministry, but as a trainer of ministers.[5] This gives the idea of the pastor as a rancher, rather than a shepherd. The main difference between the shepherd and the rancher is "who takes care of the sheep. The shepherd must do it personally; the rancher delegates the pastoral care to others."[6] There are three prominent symbols of the shepherd mode: home visitation, hospital visitation, and personal counseling. The church people should be taught not to expect to get all of that from the pastor and still appreciate his or her leadership. They should be taught that the pastor is ultimately responsible for seeing to the excellent care that they are receiving by a pastoral-care team. The members of the church should receive high-quality pastoral care, but not necessarily directly from the pastor.

RECLAIMING

In Luke 15 Jesus stressed the need to care for the lost. When 1 percent of the flock is lost, the Good Shepherd searches tirelessly and relentlessly until the sheep is found (Luke 15:1-7). In the parable the shepherd goes out to search for one sheep—the very least that can be numbered. "So if there had been but one lost soul, Christ would have died for that one."[7] As a church, we have a challenge—we need to improve our efforts in caring and nurturing our members into a discipleship path.

In one of his speeches, Martin Luther King, Jr., said that "if a man hasn't discovered something he will die for, he isn't fit to live." Jesus Christ came to this world with a mission, "to seek and to save the lost" (Luke

19:10, NIV). He sacrificed for us by dying on the cross; we sacrifice by living a life of self-denying service for Him.

Many times I have heard church leaders saying, "We are planning to have evangelism during the summer." Those kind of statements have troubled me. If the Christian church business and the main goal of the Great Commission is to win souls by making disciples, how can we dedicate just a part of the year to the activity that supposed to be our main pursuit? If you mean by that expression to hold evangelistic meetings for reaping, then it could be acceptable.

The New Testament church could not even imagine a Christian who was not involved in ministry. "It was impossible for New Testament believers not to be involved in meaningful ministry in harmony with their spiritual gifts. In fact, the whole context of Romans 12 is a discussion of spiritual gifts. The involvement of every member in ministry in harmony with their spiritual gifts was the norm for the first-century church, and this likewise must become the norm of God's last-day church."[8] "I have been crucified with Christ; it is no longer I who live, but Christ lives in me; and the life which I now live in the flesh I live by faith in the Son of God, who loved me and gave Himself for me" (Galatians 2:20, NIV).

In this volume you have had the opportunity to review some of the most important presentations presented during the 2019 General Conference Nurture and Retention Summit. As we reflect on these topics, we hope you will be challenged to reconsider your priorities, to strength your disciple-ship processes, and to mobilize your church for service and mission.

GERSON P. SANTOS
Associate Secretary
General Conference Nurture
and Retention Committee Secretary

ENDNOTES

1   C. William Pollard, in F. Hesselbein, M. Goldsmith, and R. Beckhard, *The Leader of the Future* (New York: Jossey-Bass Publishers, 1996), p. 246.

2   Ellen G. White, *Christian Service* (Washington, D.C.: Review and Herald Pub. Assn.,1925), p. 59.

3   Ellen G. White, *Christ's Object Lessons* (Washington, D.C.: Review and Herald Pub. Assn., 1900, 1941), p. 326.

4   Ellen G. White, *The Acts of Apostles* (Mountain View, Calif.: Pacific Press Pub. Assn., 1911), p. 9.

5   Russell Burrill, *Revolution in the Church* (Fallbrook, Calif.: Hart Research Center, 1993), p. 47.

6   C. Peter Wagner, *Strategies for Church Growth* (Ventura, Calif.: Regal Books, 1989), p. 134.

7   E. G. White, *Christ's Object Lessons*, p. 187.

8   Burrill, pp. 25, 26.

2013 Nurture and Retention Recommendations

1. The GC to have a dedicated Associate Secretary whose responsibilities are to monitor implementation of the global church strategic plan in general and in particular to monitor progress in the area of nurture, retention, discipleship, and reclamation; this Assoc. Secretary to be secretary of the GC Nurture & Retention Committee.
    This recommendation has been partially implemented

2. Each division and union to have a designated N&R coordinator and an N&R committee chaired by one of the officers and including the following departmental directors: Children's Ministries, Education, Family Ministries, Ministerial, Sabbath School & Personal Ministries, Women's Ministries and Youth Ministries.

    Effectively four recommendations:

    2a. Each division to have a designated Nurture & Retention coordinator
    Successfully implemented

    2b. Each division to have a Nurture & Retention Committee chaired by one of the officers and with departmental representation
    Uncertain: probably only partially implemented

    2c. Each union to have a designated Nurture & Retention coordinator
    No data: anecdotally this has been implemented by a few unions, but it mostly remains unimplemented

    2d. Each union to have a Nurture & Retention Committee
    No data: it's possible this has not been implemented by any union; certainly, by very few

3. Each division to have an overall plan to improve the audited membership retention rate by x percent, the percentage to be selected by each division and then communicated to the General Conference.
    No data: possibly not implemented by any division

4. Each division and union to have and implement an active discipleship plan, along the lines of the "Growing Fruitful Disciples" model.
    Adopted as a KPI of the Reach the World 2015–2020 plan
    Unachieved. At the division level, implementation uncertain; there has been limited implementation at the union level, but no data are available

5. General Conference Departments, in collaboration with one another and consultation with division leaders, to create materials that meet expressed needs in the areas of nurture, retention and discipling, avoiding multiplicity of initiatives and approaches.
   Adopted as a KPI of the Reach the World 2015–2020 plan
   No data on implementation

6. Each division to hold conferences on nurture, retention and discipling: one involving administrators and academics (along the lines of the global summit), then further conferences sharing data and good practice with pastors and elders.
   Adopted as a KPI of the Reach the World 2015–2020 plan
   Some progress towards implementation: IAD, NSD, SSD, and TED held division-wide conferences—NSD annually; unions in IAD and TED (and perhaps elsewhere) have held conferences for pastors

7. Comprehensive, widespread and practical training in conflict resolution and reconciliation to be implemented throughout the worldwide Church.
   Adopted as a KPI of the Reach the World 2015–2020 plan No data on implementation; anecdotally: very few unions; possibly none

8. Approved membership software to be used in all fields to improve records of local church membership.
   Adopted as a KPI of the Reach the World 2015–2020 plan— but as "Widespread adoption of membership software" KPI achieved. Summit recommendation not yet achieved, but implementation taking place, gradually, throughout the world field

9. Specific training in nurture, retention and discipling to be part of all ministerial and theological education programs.
   No data; implemented by a few colleges on an ad hoc basis

10. A new section to be added to the Church Manual on discipleship at the local church level (and the Minister's Manual and Elder's Handbook subsequently to be amended appropriately).
    Successfully implemented!
    (Voted at 2015 GC Session)

Conclusions

Whatever recommendations are made by the 2019 Summit, they should include a reporting mechanism. As for many of the recommendations/goals, little or no data are available on implementation; but this reflects the fact that no reporting mechanism or responsibility was established.

This review was presented at the 2019 Nurture and Retention Summit by Anthony Kent and David Trim with an analysis of what had been implemented.

2019 Nurture and Retention Summit Recommendations

WE HAVE BEEN CALLED BY CHRIST to fulfill the Great Commission to make, not merely members, but disciples. With this goal in view, local churches should aim to create a warm and caring environment for spiritual growth, in which youth, adults, and visitors feel loved and supported. All ministries of the church must be united together in the mission of making mature and faithful disciples. A healthy church develops a nurture plan with respect to the cultural context. This plan includes equipping every member to be active and personally involved in disciple making using his or her talents and spiritual gifts. Plans for nurturing and training disciples may also include networks and small groups that provide opportunities for members to grow in Christ, serve people, and express their faith through various skills and interests.

RECOMMENDATIONS FOR THE LOCAL CHURCH

1. **Implement a systematic process of discipleship with clear and practical steps:**

   - Prepare new Adventist believers before baptism and integrate them into church life
     (train new Adventist believers through baptismal classes, Bible studies; involve them into church life through small groups, Pathfinder, Youth Alive activities, prayer, social and other meetings; Adventist Recovery programs, iCOR and other programs and ministries)

   - Integrate new members into church life and ministries
     (invite new disciples to church events and programs outside of Sabbath worship; involve them in prayer, small groups, Pathfinder, Youth activities, Alive and other meetings,etc.; recognize individual skills and spiritual gifts of the Holy Spirit; help people find ways to express their faith through different services to community and ministries in the church; help each one become a part of a ministry team or small group)

   - Develop spiritual habits
     (train and mentor members on how to develop spiritual habits,

including personal devotions, regular prayer life, personal Bible study and Sabbath School lessons, reading Ellen White's writings, faithful tithing, Sabbath School and church worship attendance, etc.)

- Foster growth in biblical & doctrinal understandings
  (conduct special series on Adventist doctrines, prophecy seminars; provide tools for personal Bible studies as In Step with Jesus and others; involve members in small groups and evangelistic events to deepen their biblical/doctrinal knowledge and witnessing skills; etc.)

- Train and involve new converts in personal witnessing and mentoring others:
  (train members in soul-winning and mentoring; involve them in different evangelistic initiatives; provide a practical tool to aid them in mentoring all new members, e.g., Discipleship Handbook or similar tools)

2. **Create a warm and nurturing atmosphere in the congregation:**

- Encourage members to be kind and welcoming, and to take an interest in others
  (train members how to demonstrate friendliness, acceptance, sensitivity, interest in visitors, and conflict resolution; set up a welcoming ministry with all ages involved; etc.)

- Create small groups and train/equip elders, Sabbath School leaders, and church members in mutual nurture and care in small groups

- Establish a culture of hospitality and member care
  (identify and assign gifted members and leaders to connect with visitors and include them in service projects based on their comfort level and interest; invite members to adopt a visitor, neighbor, co-worker and regularly invite them into their homes for fellowship; have a visitation plan—each member/family visited with once a year; ministry to homebound members; etc.)

- Develop active social and prayer ministries
  (create a prayer list for church needs; have an active social calendar; etc.)

- Move congregation toward being a missional community
  (build relationships with and provide services to the community outside the church, create comfortable environments for members' witnessing and services)

3. **Develop and implement a strategy of reclaiming former and inactive members:**

   - Regular membership audit process and plan
     (Develop and implement a system for the periodic review of the church membership list to identify those who may require transfer due to moving away, removal due to death, or redemptive ministry due to no longer attending or supporting the church etc.)

   - Former and inactive member ministry plan
     (Identify and assign gifted members and leaders to connect with former and inactive members by using a step-by-step process based on building strong relationships, implementing a visitation plan, and holding reclamation events such as music concerts, holiday programs, reunion or homecoming day, etc.)

4. **Monitor and evaluate discipleship, nurture, and reclamation efforts:**

   - Utilize an assessment and planning tool to identify and develop key ministries
     (Assess the strength of your church's ministry in each area listed in the above recommendations by using the provided sample or a similar instrument)

   - Utilize an evaluation tool to periodically review disciple-making effectiveness
     (Beyond merely tracking baptisms and attendance, assess the effectiveness of your congregation's discipleship plan: by examining spiritual growth, especially of those recently baptized, and their involvement in different aspects of Christian life.)

RECOMMENDATIONS FOR ADMINISTRATION

1. The GC to have a dedicated Associate Secretary whose responsibilities are to monitor progress, especially achievement of goals in the area of nurture, retention, discipleship and reclamation; this Associate Secretary to be secretary of the GC Nurture & Retention Committee.

2. A new section to be added to the Church Manual on the following:

   - Conducting periodical/annual membership audit from a redemptive/pastoral care perspective

- The need for local churches to craft and implement a customized strategy to move the congregation towards being a missional community that builds relationships with one another and with the community in order to create comfortable environments wherein they can—through service—share their faith and their testimonies of God's love and grace.

- Intentional mentoring of young people and newly baptized.

- Training in conflict resolution and reconciliation to be implemented in the local church.

3. Clarify the meaning of evangelism and discipleship in the Church Board section of the Church Manual.

4. Add to the Sabbath School section of the Church Manual regarding the vital role of Sabbath School in discipleship.

5. Each division to have an active discipleship plan, tailored to their local context and drawing on resources prepared by GC and division departments.

6. Each union to actively encourage the adoption by their local churches of a clear strategy on how they are going to nurture and train their disciples and reclaim missing members.

7. Adventist Church leaders and educational institution leaders to establish initiatives to increase the availability of Adventist education to children and youth, given the relationship between attendance at an Adventist school and retention of youth in the Church.

8. Specific training in nurture, retention and discipling to be foundational of all ministerial and theological education programs.

Appendix C

SAMPLE SURVEY FOR THE LOCAL CHURCH

Self-assessment of the Implementation of the 2019 Summit Recommendations

1. **Does your congregation have an active discipleship plan?** ○ Yes ○ Not sure ○ No

2. **Does your church have a thorough baptismal preparation process for new converts?** ○ Yes ○ Not sure ○ No

3. **Which of the following options is more common for your church in preparation of new converts for baptism?**
   ○ Baptismal preparation studies (class or personal
   ○ Evangelistic meetings
   ○ Other (please specify)

4. **Does your church have a small-group network to nurture members and promote wholistic spiritual care?** ○ Yes ○ Not sure ○ No

5. **How does your church integrate new converts into church life and ministries?**

6. **Does your church provide intentional training for new members in the following areas?**
   - Development of spiritual habits (e.g., personal devotions, regular prayer life, faithful tithing, church attendance, etc.? ○ Yes ○ Not sure ○ No
   - Personal witnessing and soul-winning ○ Yes ○ Not sure ○ No
   - Mentoring others ○ Yes ○ Not sure ○ No
   - How to create a warm and welcoming atmosphere in the church ○ Yes ○ Not sure ○ No
   - Conflict resolution ○ Yes ○ Not sure ○ No

7. **Do you have in your church:**
   - Welcoming ministry? ○ Yes ○ Not sure ○ No
   - Hospitality ministry? ○ Yes ○ Not sure ○ No
   - Member visitation/personal contact plan (each member/family visited or met with once a year)? ○ Yes ○ Not sure ○ No
   - Regular prayer ministry? ○ Yes ○ Not sure ○ No
   - Regular membership audit? ○ Yes ○ Not sure ○ No
   - Former and inactive member ministry plan? ○ Yes ○ Not sure ○ No

8. **In your church, do you have an evaluation tool to monitor the effectiveness of your:**
   - Discipleship plan? ○ Yes ○ Not sure ○ No
   - Nurture and welcoming atmosphere? ○ Yes ○ Not sure ○ No
   - Reclamation efforts? ○ Yes ○ Not sure ○ No